Teen
Legal
Rights

TEEN
LEGAL
RIGHTS

A Guide for the '90s

KATHLEEN A. HEMPELMAN

Greenwood Press
Westport, Connecticut · London

Library of Congress Cataloging-in-Publication Data

Hempelman, Kathleen A.
    Teen legal rights : a guide for the '90s / Kathleen A. Hempelman.
        p.   cm.
    Includes bibliographical references and index.
    ISBN 0–313–28760–0 (alk. paper)
    1. Minors—United States.   2. Teenagers—Legal status, laws, etc.—
United States.   3. Childrens' rights—United States.   I. Title.
KF479.H46   1994
346.7301'35—dc20
[347.306135]   93–37509

British Library Cataloguing in Publication Data is available.

Library of Congress Catalog Card Number: 93–37509
ISBN: 0–313–28760–0

First published in 1994

Greenwood Press, 88 Post Road West, Westport, CT 06881
An imprint of Greenwood Publishing Group, Inc.

Printed in the United States of America

The paper used in this book complies with the
Permanent Paper Standard issued by the National
Information Standards Organization (Z39.48–1984).

10 9 8 7 6 5 4 3 2

For my parents,
Geraldine and Richard Hempelman

Contents

Acknowledgments xiii

Introduction: What Teen Rights Are All About xv

Chapter 1   Behind the Wheel 1

Obtaining a Driver's License 1

Responsibility for Accidents 5

Auto Insurance 6

Traffic Offenses 10

Curfews 11

Owning and Renting a Car 12

Chapter 2   At School 15

Attendance and Grades 15

Freedom of Expression 19

Distributing Materials on School Grounds 22

Student Newspapers 24

Clothes as a Form of Expression 25

School Libraries and School Books 26

Freedom of Assembly 27

Religion and School Prayer 29

Discipline and Due Process 31

Corporal Punishment 36

	School Searches	37
	Weapons	39
	Students and the Police	40
	Sports	41
	Testing	42
	Other Discrimination Issues	43
	Student Records	45
	Private Schools	46
Chapter 3	**At Home**	49
	Teens, Parents, and Money	49
	Discipline	50
	Tobacco	52
	Adult Books and Adult Movies	53
	The Age of Majority	53
	Legal Guardians	54
	Termination of Parents' Rights	55
	Other Family Issues	58
Chapter 4	**On the Job**	61
	Teens and the Job Market	61
	The Minimum Wage	65
	Summer Jobs	65
	The Obligations and Benefits of Employment	66
	If You Lose Your Job	68
	Income Taxes	69
	Privacy	70
	Discrimination in Employment	70
	Job Safety	74
Chapter 5	**On Your Own**	77
	Emancipation	77
	Having Your Own Apartment	80
	Serving Your Country	80
	The Right to Vote	81
	Holding Public Office	81

Chapter 6 Your Personal Appearance 83

At Home 83

At School 83

At Work 84

In Public 85

Chapter 7 If Your Parents Divorce 87

Custody 87

Child Support 90

Grandparents and Stepparents 92

Other Issues Relating to Divorce 93

Chapter 8 Your Sexual Life 97

Birth Control 97

Abortion Rights 99

Sexually Transmitted Diseases 104

Rape 104

Chapter 9 Marrying and Having Children 107

Parental Consent for Marriage 107

Other Teen Marriage Issues 110

The Rights of Teenage Parents 111

Financial Help for Young Families 113

Chapter 10 Your Right to Be Healthy and Safe from Abuse 117

Abuse and Neglect 117

Sexual Abuse 127

Medical Care 129

Other Issues Relating to Abuse and Neglect 131

Mental Health Issues 132

Foster Care 133

Chapter 11 Alcohol and Drugs 139

The Legal Drinking Age 139

Drinking and Driving 140

Illegal Drugs 142

Chapter 12   Teens and Crime   147

    Arrests   147

    The *Miranda* Warning   149

    When Minors Are Arrested   151

    Searches and Seizures   153

    Intake   155

    Pretrial Detention   157

    Juvenile Court Hearings   158

    Minors in Adult Court   162

    Sentencing   163

    Probation   165

    Treatment in an Institution   166

    Juvenile Court Records   167

Chapter 13   Age, Race, and Sex Discrimination   171

    Age Discrimination   171

    Race Discrimination   172

    Sex Discrimination   176

Chapter 14   Gay and Lesbian Teens   179

    Is It Legal?   179

    Family Matters   180

    At School   181

    In Public   183

Chapter 15   Property Rights and Crimes Against Property   185

    Earnings   185

    What Can a Minor Own?   185

    When Parents Die   187

    When Minors Die   190

    The Property of Others   191

    Trespassing and Property Damage   191

Chapter 16   Entering into Contracts   195

    The Basics   195

    Disaffirming Contracts   196

    Necessaries   197

Chapter 17	**Taking Matters to Court**	199
	The Vocabulary of a Lawsuit	199
	Why People Go to Court	199
	Minors as Plaintiffs	201
	Minors as Defendants	203
	Lawyers	204
	Small Claims Court	205
	Bringing a Lawsuit	205
	Preparing a Civil Case	207
	Trials	208
	Damages	210
	Appealing a Court Decision	211
Chapter 18	**How to Find the Law**	213
Glossary		217
Index		227

Acknowledgments

I would like to thank attorneys Jane Hudson, Becky Winterscheidt, Jane Beach, Lee Cormier, and Mark Roelke, and also Hal Martin Fogel, Ron Schumaker, and Deborah Merritt, for their valuable and important suggestions on substantive issues in this book. I would also like to thank Sarah Chilton for her research on legal issues relating to reproductive rights, and David Rauch for his work on the chapter relating to civil courts and civil lawsuits. I wish them luck in their careers as lawyers.

For assisting and supporting me in other ways, I thank Shari Lightstone, Jane Hudson, Commissioner Thomas Jacobs of the Maricopa County Juvenile Court, Gordon Kirk, Ph.D., and Ron Rinehart of the *Arizona Republic*. The list also includes my brother, Ed Hempelman. Special thanks go to Hal Martin Fogel for permitting me to use a number of his photographic images.

I hasten to extend special thanks to Barbara Rader and the staff of Greenwood Publishing Group, Inc. Working with Barbara and her colleagues was sheer pleasure. These bright people taught me more about writing.

My father did not live to see this book in print, although he supported my efforts in the writing of it. I thank both my parents for encouraging me during the course of this special project.

Finally, I thank Barbara and Ben Shearer. Had it not been for this sparkling couple, I would not have had the opportunity to write this book. They already know how grateful I am to them; I hope they know how grateful I always will be.

Introduction: What Teen Rights Are All About

The purpose of this book is to inform teens, teachers, high school counselors, and parents of the legal rights of young people in the 1990s and to explain areas of modern American law that teens want to know about.

Minors had no legal rights to speak of at the beginning of the twentieth century. They had no recourse against family abuse and neglect, including sexual abuse. Many labored in sweaty textile mills at the age of 6. The poorest survived as orphans on the mean streets of America's great northern cities. A juvenile delinquent might spend years in a juvenile hall or asylum for stealing a dollar or a loaf of bread.

The rights of young people increased in the decades that followed, but it is in the last 25 years that these rights have expanded dramatically. Today young people are major figures on the American legal scene—they no longer are ignored. Not only do state child protective agencies and child labor laws now protect minors; young people now have constitutional ''due process'' rights in juvenile court, First Amendment and other constitutional rights in public schools (but only as of 1967), and privacy rights in the area of birth control and abortion. But that is just the beginning.

Teen Legal Rights: A Guide for the '90s explains the rights and responsibilities of teens in all areas of law that play a role in their lives. In question-and-answer format, it covers the expanding rights of young people at home, at school, on the job, and behind the wheel, and discusses their constitutional rights in juvenile court. This comprehensive review also addresses legal rights relating to teen sex, including birth control, abortion, and homosexuality. Among other issues covered are minors' rights in parents' divorce proceedings and minors' property rights.

Teen Legal Rights: A Guide for the '90s is a beginning point for understanding the rights and responsibilities of today's young people. Although the rights and responsibilities discussed in this book apply to "minors"—a legal term for young people under age 18—"teen" and "teenager" are used in a general sense to apply to minors as well. The term "children" is used when the issue discussed relates to the relationship of parent and child.

In the legal arena of minors' rights, an important point needs to be made. Although many rights of young people now are protected, enforcing these rights is another matter. High school students still are searched illegally and are punished for exercising recognized First Amendment rights, and police officials and juvenile courts often proceed illegally against minors of all ages. Legal advocates for young people still are few and far between. Despite the unrelenting expansion of minors' rights in American courts today, those same rights will continue to be abridged without legal remedy or redress unless public interest organizations, government agencies, private attorneys, and parents are plaintiffs in cases brought in behalf of minors.

Teen
Legal
Rights

— 1 —

Behind the Wheel

OBTAINING A DRIVER'S LICENSE

At what age can a young person obtain a driver's license?

Usually at age 16. Most states require teens to drive on a learner's permit before they can take the test for a regular driver's license. With a learner's permit, a young person can operate a vehicle only if a licensed adult driver is also in the front seat. After the permit holder has driven on a learner's permit for a specified number of weeks or months, he or she then can apply for a regular license.

Some states require young people to pass a driver's education course before applying for a driver's license. Whether or not a driving course is required, a teen who passes a driving course usually is able to obtain car insurance at lower rates.

See Table 1 for a summary of state licensing laws for driving.

Is driving without a license always illegal?

Yes. Both adults and minors must have a driver's license to drive a vehicle, and the license must be in the driver's possession while behind the wheel.

Can a parent prevent a minor child from obtaining a driver's license or learner's permit?

Yes. In most states a parent must sign the minor's driver's license or

Table 1
Driver's License Laws, by State, 1993

	Age for Driver's License			Driver's License Duration and Expiration Date	Fee
	Regular	Learner's	Restrictive		
Alabama	16	15[8]	14[9]	Four Date of Issuance	$15.00
Alaska	16	14	14[2,9]	Five Birthday	$10.00
Arizona	18	15/7 mo. [2,8]	16[2]	Four Birthday	$7.00
Arkansas	16	14-16[8]	14[2,5]	Four Birthday	$14.25
California	18	15[1,7]	16[1]	Four Birthday	$12.00
Colorado	21	15 yrs. 9 mo.[8]	15.5[1]	Five Birthday	$15.00
Connecticut	16[1]	16[1]	16[1]	Two, Four Birthday	$28.50-$43.50
Delaware	18	15/10 mo.[2,8]	16[1,2]	Five Birthday	$12.50
District of Columbia	18	[7,8]	16[2]	Four Date of Issuance	$20.00
Florida	16	15[8]	15[2]	Four or Six Birthday	$20.00
Georgia	21	15	16[2]	Four Birthday	$4.50
Hawaii	18	[8]	15[2]	2 if 15-24 or over 65, others-4 Birthday	2 yr./$6 4 yr./$12
Idaho	16[1]	16[18]	15[1]	Four Birthday	$19.50
Illinois	18	[8]	16[2,1]	Four, Five Birthday	$10.00
Indiana	18	16[6,13]	16 & 1 mo.[2,1]	Four, Three Yr. over 75 ($3) Last Day Birth Mo.	$6.00
Iowa	18	14	14[1,2]	Over 18 and under 70-4, others-2 Birthday	2 yr./$8 4 yr./$16
Kansas	16	[8]	14	Four Birthday	$8.00-$14.00
Kentucky	18	[8]	16[2]	Four Last Day Birth Mo.	$8.00
Louisiana	16	16[2]	17[14]	Four Birthday	$18.00
Maine	17	[8]	16[1]	Four Birthday	$20.00
Maryland	18	15/9 mo. [8,13]	16[2,1]	Five Birthday	$20.00
Massachusetts	18	[8]	16.5[2,1]	Five Birthday	$63.75

Table 1 (continued)

	Age for Driver's License			Driver's License Duration and Expiration Date	Fee
	Regular	Learner's	Restrictive		
Michigan	18		16[2,1]	Two, Four Birthday	2 yr./$6.00 4 yr./$12.00
Minnesota	18	8	16[1]	Four Birthday	$15.00-$34.00
Mississippi	15	8		Four Birthday	$20.00
Missouri	16	15[7]	15.5[15]	Three Date of Issuance	$7.50
Montana	18	8	15[2,1]	Four Birthday	$16.00-$24.00
Nebraska	16	15[7]	14	Four Birthday	$10.00
Nevada	18	15.5[8]		Four Birthday	$14.00 $19.00
New Hampshire	18		16[1]	Four Birthday	$30.00 $32.00
New Jersey	17		16	Four Date of Issuance	$16.00 $17.50
New Mexico	16	15[1]	14[13]	Four 30 days after birthdate	$10.00
New York	17[1]	16	16[2]	Four Birthday	$22.25
North Carolina	18	15[1,2,13]	16	Four Birthday	$10.00
North Dakota	16	8	14[2,1]	Four Birthday	$10.00
Ohio	18	16[2 8]	14[9]	Four Birthday	$6.50
Oklahoma	16	6	15.5[1]	Four Date of Issuance	$18.00
Oregon	16	15[8]	14	Four Birthday	$26.25
Pennsylvania	16	16[2,7]	16[2]	Four Last Day Birth Mo.	$22.00
Rhode Island	16	8	16[1]	Five Birthday	$30.00
South Carolina	16	15[5]	15	Four Birthday	$10.00
South Dakota	16		14[5]	Four Birthday	$6.00
Tennessee	18	15[7]	15	Four Birthday	$16.00
Texas	16[1]	15	15[1,7]	Four Birthday	$16.00
Utah	16[1,2]	16	15 yrs. & 9 mos.[3,5]	Five Birthday	$15.00-$20.00

Table 1 (continued)

	Age for Driver's License			Driver's License Duration and Expiration Date	Fee
	Regular	**Learner's**	**Restrictive**		
Vermont	18	15[13,8]	16[7]	Two or Four Birthday	$12 or $20
Virginia	18	15-8 mo.[2,8,7]	16[2,1]	Five Last day birth mo.	$12.00
Washington	18	15[6]	16[1]	Four Birthday	$14.00
West Virginia	18	15[8]	15[2]	Four Date of Issuance	$10.50
Wisconsin	18[1]	15.5[8]	16[1,2]	Four Birthday	$15.00
Wyoming	18	15[2,7]	15[2,7]	Four Birthday	$10.00

1. Must have completed approved driver education course.
2. Guardian's or parental consent required.
3. For use while enrolled in driver education course. Must be accompanied by instructor.
4. Upon proof of hardship.
5. Driver with learner's permit must be accompanied by locally licensed operator 21 years or older.
6. Must be enrolled in driver education course.
7. Driver with learner's permit must be accompanied by locally licensed operator 18 years or older.
8. Learner's permit required.
9. Restricted to mopeds.
10. All persons under 17 are prohibited from operating vehicles between 11 p.m. and 5 a.m.
11. If 65 or over, fee, $4.
12. To and from school or transporting handicapped.
13. Must be accompanied by licensed operator 25 years of age or older or a school driver-training instructor.
14. Hours of operation restricted.
15. Driver with learner's permit must be accompanied by licensed parent or guardian.

Source: American Automobile Association, *58th Edition of AAA's Digest of Motor Laws*, 1992.

learner's permit application. If the parent refuses, the minor can't obtain a driver's license, and, therefore, can't legally drive.

If a guardian or foster parent is legally in charge of the minor's care and upbringing, he or she is the one who must sign (and may refuse to sign) the application. For more about guardians, see Chapter Three, "At Home," and for more about foster parents, see Chapter Ten, "Your Right to Be Healthy and Safe from Abuse."

If state law requires parental consent for a young person to obtain a driver's license, at what age is consent no longer needed?

Usually at age 18, which is the age of majority in most states. For more about the age of majority, see Chapter Three, "At Home."

Can a parent revoke a minor's license or learner's permit?
It depends on the state's driving laws. Whether or not a state permits this, it is clearly within the authority of parents to forbid a minor to drive.

RESPONSIBILITY FOR ACCIDENTS

What should a teen do if he or she has a traffic accident?
The first rule is *stay at the scene*. A minor who is involved in an accident should immediately ask another person to call the minor's parents and also the police. The police officer will undoubtedly ask the drivers and all passengers for their names and addresses and will want to see driver's licenses from everyone. In addition, the officer will ask a number of questions for the basic purpose of completing his or her police report. All requests should be complied with promptly and courteously.

In most states, refusing to produce identification or leaving the scene of an accident before the police arrive is a crime. For more information about police questioning, see Chapter Twelve, "Teens and Crime."

If a minor injures someone or damages property through his or her own fault while driving, who is financially responsible?
Usually the minor's parents. In every state, one of the conditions for obtaining a driver's license or learner's permit is that the applicant agree to be financially responsible for injuries or property damage he or she causes as a result of negligent or reckless driving. If a parent is required to sign a teenage child's application for a license or permit, most states hold *both* parents responsible for injuries or property damage caused by the minor's negligent or reckless driving, even if only one parent actually signed it.

Parents can be held liable for injuries or damage caused by a minor child while driving a parent's car for either personal enjoyment or a family purpose such as running an errand. They also can be held liable for permitting a minor child to drive without a driver's license or learner's permit.

Does this mean a teenage driver can't be held liable for injuries or property damage caused by his or her acts behind the wheel?

No. Almost anyone, including minors, can be taken to court for negligently or recklessly causing injuries or property damage. However, minors usually are "judgment proof," which means they normally don't have the money to satisfy a court-ordered judgment for damages. This is why state driving laws hold parents financially responsible for injuries or property damage caused by the careless acts of their minor children. For more about court actions to recover money, see Chapter Seventeen.

If a teen's parents are divorced, who is held liable for injuries caused by the teen while driving?

Usually both of the parents, regardless of who retains custody. If a minor's parents divorce *before* the minor is granted a license, in many states parental liability depends on which parent has custody on the date of the application. In joint custody situations, both parents continue to be liable. For more about custody in divorce situations, see Chapter Seven, "If Your Parents Divorce."

Can parents avoid being held liable for a minor child's careless acts while driving?

Sometimes. In many states if a minor has a decent income and owns property, the parents can file a statement with the state department of motor vehicles attesting to the minor's separate financial responsibility. Once they do, they can't be held liable for injuries or property damage caused by the minor's negligence or recklessness while driving, except when their actions contribute to the cause of the accident.

In certain states, parents can't be held responsible for a minor child's negligence or recklessness if the minor buys a car with his or her own money and the title to the car is in the minor's name.

If a young person lends the family car to a friend or lets someone else do the driving, can the minor's parents be held responsible for injuries or property damage caused by the other driver?

Yes.

AUTO INSURANCE

How does auto insurance work?

When a person has auto insurance, an insurance company has agreed to pay for property damage and medical care in connection with the ownership and operation of a particular vehicle. The company's agreement to pay under the terms of its insurance policy is conditional upon the payment of a "premium," which is simply the cost of the insurance coverage.

When it comes to families, the auto insurance buyer—the "policy-holder"—usually is an adult driver of the family car. A spouse and any children under age 21 can be insured under the same policy.

Is a minor required to have auto insurance?

In most states, all drivers must have a minimum amount of auto *liability* insurance, which insures against damage caused by the insured driver's negligence or recklessness. Proof of auto liability insurance in the legally required amount is the standard way for a person to establish financial responsibility. In many states it is the *only* way.

Can minors buy their own auto insurance?

Usually they are unable to. Insurance companies have calculated that teen drivers are very poor insurance risks. The companies can't profit by insuring teen drivers separately unless exorbitant premiums are charged, because teens as a group have a high accident rate and many insurance claims. (Teenage women are a safer risk than teenage men, but only by a slight margin.)

But as stated earlier, auto insurance companies permit teen drivers to be covered under their parents' policy. The additional premium to cover a minor under an adult policy is high, but at least it is affordable. This is the way most teen drivers are insured, and again, the way their parents' financial responsibility is established when the teen applies for a driver's license.

Is there anything a teen can do to reduce the premium charged for his or her part of the car insurance?

Yes. Many insurance companies reduce the premium for teen drivers if the teen doesn't smoke. Some companies also reduce the premium if the teen maintains good grades.

If a minor's parents are divorced, which parent's policy is he or she covered under?

Usually the custodial parent's policy, although if the minor is permitted to drive both parents' cars, each must cover the minor.

What "risks" does auto insurance cover?

Quite a variety. The types of coverage included in a standard auto insurance policy are:

1. "Collision" insurance, which covers damage to the insured car when an insured driver isn't at fault;

2. "Comprehensive" insurance, which covers damage to the insured car resulting from fire, theft, vandalism, hail, falling objects, windshield breaks, and collisions with animals;

3. "Medical payments" insurance, which covers medical expenses that an insured driver and any passengers incur in a traffic accident. It also covers injuries suffered by an insured person while riding in another car, or walking.

4. "Bodily injury liability" insurance, which pays for claims against an insured resulting from injuries to passengers, pedestrians, and persons in other vehicles. Bodily injury liability insurance also pays for legal expenses incurred to defend the insured in a lawsuit. If an injury is serious or fatal, liability claims for bodily injury can add up to many thousands of dollars.

5. "Property damage liability" insurance, which pays for claims against an insured when the insured car causes damage to someone else's property. Usually the damaged property is another driver's car, but it also might be damage to a building, telephone pole, or lamppost.

6. "Uninsured motorist" insurance, which pays medical costs of an insured's bodily injuries and car damage when another person is at fault but that person doesn't have liability coverage. Uninsured motorist coverage often pays for auto damage and bodily injuries in "hit-and-run" situations.

What is "no-fault" insurance?

It is a type of auto liability insurance in which each party collects from his or her own insurance company, regardless of who caused the accident. Under state no-fault insurance laws, the injured party doesn't have to prove negligence or recklessness before an insurance company pays up. About half the states have no-fault insurance laws.

How does no-fault insurance differ from traditional car insurance?

Basically in the manner in which the innocent party collects payments. With regular auto insurance, an accident victim must make a claim against the other driver's insurance company. Before that insurer will pay, the accident victim must prove that the other driver was negligent or reckless. This may be difficult if the cause of the accident is tough to determine.

If the other driver's fault is established, the amount payable to the

On the road somewhere out West. Photo: Hal Martin Fogel. Reprinted with permission.

accident victim must be calculated. The amount depends on such factors as the victim's medical expenses, property damage, lost wages, and pain and suffering. Added to these are the lawyer's fees for proving who was at fault.

For more about lawsuits, including how to calculate damages in personal injury cases, see Chapter Seventeen, "Taking Matters to Court."

TRAFFIC OFFENSES

If a person commits a minor traffic offense, is he or she placed under arrest?

No. The person is simply cited for violating a traffic law.

If a minor commits a traffic offense, does the case go to juvenile court?

Not usually. In most states, all minor traffic offenses go to the state's adult traffic court. But juvenile courts have the power to suspend a minor's driver's license if the minor commits a delinquent act involving a car. For more about juvenile courts, see Chapter Twelve, "Teens and Crime."

What kinds of punishment can a teenage driver receive for a traffic offense?

It depends on the nature and severity of the offense and also the state in which the offense was committed. In any traffic court, fines can be swiftly imposed and licenses can be suspended or revoked.

Can a minor's license be revoked because of too many traffic tickets?

Yes. In every state both teen and adult drivers can lose their licenses if they are "habitual violators." This happens most often when the offense is DWI.

What is the punishment for DWI (driving while intoxicated)?

It varies from state to state, but for a first offense the license of the drunk driver usually is suspended or revoked. Sometimes the offender will receive a restricted license that allows him or her to drive to work but nowhere else. Weekend detention is often given. Repeat offenders are always punished more severely.

See Chapter Eleven, "Alcohol and Drugs," for more about the legal aspects of drinking and driving.

Does a police officer need a search warrant to search a car?

It depends on the case. When a person is arrested for a serious offense involving a car, both the car and the arrested person can be searched. This is called a "search incident to an arrest." When this happens, the police must limit their search to areas within the arrested person's reach just before the arrest, and to items in "plain view." If the car is seized by the police—if they "impound" the car—they can only search the rest of it after obtaining a search warrant.

Why might the police impound a car?

To preserve evidence of a crime involving the car. For more about police searches and search warrants, see Chapter Twelve, "Teens and Crime."

Can a minor be arrested for having a weapon in the car?

In most states virtually anyone can be arrested for carrying a concealed weapon, and in many states a person can be arrested for having a weapon within easy reach inside a vehicle. These arrests can be made without a warrant.

Is hitchhiking illegal?

It depends on state or local law. Some states and cities prohibit hitchhiking altogether, some don't regulate it at all, and others permit it only when the hitchhiker is standing at a certain location near the roadway. For example, some states prohibit hitchhiking on freeways, urban roadways, bridges, and highway on-ramps and off-ramps, but permit it on other roads and streets.

CURFEWS

What is a curfew?

It is a state or local law that prohibits individuals from being on the street between specific hours after dark. Curfews usually apply to young people, but they have been applied to adults, and have also been used illegally against racial and ethnic minorities.

Under curfew laws, being on the street includes riding or sitting in a car. But a minor usually isn't in violation of a curfew law, whether on the street or in a car, if he or she is with an adult.

When are curfews illegal?

When the state or local curfew law is too vague or too broad. As explained in Chapter Twelve, a law must be written clearly and specifically, so citizens have fair notice of exactly what actions the law prohibits. Many courts have ruled that curfew laws that simply prohibit "loitering" or "vagrancy" are unenforceable because they forbid perfectly legal acts such as having a smoke outside a restaurant that enforces a "no smoking" policy.

In a 1971 case from the state of Washington, a city ordinance that simply declared "loitering" and "wandering" illegal was declared unconstitutional after a high school senior was pulled over at 4:30 A.M. by the police for violating it. The young man was returning from a party and wanted to take a drive along the beach near downtown Seattle before going home. The statute was declared unconstitutional because its wording made his perfectly innocent behavior illegal.

On the other hand, many states have upheld well-drafted curfew laws as a way to reduce juvenile crime late at night.

What happens if a minor violates a curfew?

The police have a number of options. If the minor has a legitimate reason for being out, the police officer might send the minor home with a stern warning. In other cases the minor might either be taken home, cited for a minor traffic violation, or transported to the police station and "booked" for committing another more serious act.

The best way to find out if a city or state has a curfew is to ask a police officer, call the police station and inquire, or go to the public library and read up on local curfew laws. A reference librarian will always provide assistance in finding the law.

OWNING AND RENTING A CAR

Can a teen buy a car?

Nothing in the law prevents a minor from buying a car or other expensive item. But some car dealers refuse to sell to minors, for one basic reason. As discussed in Chapter Sixteen, "Entering into Contracts," minors are permitted to walk away from or "disaffirm" most contracts, provided they do so soon after the sale. This rule of law, which strikes many as out-of-date and even unfair, is meant to protect minors from unscrupulous salespeople.

This means, for example, that if a minor buys a car but then decides the purchase was a bad idea, the dealer can't refuse to take the car back even if the minor paid full price. (However, the dealer can reduce the refund to reflect any damage or wear and tear to the car while in the minor's possession.) Basically, the law makes the risk of financial loss fall on the dealer and not the minor.

In some states, minors can only disaffirm contracts until age 16.

If a teen does buy a car, it must be titled, registered, and licensed, and in most states the teenage driver must have auto insurance.

Can a teen take out a car loan?

That would be difficult. In order for a teen to obtain a car loan, he or she would have to be earning enough money to make monthly loan payments without a lot of effort. Most teens don't earn this much. Besides, most lenders have a basic policy of rejecting all loan applications from minors.

Can a teen rent a car?

Whether a minor can rent a car always depends on whether the car rental agency is willing to rent cars to minors. Few will rent to persons under age 25.

FOR FURTHER READING

Bailard, Biehl & Kaiser, Inc. *How to Buy the Right Insurance at the Right Price*. Homewood, Illinois: Dow Jones-Irwin, 1989.

Glass, James. *Traffic Court: How to Win*. Arcadia, California: Allenby, 1988.

Marks, James R. *Sharing the Risk: How the Nation's Businesses, Homes and Autos Are Insured*. New York: Insurance Information Institute, 1989.

Table 2 (continued)

STATE	LAW
South Dakota	Minor May Decide[1]
Tennessee	Minor May Decide[1]
Texas	Minor May Decide[4]
Utah	Not Applicable[3]
Vermont	Minor May Decide[1]
Virginia	Not Applicable[3]
Washington	Minor May Decide[10]
West Virginia	Minor May Decide[1]
Wisconsin	Minor May Decide[1]
Wyoming	Minor May Decide[1]

1. Minor must be 16 or older. In Vermont a minor under age 16 may drop out after completing the tenth grade.
2. Minor may drop out at age 16 if employed, and in the District of Columbia after completing the eighth grade.
3. State law does not allow a minor to drop out before graduation.
4. Minor must be 12 or older.
5. Age will change to 18 in the year 2000.
6. Minor must have completed eighth grade.
7. Minor may drop out if authorized by the local school board.
8. Minor must be 17 in New York City.
9. Minor may drop out at age 16 if employed.
10. Minor may drop out at age 15 if employed or if the school superintendent determines that the minor is proficient in grades 1–9.

Source: Reproduced with the permission of The Alan Guttmacher Institute from Patricia Donovan, *Our Daughter's Decisions: The Conflict in State Law on Abortion and Other Issues,* 1992.

varying results. Some have ruled it isn't improper to grade "truants" or "tardies" more harshly, because learning to be responsible is consistent with the overall goals of a school curriculum. Others say that lowering grades for poor attendance or misconduct misses the point of what grades are really for.

In one case a Kentucky high school was forbidden to lower a student's grades for absences due to a suspension. Since the student was denied credit for work he missed during his suspension, additional grade reductions for his absences were said to be "overkill."

If a school has a policy of lowering grades for truancy, the school should tell the students at the beginning of the year how many absences will result in reduced grades, and whether the rule applies to both excused and unexcused absences. If grades can also be lowered for misconduct, students should be told what kinds of behavior might actually result in lowered grades.

Can a student flunk out of public high school?

"Flunking out" is a phrase usually associated with college, but it does have an equivalent in the high school setting.

If a student doesn't fulfill the requirements of a particular course of study, he or she won't be able to graduate. The student can repeat courses until reaching the maximum age for attending high school, but has to leave upon reaching that age if he or she doesn't graduate first. After that the student can obtain a graduate equivalency degree, or "GED," but generally would be unable to receive a high school diploma in the absence of a special state law or state program.

Are married students required to stay in school? Can married students be kept out of school?

In answer to the first question, married students usually are "emancipated" from the obligation of having to attend high school, even if they otherwise are too young to quit. As to the second question, the Constitution requires that all students be permitted to attend classes and participate in their high school graduation ceremonies regardless of marital status.

For more about emancipation see Chapter Five, "On Your Own," and for more about teen marriages see Chapter Nine.

Can a pregnant teen be prevented from attending high school? Can students with children be prevented from attending high school?

The answer to both questions is no. In times past, pregnant students either dropped out of high school or were told to leave, and, of course, many never went back. But these days, pregnancy and parenting can't keep a student from completing high school.

Can students who have HIV/AIDS (human immunodeficiency virus/acquired immunodeficiency syndrome) be prevented from attending high school?

Some school boards have tried to bar students with HIV/AIDS from attending classes, but courts have ordered them enrolled once health officials certify that the student isn't likely to infect others.

HIV is the virus that causes AIDS. It can be transmitted during sexual intercourse. Although HIV/AIDS is life-threatening, research shows that it can't be transmitted through casual contact. Several states have policies requiring students with HIV/AIDS to be permitted to attend school unless they have open cuts, display dangerous behavior such as biting, or can't control their bodily discharges.

FREEDOM OF EXPRESSION

> Congress shall make no law . . . abridging the freedom of speech, or of the press.
>
> —First Amendment,
> U.S. Constitution

Do students have free speech rights at school?

Yes. The constitutional guarantee of free expression extends to high school students. However, these rights can be limited in certain school situations, as this section explains.

The right of students to express their opinions freely is guided by an important United States Supreme Court case, *Tinker v. Des Moines Independent School District*. This 1969 case made it clear that students don't forfeit their constitutional right of free expression when they step onto school property.

In *Tinker*, the Supreme Court upheld the right of students at an Iowa public high school to wear black armbands to protest America's involvement in Vietnam. Because the armbands were a means of communicating an idea and not just an item of dress—because the armbands were a form of "symbolic speech"—wearing them raised a First Amendment issue.

The Supreme Court established in *Tinker* that in order to limit student expression, school authorities must prove that the expression either "materially and substantially" disrupts school work and school discipline or collides with the rights of others. The school must base its decision to limit speech on concrete facts showing that the expression would probably cause "substantial and material" disruption at school. Its decision must be motivated by more than the desire to prevent the discomfort which often accompanies an unpopular viewpoint.

According to the Supreme Court, the student armbands in *Tinker* didn't create any problems that substantially interfered with either school activities or the rights of the other students. Because the school rule couldn't be justified as a valid restriction on First Amendment rights, the Supreme Court declared it unconstitutional.

The basic analysis set out in *Tinker* applies to this day to cases involving the free speech rights of students.

What types of student expression does the First Amendment regulate?

Virtually every kind of communication, both verbal and nonverbal, including speeches, essays, leafleting, armbands and buttons, books in the library, school newspapers, underground newspapers, walk-outs, and sit-ins.

In the area of free expression, what does "material and substantial" disruption really mean?

Consider the following situations. Students could probably distribute handouts between classes unless doing so would seriously interfere with hall traffic. On the other hand, students could be prohibited from distributing such materials during class time. School officials could refuse to let students use the school's photocopiers to duplicate handouts if the students planned to use them instead of going to class. But the school would probably be required to let students use the copiers after school, whether or not school officials agree with the content of the handouts. Students would be able to post written materials such as newspaper articles and meeting announcements on school bulletin boards whether or not the subject matter is controversial, provided the posted material isn't vulgar by standards that the community generally adheres to.

Can students be punished for openly criticizing a teacher or school policy?

Only if the criticism or manner of expression either materially and substantially interferes with school activities or offends the rights of others. In a 1973 case, a court upheld a high school's decision to confiscate signs that students planned to distribute to protest a certain teacher's dismissal. The court believed the school had a realistic basis for believing that the protests would interfere with school work and school discipline.

Although the school claimed victory in this situation, students have won many First Amendment cases. In 1972, an Illinois court upheld the actions of high school students who published and distributed an underground newspaper criticizing certain school officials. The newspaper, styled on the *National Lampoon,* urged the student body to discard reading materials relating to school policy that they had been told to give to their parents. The students prevailed because the school couldn't prove that the newspaper caused material and substantial disruption or offended the rights of others.

Does the First Amendment protect students who libel or slander school officials?

The First Amendment doesn't protect anyone who libels or slanders.

Libel is a written, published statement that the writer either knows or should know is untrue. *Slander,* on the other hand, is a spoken statement that the speaker either knows or should know is untrue. Libel and slander are types of "defamatory" statements, and statements such as these are said to "defame" people. Defamatory statements are never protected by the First Amendment, and persons who defame others can be sued for damages caused by their defamatory acts.

School authorities always have the power to censor libelous material written by students. In addition, school officials can punish students who make slanderous statements and can stop the distribution of libelous material, whether or not the material was prepared at school.

Can school officials prohibit obscene language on school grounds?

Yes. School officials have extensive authority to determine what kind of language is obscene and to discipline students for using it. Schools are said to have an interest in teaching students the boundaries of socially appropriate behavior, including their manner of speech.

This rule doesn't apply just to "four-letter" words, and, in fact, the language that schools often prohibit wouldn't strike every high school student as vulgar or obscene. Consider the following speech, which a student gave before a high school assembly:

> I know a man who is firm—he's firm in his pants, he's firm in his shirt, his character is firm—but most . . . of all, his belief in you, the students of Bethel, is firm.
>
> Jeff is a man who takes his point and pounds it in. If necessary, he'll take an issue and nail it to the wall. He doesn't attack things in spurts—he drives hard, pushing and pushing until finally—he succeeds.
>
> So vote for Jeff for A.S.B. vice-president—he'll never come between you and the best our high school can be.

The speaker was given a two-day suspension for this speech, and the United States Supreme Court sided with the school. If this ruling seems harsh, it is important to know that the situation in the case was unique. The speaker's audience consisted mostly of 14-year-olds. Upon hearing the speech, some of them hooted and yelled, and others were bewildered and embarrassed. According to the Supreme Court, because the speech disrupted classes and confused many of the students, the school didn't violate the First Amendment when it disciplined the speaker. However, it said the speech might have been protected if the student had delivered it in a different setting, and to older students.

Schools may always prohibit the distribution of materials that are generally considered obscene and may legally confiscate obscene materials.

DISTRIBUTING MATERIALS ON SCHOOL GROUNDS

Can school authorities legally enforce a rule prohibiting students from distributing written materials on school property before, during, and after school?

No. School officials can only enforce such a rule if they can show that distributing written materials at school could *always* interfere with school activities or the rights of others. That would be a tough case to win.

Can school authorities legally enforce a rule permitting students to distribute written materials before and after classes but not during school hours?

Only if the school is able to prove that leafleting during school hours is *always* likely to disrupt school work or school discipline materially. School officials would have to prove, for example, that the student leafleters would always block the halls, disrupt classes, cause damage to school property, or interfere with the legal rights of others. That would be another tough case.

Can a school legally enforce a rule prohibiting students from bringing "controversial" or "distasteful" materials on school property, regardless of the subject matter?

No, for an important constitutional reason. Because blanket rules like these fail to let students know what kinds of materials *in fact* are prohibited and what kinds of materials *in fact* are acceptable, the Constitution says they are "overbroad" and therefore "void for vagueness." If rules such as these could legally be enforced, a school could prohibit materials that the most oversensitive teacher or administrator might happen to have a problem with. The limits on the constitutional right of free speech don't reach this far.

If certain students distribute materials in an orderly manner but others react disruptively, can the school step in? *Should* **the school step in?**

These questions raise an important issue because the disruption isn't being caused by students who are attempting to exercise their free speech rights, but by the reactions of others. In these situations the school has a duty to protect the leafleters.

The school would be permitted to regulate the "time, place, and manner" of the students' leafleting activities to make certain that their right to distribute the materials isn't diminished. It may have to provide extra protection for the leafleters. However, it can only stop the leafleting if serious problems occur, or if it tends to aggravate an already touchy situation.

Can a school forbid all leafleting on a particular issue altogether?

No. This would be an unconstitutional restraint on the First Amendment rights of *all* students.

In one important case, a school policy prohibited the use of school facilities for all political activities, including activities relating to presidential politics. When a number of students were punished for distributing materials supporting Senator George McGovern's 1972 bid for the presidency, some of their parents took the issue to court.

The parents won. The state supreme court refused to uphold the school's restrictive policy, stating that it violated the First Amendment rights of the entire student body.

If a school policy requires prior approval of materials to be distributed, how would a student go about obtaining it?

Ask a teacher for a copy of the school's approval procedures. These guidelines should always be in writing and should be precise. If they aren't clear enough or don't address important issues, the student should ask a school official for a more detailed explanation.

The approval procedures should require the school to decide on the student's materials right away. They shouldn't permit school officials to "sit" on a request for approval until the best time for the student to exercise his or her First Amendment rights has come and gone.

Approval procedures can be illegal when they are unclear or in any way tend to discourage students from exercising their constitutional rights.

If a school refuses to approve student material for distribution, what can be done?

The student should request a written copy of the school's decision, to test the reason for its refusal against the *Tinker* case. Students always have a right to know why the school believes the rejected materials will seriously interfere with school activities or offend the rights of others.

If the student disagrees with the decision, he or she should consider appealing. Appeals are discussed later in this chapter.

STUDENT NEWSPAPERS

Can school officials censor student material in school newspapers?

They can in certain cases. In a 1988 case the Supreme Court modified *Tinker* by upholding school officials who censored stories in a school-sponsored student newspaper. The school vetoed stories written by journalism students on teen pregnancy and the effects of divorce on children. Under *Tinker* the articles probably would have been protected. However, the Supreme Court ruled that they could be censored because they conflicted with the school's overall educational goals.

Because of this decision, known as *Hazelwood School District v. Kuhlmeier*, schools across the county have begun to censor articles in school-sponsored student publications. They now may censor "poorly written, prejudiced or vulgar articles" and articles that are "not suited for immature audiences." They may censor material on teen sex and articles advocating the use of drugs or alcohol and other conduct inconsistent with the "shared values of a civilized social order." They may, according to the Supreme Court, even censor material that associates the school with "anything other than neutrality on political issues."

However, *Hazelwood* doesn't apply if the school-sponsored publication has consistently made a point of publishing student opinions—if the publication has been a "public forum" for student expression in the past. Nor does it apply if student editors have the last word on the content of the newspaper.

In light of *Hazelwood*, school officials in Nevada recently were able to prevent a Planned Parenthood advertisement from running in a school-sponsored high school newspaper, even though the school had accepted ads from casinos, bars, churches, political candidates, and the United States Army. The censorship was upheld because the school's decision to censor was shown to be in keeping with sound academic concerns, and because the newspaper hadn't been a public forum for student expression in the past.

—2—

At School

ATTENDANCE AND GRADES

Does everyone in the United States have a right to an education?

Every young person in the United States has a right to a free public education, and every young person in the United States has an obligation to attend school. Minors in most states must attend school between the ages of 7 and 16, and in some they are required to attend longer. A student can only quit school when the applicable state law no longer requires attendance.

In many states a student who misses too much school can be brought under court supervision so that his or her attendance can be monitored by a probation officer. Parents can be prosecuted for failing to keep their children in school.

See Table 2 for age requirements for school attendance in the 50 states and the District of Columbia.

Are teens allowed to remain in high school longer than it normally takes to finish?

Yes, although most states have a maximum age limit. It varies from state to state, but most set it at age 21.

Can a student's grades automatically be lowered for poor attendance or misconduct?

These practices have been tested in courts across the country, with

Table 2
Age at Which Minors May Leave School, by State, 1992

STATE	LAW
Alabama	Minor May Dedide[1]
Alaska	Minor May Decide[1]
Arizona	Minor May Decide[1,2]
Arkansas	Minor May Decide[1]
California	Not Applicable[3]
Colorado	Minor May Decide[1]
Connecticut	Minor May Decide[1,2]
Delaware	Minor May Decide[1]
D.C.	Minor May Decide[1,2]
Florida	Minor May Decide[1]
Georgia	Minor May Decide[1]
Hawaii	Not Applicable[3]
Idaho	Minor May Decide[1]
Illinois	Minor May Decide[1]
Indiana	Minor May Decide[4]
Iowa	Minor May Decide[1,2]
Kansas	Minor May Decide[1]
Kentucky	Not Applicable[3]
Louisiana	Minor May Decide[4]
Maine	Minor May Decide[4]
Maryland	Minor May Decide[1]
Massachusetts	Minor May Decide[1]
Michigan	Minor May Decide[1]
Minnesota	Minor May Decide[1,5]
Mississippi	Minor May Decide[4]
Missouri	Minor May Decide[1]
Montana	Minor May Decide[1,6]
Nebraska	Minor May Decide[1]
Nevada	Minor May Decide[4]
New Hampshire	Minor May Decide[1]
New Jersey	Minor May Decide[1]
New Mexico	Minor May Decide[1,7]
New York	Minor May Decide[1,8]
North Carolina	Minor May Decide[4]
North Dakota	Minor May Decide[1]
Ohio	Not Applicable[3]
Oklahoma	Not Applicable[3]
Oregon	Minor May Decide[9]
Pennsylvania	Minor May Decide[4]
Rhode Island	Minor May Decide[1]
South Carolina	Minor May Decide[1]

The answer to this question is unclear. Under *Pico,* probably not, although under the *Hazelwood* case, discussed earlier, this probably could happen.

The American Library Association's Bill of Rights prohibits libraries from discriminating on the basis of age when lending books. This document doesn't have the force of law, but it does assert an important First Amendment position.

Can school boards constitutionally restrict the types of reading material that teachers may use in class?

Yes. Although school boards can't have books removed from school libraries because of the ideas in them, they can prohibit the use of teaching materials that are considered vulgar or obscene by community standards.

In 1989, a federal appeals court in Florida upheld a high school's decision to remove a collection of essays from a school reading list because certain parents thought some of the essays were vulgar. The selections objected to were *Lysistrata* by the ancient Greek Aristophanes and "The Miller's Tale" from Chaucer's *Canterbury Tales.* Both selections contain references to sex.

After the school board sided with the parents, other parents took the matter to court, claiming violations of the First Amendment. The judge said he had trouble understanding how Aristophanes and Chaucer could cause eleventh and twelfth graders in modern America any harm. Even so, he let stand the school board's decision because, he said, striking the books from the reading list was related to legitimate curriculum concerns of the school board.

These two cases point to an odd distinction in the law, and one that is troublesome to many. Removing books from the shelves of a school library because someone disapproves of the ideas in them is a First Amendment violation. On the other hand, public schools may exercise almost total control over their curricula. Courts have permitted schools to prohibit even mildly offensive reading material from their lesson plans.

FREEDOM OF ASSEMBLY

> Congress shall make no law . . . abridging the right of the people peaceably to assemble.
>
> —First Amendment,
> U.S. Constitution

Can a school prevent students from forming a club at school that promotes an unpopular point of view?

Courts in some states have ruled that school facilities can be used only for activities relating directly to the curriculum. In these states, classrooms and meeting halls can be used only by organizations such as honor societies and foreign language clubs. In others, any club can meet unless its activities cause material and substantial disruption or deprive other students of their legal rights.

The law in this area is unclear. In 1983 a Pennsylvania high school was able to prevent a student group, the Student Coalition for Peace, from using school facilities for an antinuclear presentation. The school board's stated goal was to "keep the podium of politics off school grounds." But a number of years earlier, a Michigan state court stated that "absent a threat to the orderly operation of the school, to deny recognition to a student group because it advocates 'controversial' ideas is unconstitutional."

Unless the Supreme Court takes up this issue, the "freedom" in "freedom of assembly," at least with respect to club meetings on school grounds, will continue to vary from state to state.

Can school officials legally stop sit-ins, walk-outs, and protest marches on school property?

It depends on the situation. Demonstrations raise free speech issues and also free assembly issues, and this makes them subject to the ruling in the *Tinker* case (discussed earlier in this chapter).

Demonstrations and walk-outs can indeed disrupt school work and school discipline, and when they do, school authorities can and should intervene and may legally suspend students for participating. However, some courts have said that students should be given less punishment for participating in nonviolent demonstrations, if punished at all, given the importance of free speech in our society.

Sit-ins aren't necessarily illegal because they occur inside school, but any demonstration has a better chance of coming within the First Amendment's right to assemble peaceably if it occurs outdoors and before or after school. School officials have the right to stop protests that block halls or make students miss class and may discipline students who damage property or cause injuries. Students can be arrested if a situation becomes so serious that laws are broken. But a school violates the Constitution if it enforces a rule banning demonstrations altogether.

Have students been able to organize gay or lesbian rights clubs in high school?

Some high schools permit them, and federal law appears to limit the power of schools to prevent them. Under the Equal Access Act of 1984, a national law, if a public high school receiving federal assistance permits any student group to meet after hours on matters outside the regular curriculum, it can't forbid any other group from forming because of its religious, political, or philosophical beliefs. What this means is that if a school permits any non-curriculum-related groups to organize, it probably can't forbid a gay or lesbian rights club from forming. For more information on gay and lesbian rights see Chapter Fourteen.

RELIGION AND SCHOOL PRAYER

> Congress shall make no law . . . respecting an establishment of religion, or prohibiting free exercise thereof.
> —First Amendment,
> U.S. Constitution

Can public schools prevent students from praying during school hours?

Nobody can prevent anybody from praying.

Can schools set aside a time for students to pray or observe a moment of religious silence?

No. Under the Establishment Clause of the First Amendment (shown above), public schools can't take actions that appears to advance religion. For this reason, giving students a special time during the day to pray or observe a moment of prayerful silence is unconstitutional. On the other hand, public schools may allow students a moment of silent meditation, and many do.

School prayers and Bible readings in school also are prohibited under the Establishment Clause, even if participation is voluntary.

Can religion instructors hold class in a public high school building after hours?

No, even if the school is willing to give *all* religions a chance to hold class in the building.

Can schools release students from school during the day for religion classes?

In fact, yes. Schools may "accommodate" religion by letting students leave school for religious instruction. According to the courts, these "release-time" programs don't advance religion illegally even though they do help students to practice their faith.

Schools may also release students from sex education classes for religious reasons, but only if there are other ways (such as a health class) to satisfy the overall requirements of the class.

Why don't rules limiting religion in public schools violate the First Amendment right to the free exercise of religion?

Because in public schools the rule against government involvement in religion overrides the right of young people to exercise the religion of their choice. (The First Amendment, including the Free Exercise Clause, is shown above.) To permit a student or teacher to practice his or her religion openly in public school would infringe on the personal religious rights of others.

The tension between these two rights has arisen when teachers have tried to promote their religious beliefs in class. For example, a public school teacher in Pennsylvania was dismissed for opening class with the Lord's Prayer and a Bible story. The teacher took the issue to court, arguing that he was dismissed because he had exercised his rights under the Free Exercise Clause. The court upheld the teacher's dismissal, saying his right to practice his religion didn't entitle him to promote his personal beliefs in class.

May student religious groups use public school facilities for meetings?

In the past, student religious groups weren't allowed to meet in public schools—the school would be giving the appearance of advancing religion. But under the federal Equal Access Act of 1984, if a public school permits any student group to meet after hours on matters outside the regular curriculum, it can't forbid any other group from forming for religious, political, or philosophical reasons. This means that if a school permits any non-curriculum-related groups to use its meeting rooms, it can't forbid a religious group from doing the same.

Are prayers at public school graduation ceremonies illegal?

Yes. The Supreme Court surprised many in 1992 by ruling that a high school violated the Establishment Clause when it arranged for a minister to give a short prayer at a high school graduation. In court, the school argued that the students hadn't been forced to participate in a religious event because they could have skipped the ceremony. It also argued that it had sincerely attempted to come up with a nonsectarian prayer.

The Supreme Court rejected these arguments, saying that because each graduate was undoubtedly going to attend graduation, each was also required to participate in the prayer. The school therefore promoted religion in violation of the Establishment Clause.

Are prayers at public school athletic events also forbidden?

The Supreme Court hasn't dealt with this issue, but the high school graduation case discussed earlier probably applies to prayers at athletic events as well.

Can students be punished for refusing to salute the American flag or recite the Pledge of Allegiance at school?

No, because refusing to salute the flag or recite the Pledge of Allegiance are forms of symbolic speech. Punishment by school officials would be a First Amendment violation, whether the reason for the refusal was political or religious. Anyone can also refuse to stand during the Pledge of Allegiance or the "Star Spangled Banner."

DISCIPLINE AND DUE PROCESS

> No State shall ... deprive any person of life, liberty, or property, without due process of law.
>
> —Fourteenth Amendment,
> U.S. Constitution

Do students have a right to be advised of their school's disciplinary rules?

Always. Most school districts require that their schools' disciplinary rules be written out and distributed to each student. This makes sense, because students naturally have a better chance of knowing when they've broken a school rule if they have had an opportunity to read and review it. But whether or not a public school has written rules, school officials can't punish a student for breaking a school rule if the student had no reason to know it existed.

Does a school have to advise students of the punishment for violating a particular rule?

It depends on the offense. When it comes to serious violations, schools need to spell out in advance the types of punishment a student can receive. For less serious violations, schools don't have to specify the range of possible punishments.

Is a student entitled to a school hearing before being punished?

It again depends on the seriousness of the offense. If a student faces suspension or other serious punishment, he or she is always entitled to "due process of law." This is an important concept—every adult and adolescent should know what it means.

What is "due process of law"?

Due process of law, or simply "due process," is the overall process by which a society decides whether someone's legal rights should be taken away. It means that a public body can't punish someone or take away his or her rights without following specific procedures to determine whether the "taking" would be fair. An obvious example of due process is a trial to determine whether a person has committed a crime and whether a particular form of punishment should be imposed.

What does due process mean in the high school setting?

It means that a student can't be seriously punished without being afforded at least an informal hearing to determine whether he or she actually committed the offense. The amount of due process depends on the seriousness of the possible punishment, and therefore the seriousness of the offense.

The Supreme Court established in *Goss v. Lopez* that students as well as adults have due process rights. In this well-known 1975 case, a number of students were suspended after demonstrating at their public high school in Ohio. Their student records were unclear as to why the school took action against them, and none was given a due process hearing either to deny or to explain his or her participation.

The Supreme Court ruled that the Due Process Clause of the Fourteenth Amendment required the school to advise each student in advance that he or she was being suspended. Also, it ruled that the school should have advised each student of the facts supporting his or her suspension and should have provided each at least an informal hearing, with adequate prior notice, either to deny or to defend the charges.

When does due process apply to students?

It applies whenever a student is accused of an act that could result in suspension, expulsion, a lowered grade, or other serious punishment. Due process doesn't mean the student will be found innocent. It simply means that procedures are in place, and are used, to ensure that the school treats its students fairly.

Sometimes states or school districts afford students more due process than is guaranteed under the Constitution. When this happens, the school must follow the state or school district's broader procedures.

What is the difference between suspension and expulsion?

Although school districts or individual schools establish their own time frames for suspensions and expulsions, short-term suspension usually lasts up to ten days. Long-term suspension usually lasts longer and may extend to as long as two semesters.

In an expulsion, the student normally is dismissed from school permanently. Students can be expelled for being violent at school, damaging or stealing either school property or the property of another student, or having drugs or weapons on campus.

How does due process apply to expulsions?

Formal due process procedures are required for expulsion. A student who faces the prospect of being expelled should receive adequate advance notice of the charges and adequate notice of the time, place, and nature of the hearing. The student is entitled to a fair hearing before an impartial person and may be represented at the hearing by an adult, and in some states an attorney.

The student or adult representative should be entitled to introduce evidence, cross-examine the school's witnesses, and receive a written record of the school's decision. The decision always should describe the evidence it relied on in deciding to expel.

These procedures apply to all serious offenses. They should also apply if the school has proposed long-term suspension.

What due process guarantees apply to short-term suspensions?

Short-term suspensions require less due process than expulsions and long-term suspensions. A student who faces short-term suspension has a right to oral notice of the offense, an explanation of the evidence the decision maker plans to rely on, and a chance to disprove the charges. Advance notice of the school's intent to impose a short-term suspension can be shorter than for situations that could result in expulsion or long-term suspension. Cross-examination of witnesses usually isn't allowed, and the student normally can't be represented by a lawyer.

Do students have due process rights whenever they get in trouble at school?

No. Due process is for serious school violations that may have serious consequences—for violations that could deprive a student of a valuable right and be a blot on his or her record. But, as stated, a school board may permit students to be heard on disciplinary matters that federal or state law doesn't consider serious enough for due process. School authorities should always advise the students of the types of offenses meriting due process in addition to those that could result in suspension or expulsion.

How can a student find out about the types of offenses that merit due process? How can a student find out about the school's due process procedures?

Most high schools give students a handbook explaining the school district's disciplinary rules and its due process procedures. If no such handbook exists, the student should ask a teacher or school administrator for more information on the subject.

Can a student be suspended or otherwise disciplined for an off-campus activity?

Only if school officials believe the student will pose a serious danger to other students. For example, a serious criminal charge, including a drug-related offense, can be the basis for suspension. Because suspension means that the student might be deprived of a valuable right, punishment for an off-campus activity can only occur after the student has been afforded a full due process hearing.

If a student is arrested, can he or she be suspended or expelled from school before trial?

Not for that reason alone. As Chapter Twelve explains, an arrest is simply a police officer's reasoned belief that a person has committed a crime or is in the process of committing one. But an act that results in a student's arrest can also be a school violation, and when this happens, the school can hold its own due process hearing on the offense.

Here an important concept applies. The amount of evidence needed to punish a student for a school offense is less than the amount needed to convict the student for the same offense in juvenile court. As a matter of constitutional law, to convict and sentence a person for committing a crime, the state must prove its charges "beyond a reasonable doubt." However, as in a noncriminal or "civil" case, in order to impose punishment the school only needs to prove it is "more likely than not" that the student violated a certain school rule. Its "burden of proof" is lower because the school is only punishing the student for breaking an internal rule, not a public law.

If the school meets its burden of proof at the school hearing, it can punish the student before his or her courtroom trial. In addition, the court may take the school's decision into account in reaching its own decision.

In each situation the student should be represented by a lawyer at both the disciplinary hearing and the trial.

Students can't be punished at school for the criminal acts of parents, relatives, or friends.

If a student gets in serious trouble at school, is he or she entitled to receive the *Miranda* warning from school officials?

No. Only the police give the *Miranda* warning. They recite its famous lines to persons who have been placed under arrest. As explained in Chapter Twelve, the *Miranda* warning advises "arrestees" that they have a right to remain silent, that anything they say to the police may be held against them, and that they are entitled to the services of an attorney.

School officials don't have the power to arrest under state law, so they can't give the *Miranda* warning. For more about arrests and *Miranda* see Chapter Twelve, "Teens and Crime."

If a student is found guilty of a school offense, can the school impose any punishment it wants?

No, although schools have extensive power when it comes to meting out punishment. On the other hand, courts will overturn a form of punishment that is too severe—punishment that is "arbitrary, capricious, or oppressive."

Without a due process hearing, can a student be forbidden to participate in extracurricular activities as punishment for a school offense?

No. The right to participate in extracurricular activities is valuable enough to merit a due process hearing.

Can a student appeal a disciplinary decision?

Yes, provided the offense merited due process. For example, a school's decision to suspend or expel a student can always be appealed.

How do appeals work?

A student's appeal (or an appeal by the student's parents) usually goes directly to the principal. It must be in writing. The principal must conduct an appeal hearing within a short time (usually within five school days) and is required to rule on the appeal shortly after the hearing. The decision can be appealed to the school superintendent, who must also provide a hearing and make a decision in a prescribed number of days.

If the "appellant" is dissatisfied with the decision of the superintendent, an appeal can be taken to the school board. An appeals hearing before the school board is always more formal.

If the appellant receives an "adverse" decision at every stage of the hearing process, the entire matter can be taken to federal or state court.

Any student who receives an adverse decision from the school principal should receive a written explanation of the school's rules and procedures for appealing. At every stage of the appeal process, the school's decision should be in writing.

CORPORAL PUNISHMENT

What is corporal punishment? Do school officials have a legal right to inflict corporal punishment on students?

Corporal punishment is any type of punishment directed toward a person's body. Striking a student is the most obvious example. The federal Constitution doesn't forbid corporal punishment in public schools, although sometimes it is prohibited by state law or a school rule. Without a provision ruling it out, a school district may approve its use. The laws of many states actually authorize corporal punishment, and when this happens a school board is powerless to forbid it.

Students usually aren't entitled to a due process hearing before corporal punishment is inflicted. The Supreme Court has stated that a school suspension is more serious than corporal punishment, which is why a student is entitled to due process before being suspended but not before receiving bodily punishment.

Even so, a student's constitutional due process rights were violated in a case in which his injuries resulted in ten days' hospitalization, and in another in which a student was injured after a teacher tied him to a desk. In both cases the school intruded on the student's personal privacy to the extent of committing a "taking" without due process of law.

Schools should rule out corporal punishment as a way to deal with problems. Clearly, teachers should exhaust all other means of disciplining a student before resorting to it. If corporal punishment is used, it should be witnessed by a second school official, and in addition, parents should receive a written explanation of the nature of the punishment and a thorough explanation of why it was used.

SCHOOL SEARCHES

> The right of the people to be secure in their persons, houses, papers, and effects, against unreasonable searches and seizures, shall not be violated, and no Warrants shall issue, but upon probable cause, supported by Oath or affirmation, and particularly describing the place to be searched, and the persons or things to be seized.
>
> —Fourth Amendment,
> U.S. Constitution

May school authorities legally search a student's clothing, backpack, gym bag, or purse?

In certain circumstances, yes, although such searches *do* intrude on students' privacy. To search a student legally, two requirements must be met. First, there must be reasonable grounds for suspecting the search will turn up evidence that the student broke the law or a school rule. Second, the search can't intrude on the student's privacy more than is needed to carry out the purpose of the search.

This is a constitutional test, established in 1985 in the Supreme Court case of *New Jersey v. T.L.O.* The basis of the test is "reasonable suspicion." If the search isn't based on reasonable suspicion, it violates the Search and Seizure Clause of the Fourth Amendment (shown earlier).

In the *T.L.O.* case a female student's purse was searched by her high school principal after she was caught smoking in a rest room. As the principal was removing a pack of cigarettes from her purse, he saw a package of rolling papers. He searched further and found some marijuana, a pipe, some empty plastic bags, a number of dollar bills, a list of students who apparently owed the student money, and two letters suggesting she might be selling drugs.

The Supreme Court ruled that because the school had "reasonable suspicion," the student's privacy rights hadn't been violated. This made the search legal. It said that although students do have privacy rights, these rights must be balanced against the need of their schools to maintain order. According to the Supreme Court, this special balance is achieved by applying the "reasonable suspicion test" to school searches.

What does "reasonable suspicion" really mean?

Reasonable suspicion exists when the school's suspicion is based on the circumstances surrounding the offense, the adequacy of the evidence, the source of the information, and the student's age, gender, and school records. In all cases the school's suspicion must be based on more than a mere hunch.

Consider the following example. A student's locker was searched for alcohol after a fellow student tipped off a school official. The search turned up evidence of drug use, but no alcohol. The state appeals court determined that the evidence was obtained upon reasonable suspicion even though the school officials weren't searching for drugs. Since the search was legal, the school could discipline the student for having drug paraphernalia on school grounds.

Does this mean school officials can legally search lockers and desks?

Yes. Students are said to share control over their lockers and desks with school officials, so their privacy rights with respect to them are lower. Even so, reasonable suspicion usually is needed for a locker or desk search. Under the laws of some states, lockers and desks may be searched at any time and for any reason, which means that students in these states have no privacy rights in desks and lockers whatsoever.

Can school officials use improperly obtained evidence against a student in a school disciplinary hearing?

In many states, yes. The *T.L.O.* case didn't go so far as to make the use of improperly obtained evidence illegal.

Most high school districts have explicit rules in their student handbooks about desk and locker searches, but not always. Whether or not published rules exist, a student should never keep anything in a locker or desk that he or she doesn't want someone else to see.

See Chapter Twelve for information about the legal limits on the use of evidence obtained in an illegal search.

Can school officials conduct strip searches?

In theory, yes, although a strip search conducted on school property is a very serious matter. As a rule, the more intrusive the search, the more individual suspicion is needed to justify it. School officials may only need reasonable suspicion to ask a student to empty his or her pockets, but they would find it almost impossible to justify a body search without full "probable cause" to believe that the student has evidence on his or her person that a law or school rule has been broken.

Body searches should be left to the police. For more about probable cause see Chapter Twelve, "Teens and Crime."

Are mass searches of students legal?

No, because under the reasonable suspicion test for searches the school's suspicion must always relate to a particular individual. In one case, school authorities did not have individual suspicion and therefore made unreasonable searches violating the Search and Seizure Clause of the Fourth Amendment, when they inspected each student's luggage as a condition of going on a school-sponsored field trip. In another case, strip searches of each member of a class to discover who stole three dollars were also made without reasonable suspicion.

Can a school require the entire student body or an entire class to take blood or urine tests to check for drug use?

No. Making students submit to urine or blood tests without individual suspicion puts all of their privacy rights in jeopardy. In a 1985 case a New Jersey high school made each student submit to a urine test for 26 different drugs. When the matter went to court on a Fourth Amendment argument, the judge ruled that the school had conducted "searches" without reasonable suspicion, which meant the tests were illegal.

Can an individual student be required to take a urine test if the school suspects he or she has been using drugs?

Yes, provided the student is allowed to give the urine sample in the privacy of a bathroom stall. Drug testing programs for high school athletes are also legal.

WEAPONS

What happens if a student brings a gun or other weapon to school?

Carrying a weapon is always against school policy. The consequences of having a weapon on school property can range from short-term suspension to automatic and permanent expulsion from the school district.

Schools can require students to pass through a metal detector before entering the school building and may legally "stop and frisk" a student who appears to be concealing a weapon. For more about stop-and-frisk searches see Chapter Twelve, "Teens and Crime."

In school weapons cases, as in all serious disciplinary matters at school, the student is entitled to a due process hearing before being suspended, expelled, or otherwise punished.

STUDENTS AND THE POLICE

Can the police question students on school property?

Police have the right to question students anywhere, and school officials don't have the power to prevent it. However, schools can legally require the police to give advance notice to a principal or teacher of their intent to question a student or interrupt class.

In fact, school authorities usually cooperate with police officers when it comes to student questioning. Students can be taken from school by the police for questioning and can be arrested on school grounds. The arrest must be based on probable cause to believe that a crime has been committed or is being committed and that the "arrestee" is the one who committed or is committing it.

If the police begin questioning a student, what should the student do?

Students aren't required to answer police questions. If a student is the target of police questioning, the best thing to do is remain silent, except to give a name and address. The student's parents should be called—the student should request permission to call a parent right away. If the student is placed under arrest, he or she has a constitutional right to contact a lawyer, but should say nothing to either the police or any school official until both a parent and a lawyer arrive.

School officials shouldn't discourage a student from calling a parent or lawyer and should never encourage a student to answer police questions. Not only would doing so put the school in a bad light, it might also make the student's confession inadmissible in court. School officials should always leave such matters to the police and the student's attorney.

What if the student thinks he or she can answer police questions competently?

The student should still remain silent. Young people often think they can clear up problems on their own by answering questions or trying to explain what happened. Usually they are wrong. Their most carefully phrased explanations often damage their case rather than help it. Never forget that the *Miranda* warning, discussed in Chapter Twelve, reminds every criminal suspect, including teens, that "anything you say may be used against you."

Can the police personally search a student on school property?

They can, but they need more than reasonable suspicion to do so. To conduct a personal search, the police must have probable cause to believe a crime has been committed or is being committed, and that the student committed or is committing it. The same rule applies to police searches of lockers and desks. (Some courts have ruled that if the police are simply assisting school officials in a search, they don't need full probable cause.) If the police turn up evidence of a criminal act, it can be used in court.

For more about probable cause see Chapter Twelve, "Teens and Crime."

Can student property that school officials find in a search be used in a criminal investigation?

School officials are always free to turn over evidence of a crime. In some states, even evidence uncovered in an illegal school search can be used in a later criminal investigation.

SPORTS

> No state shall deny to any person within its jurisdiction the equal protection of the laws.
>
> —Fourteenth Amendment,
> U.S. Constitution

Are all-male and all-female high school athletic teams ever illegal?

Yes. If the school doesn't have a separate-sex team for a sport that doesn't involve bodily contact, schools can't prohibit women students from participating, or from at least trying out. Track, ski, golf, and tennis are examples of such sports.

Does this mean that separate-sex teams for noncontact sports can be legal?

Yes.

Can women students play contact sports such as football or basketball on the same team as the men?

The answer to this question currently is unclear. Courts in a number of states have ruled that when it comes to contact sports, if no separate-sex team exists and the women can effectively compete against men, they can't be prohibited from playing unless doing so places their health and safety at risk. But if all the men who try out for a contact sport are better than all the women, the women who don't make the team haven't been discriminated against on the basis of gender.

A New York court recently faced the question of whether a woman student could try out for junior varsity football. It ruled that the school district failed to prove that prohibiting mixed competition serves any important objective. Although the school claimed the policy was needed to protect the health and safety of women students, its argument failed because no woman athlete was given the chance to prove that she was as fit as, or more fit than, the weakest man on the team.

If the women shouldn't be competing in mixed play because of health or safety risks, a separate-sex team must be formed. The women's team must be equal to the men's team in terms of funding, available facilities, and coaching staff.

Can a woman be required to play on a women's team that plays a contact sport if she is as good as the men?

Yes, for a practical reason, which is that separate-sex teams increase total participation in high school sports, especially the participation of women.

Can a man be prevented from playing on a women's sports team?

Yes. Rules preventing discrimination in high school sports work in favor of students who want more physical challenge, not less.

TESTING

Is tracking legal?

Tracking—placing students in different classes, usually on the basis of test scores—has been challenged in the courts as unfair to minorities.

The challenges claim that the tests are "culturally biased," which means that when they are drafted by members of a particular group, students from that group too often are the highest scorers. If it is proved that the tests are biased and therefore discriminate against minorities, the tracking system discriminates illegally.

A California court recently ruled that too many black students were placed in special education classes after the results of an IQ test were used to place them. On the basis of its finding, the court said the school's tracking system was discriminatory, and therefore illegal.

Courts in at least two states have ruled that after forced school desegregation is ordered, schools can't group minorities in lower tracks until the disadvantages of their earlier discriminatory education have been corrected. Some courts have ruled that a minority student can't be put into a special class without first receiving a due process hearing.

Is competency testing discriminatory?

It can be. Minimum competency tests, or "MCTs," are used by many schools to decide whether a student should pass to a higher grade or be awarded a diploma. Competency tests can be discriminatory if they are introduced into a school when, because earlier public schooling was inadequate, minority students can't make passing grades. When this has happened, students have been permitted to advance to the next grade without taking the test.

States with MCTs often build in a series of required skills tests in earlier grades and make schools provide remedial help to students who don't pass. On the basis of these early tests, schools are able to develop improvement plans for students who are behind, focusing on areas where a particular student needs special help.

What happens if a student is denied a high school diploma because he or she can't pass the school's competency tests?

If the tests aren't discriminatory, the student would have to study for a graduate equivalency degree, or "GED." For more about GED tests, see the discussion at the beginning of this chapter.

OTHER DISCRIMINATION ISSUES

Are male-only or female-only classes still permitted in public high schools?

No. Except for gym, classes that used to be offered only to male students can no longer be off-limits to females, and vice versa. Women can't be denied the chance to take a class in auto mechanics, and men can't be prohibited from enrolling in a course in secretarial skills or home economics. Student clubs that limit their membership to one gender or the other also are illegal.

Do illegal aliens have a right to attend public high school in America?

Yes. They have just as much right to attend public high school as native born young people. To attend school, an illegal alien just needs to live within the school's geographic boundaries.

Are schools required to offer classes in a student's native language if the student can't understand English?

No. Bilingual education—classes taught in one's own language while the same classes are taught in English—isn't a legal right. However, public schools must at least provide English language classes for non-English-speaking students to bring down obvious language barriers. Bilingual education is one of many options under federal law that a school can use to educate limited-English proficiency or "LEP" students.

States with high numbers of non-English-speaking students have broad programs to eliminate language barriers in public schools.

Are handicapped students entitled to special benefits at school?

Yes, if they need them. Under important federal laws, public schools must provide for students who, because of a disability, can't learn their lessons through regular teaching methods. Each handicapped student must have a "free appropriate public education," given his or her special needs. States must establish programs to identify handicapped students and use nondiscriminatory tests to determine their achievement levels. If schools discriminate, they risk losing financial assistance from the federal government.

Can handicapped students always take classes with nonhandicapped students?

Handicapped students must be integrated with nonhandicapped students as much as possible, at the same time that their special needs are being provided for. This is called "mainstreaming."

To mainstream a student, a teacher may need special learning materials, speech services either in or out of the classroom, or maybe an aide to take care of the student's unique physical needs. Handicapped students include those with hearing problems, speech problems, and emotional disturbances, for example.

What happens if a handicapped student doesn't adapt to mainstreaming?

He or she usually is transferred from regular classes. But the student is still entitled to a "free and appropriate education"—at a special school or perhaps at home.

Are students with human immunodeficiency virus/acquired immunodeficiency syndrome (HIV/AIDS) considered handicapped under these special laws?

Courts in a number of states have ruled that HIV/AIDS students must be regarded as handicapped under the federal laws noted previously. In these states, HIV/AIDS students can't be discriminated against at school because of their condition. Students with hepatitis B also are protected.

STUDENT RECORDS

Can parents see their children's high school records? Can high school students see their own records?

The answer to the first question is yes. Under federal law, parents must be able to review their children's school records and transcripts. As to the second question, students may see their records when they reach age 18, although schools may elect to allow underage students to view them.

Public schools can't give out student records without parental consent, and state laws often provide additional safeguards to keep student records private. These laws often apply to student records in private schools as well.

Can a student do anything about damaging information in his or her student file?

Sometimes. Negative information in a student file shouldn't necessarily be removed or changed. Schools have a duty to record information about students and provide information to colleges and technical schools when students apply to them for admission.

But school records shouldn't be gossip columns. To ensure that a school keeps fair and accurate records, a good rule of thumb would be for parents to inspect their children's records once a year. If information in a student file is incorrect, misleading, petty, or vicious, the parents should ask the school to remove or correct it. If the school decides not to take action on the request, the parents are entitled to a due process hearing. If the school wins, the parents can appeal the decision through the appeal process described earlier.

Can outsiders such as the police see student records?

Law enforcement officials can't view a young person's academic file simply on request, although student records can be demanded or "subpoenaed" by a court. In addition, parents have the power to authorize persons such as relatives, lawyers, guardians, or psychologists to review their children's records.

PRIVATE SCHOOLS

Are private schools subject to state education laws?

To a great extent, yes. State laws regarding high school attendance, student health, and teacher certification apply to private as well as public schools.

Do students in private schools have the same kind of constitutional rights as public high school students?

No. Due process under the federal Constitution only protects students in public schools—only when "state action" is involved. Operating a private school is not a type of state action, so due process isn't a constitutional right. However, state constitutions, state laws, and private school policies sometimes grant due process rights to students in private schools.

Can a private school discriminate on the basis of race or gender?

A private school may not deny admission on the basis of race, gender, or nationality. If it does, it loses its tax-exempt status, which means it forfeits important tax advantages of operating as a nonprofit organization under the federal tax laws.

Can a private school discriminate on the basis of a handicap?

Again, if a private school receives federal funds for a particular program (and many do), it may not discriminate on the basis of a handicap while administering it.

FOR FURTHER READING

In General

McCarthy, Martha M., and Nelda H. Cambron-McCabe. *Public School Law: Teachers' and Students' Rights.* 3rd ed. Needham Heights, Massachusetts: Allyn and Bacon, 1992.

Meltzer, Milton. *The Bill of Rights: How We Got It and What It Means.* New York: Thomas Y. Crowell, 1992.

Price, Janet R., Alan H. Levine, and Eve Cary. *The Rights of Students: The Basic ACLU Guide to Student's Rights.* 3rd ed. Carbondale: Southern Illinois University Press, 1988.

Salomone, Rosemary C. *Equal Education Under Law.* New York: St. Martin's Press, 1986.

Starr, Isidore. *Justice: Due Process of Law.* St. Paul, Minnesota: West Publishing, 1981.

First Amendment Issues

Evans, J. Edward. *Freedom of Speech.* Minneapolis: Lerner Publications, 1990.

Gora, Joel M. *The Right to Protest: The Basic ACLU Guide to Free Expression.* Carbondale: Southern Illinois University Press, 1991.

Lieberman, Jethro. *Free Speech, Free Press, and the Law.* New York: Lothrop, Lee and Shepard, 1980.

Mayer, Michael F. *What You Should Know About Libel and Slander: Famous and Infamous Cases of Defamation.* New York: Arco, 1968.

Rogers, Donald J. *Press Versus Government.* New York: Julian Messner, 1986.

Sherrow, Victoria. *Separation of Church and State.* New York: Franklin Watts, 1992.

Students with Disabilities

DuBow, Sy, et al. *Legal Rights of Hearing Impaired People.* 3rd ed. Washington, D.C.: Gallaudet College Press, 1986.

Hoffa, Helynn, and Gary Morgan. *Yes You Can: A Helpbook for the Physically Disabled.* New York: Pharos Books, 1990.

Johnson, Mary, ed. *People with Disabilities Explain It All for You.* Louisville: The Avocado Press, 1992.

Ordover, Eileen L., and Kathleen B. Boundy. *Educational Rights of Children with Disabilities.* Cambridge, Massachusetts: Center for Law and Education, 1991.

Rothstein, Laura F. *Disabilities and the Law.* Colorado Springs, Colorado: Shepard's/McGraw-Hill, 1992.

Other School Issues

Myers, Gail Anderson. *A World of Sports for Girls*. Philadelphia: The West-minster Press, 1981.

Newton, David E. *Gun Control: An Issue for the Nineties*. Hillside, New Jersey: Enslow Publishers, 1992.

— 3 —

At Home

How much authority do parents have over their children?

Parents have the right to make decisions about what their children eat, wear, read, and watch on TV. They have the right to determine where their children will attend school and what kind of religious training they receive. Parents have broad authority to decide how to discipline a minor child. Within certain limits, they can use corporal punishment.

This chapter takes up the rights of young people at home, and the extent of their parents' authority.

TEENS, PARENTS, AND MONEY

Does a teen have a right to an allowance?

No. But parents are responsible for a minor child's support until the child reaches the age of majority, and children have a corresponding right to be taken care of.

Does a minor have a legal right to have a part-time or summer job?

No. Parents can legally forbid an unemancipated teen to work for pay outside the home. (Emancipation is discussed in Chapter Five, "On Your Own.")

Are minors legally entitled to keep the money they earn?

Not necessarily. Because parents are entitled to the services of their children, in most states they have a legal right to their children's income. If this idea seems outdated or even wrong, it is because it evolved when children were considered a type of property—when each child was regarded as another hand on the farm. If the minor was earning money instead of contributing to the upkeep of the household, his or her earnings would be the parent's pay for providing care and shelter.

Many states now have laws permitting minors to keep their earnings unless the parents notify the employer that they want to claim the earnings separately. When this happens, the employer must pay the parents, and the parents must declare the earnings on their own tax returns.

Is there any way a minor can prevent a parent from taking his or her earnings?

Yes. Parents can agree, orally or in writing, that they have no claim to their child's earnings. Or the minor's right to his or her separate earnings can be understood, although not expressly stated. Nowadays this is almost always what happens.

Are teenage children legally required to work in order to help support the family?

No. Parents are required to support their family without assistance from their children. But nothing prevents parents from requiring a teenage child to work at a part-time job. If the teen refuses to look for one, nothing in the law prohibits parents from punishing the teen in a manner that doesn't constitute abuse or neglect.

DISCIPLINE

Can a parent legally throw a teen out of the house?

No. Parents have a legal responsibility to provide for their minor children, including hard-to-handle teens. They must give each child adequate food, shelter, clothing, schooling, and medical care. Parents may never discipline a minor child in a manner that constitutes physical, sexual, or psychological abuse or use neglect as a form of punishment. In other words, teens have a right to live at home.

If parents don't live up to their responsibilities—if, for example, they force a child to live on the streets—the state can enforce the teen's

Parents come in every imaginable variety. Photo: Hal Martin Fogel. Reprinted with permission.

rights in "abandonment" proceedings in family court. (Abandonment is discussed later in this chapter.)

What should a minor do if his or her parents' discipline methods are obviously too harsh?

Discuss the matter with a teacher, minister, medical person, or adult friend, or call the state child protective agency. Action should be taken immediately.

Can parents legally prevent a child from calling the police in a family violence situation?

No. Anyone can call the police when violence erupts, although sometimes it's impossible to get to the phone before somebody gets hurt. To prevent injury and to subdue the violent family member, the police should always be called—by another family member or someone outside the family such as a neighbor or relative.

For more information about abuse and neglect at the hands of parents see Chapter Ten, "Your Right to Be Healthy and Safe from Abuse."

If a minor's parents are divorced, who is legally responsible for the minor's discipline?

Both parents remain responsible. However, unless the parents have "joint custody," day-to-day decisions regarding the child are made by the custodial parent. With joint custody, the parents continue to share these responsibilities.

For more about the rights of young persons when parents split up, see Chapter Seven, "If Your Parents Divorce."

If a minor's parents have never married, which parent is responsible for the minor's discipline?

Both are, in every state.

Are grandparents or brothers and sisters ever legally responsible for a minor?

Only if the minor's grandparents or his or her "siblings" have agreed to be responsible. This often happens when a minor's parents are elderly.

TOBACCO

At what age can teens buy tobacco products—cigarettes, chewing tobacco, and snuff?

In most states a person must be age 18 to buy any form of tobacco. Although some states prohibit minors from using tobacco in public places, it usually isn't illegal for a minor just to possess or use it.

ADULT BOOKS AND ADULT MOVIES

Why aren't laws prohibiting the sale of pornography to minors a violation of the First Amendment?
Courts have said that society has a strong interest in preventing children from seeing materials that primarily appeal to "shameful or morbid interests." In 1968 the Supreme Court upheld a New York law prohibiting the sale of pornographic materials to persons under age 17, even though some of the materials reviewed in the case weren't considered obscene for adults. The Supreme Court said that although there is no sure way to prove that a minor's exposure to pornography is harmful, New York could assume that such a link exists.

Every state controls the sale of "porn" to minors. Furthermore, each state prohibits the production and sale of child pornography, which is visual or printed material that depicts explicit sexual conduct involving children. This type of pornography is often called "kiddie porn." (Some states even make viewing child pornography illegal.)

Can minors buy or rent obscene videos?
States and cities can legally prohibit this, also.

For more about First Amendment rights under the federal Constitution see Chapter Two, "At School."

Can a minor go to an X-rated movie?
Communities usually have laws prohibiting minors from attending X-rated films, but these laws aren't always vigorously enforced. Furthermore, a theatre will rarely turn away a minor because a film is violent or sexually explicit but not X-rated. Parents do, however, have the power to forbid their children to go to all types of movies under their authority as parents.

THE AGE OF MAJORITY

What is meant by the term "the age of majority"?
It is the age at which a person legally becomes an adult. The age of majority is 18 in every state except Alabama, Mississippi, Nebraska, and Wyoming.[1]

When a young person reaches the age of majority, does all parental authority end?

Yes, but this doesn't mean the young person is entitled to all the rights of adulthood. For example, it is illegal in most states to purchase or drink alcoholic beverages before age 21, regardless of the state's legislated age of majority. In addition, states have the power to set a higher legal age for special activities such as voting in local elections and serving on a jury.

What rights does a young person gain at the age of majority?

The right to work at almost any job, enlist in the armed forces without parental consent, enter into all types of contracts, consent to all types of health care, and buy adult books. On the other hand, at the age of majority a minor no longer is subject to the ''jurisdiction'' of the juvenile court.

Can parents' legal responsibilities toward their children extend beyond the age of majority?

Yes, but these extended responsibilities are usually created by divorce courts and not public laws. In a recent Ohio case a divorce court made a well-to-do father pay for his 19-year-old son's $17,000 education at a local technical school. The court interpreted the divorce decree to require this, even though the decree said the father had to pay only for his son's *college* education.

Young people are rarely able to force well-to-do parents to pay for college when a divorce decree doesn't order it. In part this is because young persons usually can't afford lawyers.

LEGAL GUARDIANS

If parents can't care for their minor children, who helps out?

Usually it depends on factors such as the age of the children and the parents' financial worth. If the parents don't have many investments or much in savings, the children are often cared for by relatives, particularly if the children are older.

If a child is young or needs special care, a family court may appoint a ''legal guardian'' to make decisions about the child's upbringing. Decisions about the minor's education and medical care would also be made by the guardian, except in cases in which the parents still can. But the fact that a guardian has been appointed doesn't relieve the parents of their legal duty of support.

Guardians can also be appointed for minors whose parents have died, can't be found, or don't reside with the child for some other reason.

Does a minor have to obey a guardian?
Yes, unless the guardian asks the minor to do something illegal. The specific powers of legal guardians are always spelled out in state law.

How long does a guardianship last?
Until the minor reaches the age of majority, unless the court believes it should continue longer. A guardianship might be extended beyond the age of majority if, for example, the young person can't manage in the adult world because of a physical or mental disability.

Can a teen arrange for an elderly parent's medical care?
No. As a rule, a doctor can't treat a sick or injured person without his or her consent. If a parent is unable to consent to treatment, only a spouse or adult child legally may do so. However, nothing prevents a minor from calling an emergency medical team to help a sick or injured parent, and nothing prevents a minor from arranging for a parent to be taken to the emergency room for immediate care.

If a person, young or old, needs emergency treatment, that person's consent is legally *presumed.* This is why doctors and medics may give treatment in an emergency without obtaining consent from anyone.

TERMINATION OF PARENTS' RIGHTS

In cases of serious abuse or neglect, can parental rights be terminated completely?
Yes, although to do so, the situation at home must be virtually hopeless. Parental rights can only be terminated if a parent has abandoned or consistently abused a minor child.

What is abandonment?
It is a continuous failure to accept and perform parental responsibilities. Examples of abandonment include failing to keep in contact with a minor child, leaving a child with another person for a long time for no good reason, failing to provide support for a child, and ignoring a child in foster care.

Will a court only terminate parental rights when the child is an infant?

No. It often happens in the case of teens.

Why might a state seek to terminate parental rights in some cases but not others?

Because the focus of a parental rights case is not just a parent's current inability to care for a child, but whether the parent will be able to fulfill his or her obligations in the years ahead.

Can the state seek to terminate the parental rights of one parent but not the other?

Yes. This happens often.

What must the state prove in order to terminate parental rights?

It must prove that the parent repeatedly abused, continuously neglected, or intentionally abandoned a child or is unable to care for a child for some other reason. It must also show that terminating parental rights is in the minor's best interests.

Obviously, a state can only take away a child in extreme cases. Although states can take custody of a minor the first time abuse or neglect occurs at home, revoking parental rights of one or both parents after a first incident would be unusual. (In many states it would actually be illegal.) For more about the circumstances in which the state can assume custody over a minor, see Chapter Ten.

Does the state have to give assistance to a family before it can terminate parental rights?

Usually. To terminate parental rights, a child protective agency must prove to the family court that counseling was offered to the parent but that it was refused or didn't prove worthwhile. Some states skip this requirement if counseling would obviously be a waste of time.

A family court in California recently terminated a couple's parental rights after ruling that a young boy's parents had failed to improve sanitary conditions in their home. The boy needed to avoid cigarette smoke and drafts because he had serious asthma. His parents' house was filthy: dirty dishes were strewn all over, and garbage would pile up in the back yard. The parents didn't cooperate with a social worker who tried to teach them about housekeeping and hygiene, and they continued to smoke heavily around their son. After a number of months the court terminated their parental rights altogether.

In most states a court will terminate parental rights only if the parent already has been separated from the child for six months to one year. Often the minor will have been living with foster parents. (For more about foster care see Chapter Ten, "Your Right to Be Healthy and Safe From Abuse.")

Is a minor entitled to a lawyer in a parental rights case? Would the minor's lawyer be someone other than the parent's lawyer?

In most states a minor will have a lawyer, who will be someone other than the parent's lawyer. The lawyer will be court-appointed and serve at public expense. The minor has a right to separate representation because his or her position in the case might be quite different from the parent's.

Does a parent have any constitutional rights in a parental rights case?

Yes. Parental rights can be terminated only if "due process of law" has been provided—after a full hearing in family court. The parent must receive adequate notice of the hearing so he or she will have time to prepare a case opposing the termination. For more about due process see Chapter Two.

Can parents give up parental rights voluntarily?

Yes. This actually is the way parental rights are most often terminated. When a minor child is placed for adoption, the child's "birth parents" already will have agreed to give up parental rights.

Can parental rights be terminated because the parents don't have enough money—are too "indigent"—to raise the child?

The rights of indigent parents can be terminated only if there is a reason besides poverty to justify terminating their rights. Such a reason might be abandonment or consistent abuse. Failure to support a minor child will rarely be the sole reason for terminating parental rights, especially if the parent and child are close.

Can parental rights be terminated because the parent has been convicted of a serious crime?

Yes. Some states also permit parental rights to be terminated if a parent has been convicted in adult court of "debauchery" or "fornication" or if the parent has been involved in prostitution.

Can parental rights be terminated because a parent is mentally ill or has some other emotional disability?

In some states, yes, but only if the mental problem is so serious that the parent is unable to care for the child. These days, many mental disorders (even grave ones such as schizophrenia) can be treated with medications and therapy. For this reason, a family court's ruling that a parent is mentally disabled, without strong proof that he or she isn't fit to parent, won't be sufficient to terminate parental rights.

Can the parent-child relationship be terminated because the minor child would be better off in another situation such as a calmer household with fewer problems?

This is a tough question. Family courts don't exist to find perfect homes for minors—their purpose has always been to protect young persons in danger. Even so, courts in some states have considered using the child's "best interests" as the only basis for terminating parental rights.

When this approach is used, the state doesn't have to show that a parent committed a serious wrong such as child abuse or abandonment to terminate rights. It has to prove only that the child would be better off in other circumstances.

Earlier Supreme Court decisions suggest that states may violate the federal Constitution if they allow parental rights to be terminated without proof that the parents truly are unfit. Before long, the Supreme Court may have to decide whether parental rights can be lawfully terminated simply because the child's "best interests" aren't being served.

OTHER FAMILY ISSUES

Can a minor carry or use a firearm or other weapon with parental consent? Without parental consent?

The answer to the first question is a qualified yes. Federal, state, and local laws govern the possession and use of weapons. Federal law prohibits the sale of handguns to persons under age 21, and the sale of rifles and shotguns to persons under age 18. A minor can receive a handgun as a gift but can't legally buy ammunition until age 21.

States and cities regulate weapons within their borders, and the scope of their laws always includes the possession and use of firearms by young people. In certain states a minor can carry a handgun with written permission from a parent. But even in these states, if a law forbids weapons in certain places such as a retail store or public auditorium, or if a high school forbids weapons on school grounds, parental permission will never make the weapon legal.

Can a minor legally take illegal drugs at home or elsewhere with parental permission?

Never.

NOTE

1. In Alabama, Nebraska, and Wyoming, the age of majority is 19. In Mississippi it is 21.

FOR FURTHER READING

In General

Berry, James R. *Kids on the Run: The Stories of Seven Teenage Runaways.* New York: Four Winds Press, 1978.

Gilbert, Sara. *Trouble at Home.* New York: Lothrop, Lee and Shepard Books, 1981.

Kranyik, Margery A., and Karen Silverman. *Growing Up Is . . . . : Coping with Adult Problems When You're Still a Kid.* Whitehall, Virginia: Betterway Publications, 1985.

Kurland, Morton L. *Coping with Family Violence.* New York: The Rosen Publishing Group, 1990.

Reaves, John, and James B. Austin. *How to Find Help for a Troubled Kid: A Parent's Guide to Programs and Services for Adolescents.* New York: Henry Holt, 1990.

Stavsky, Lois, and I. E. Mozeson. *The Place I Call Home: Voices and Faces of Homeless Teens.* New York: Shapolsky Publishers, 1990.

Wolf, Anthony E. *Get Out of My Life: A Parent's Guide to the New Teenager.* New York: The Noonday Press, 1991.

Tobacco and Adult Books

Gorman, Carol. *Pornography.* New York: Franklin Watts, 1988.

Moretti, Daniel S. *Obscenity and Pornography: The Law Under the First Amendment.* Dobbs Ferry, New York: Oceana Publications, 1984.

Hyde, Margaret O. *Know About Smoking.* New York: Franklin Watts, 1983.

Sonnett, Sherry. *Smoking.* New York: Franklin Watts, 1977.

Legal Guardians

Koff, Gail J. *Guide to Wills and Estates.* New York: Henry Holt, 1991.

Landau, Elaine. *Growing Old in America.* New York: Julian Messner, 1985.

Larsen, David C. *Who Gets What When You Go?* New York: Random House, 1982.

MacKay, Richard V. *The Law of Guardianships.* 3rd ed. Dobbs Ferry, New York: Oceana Publications, Inc., 1980.

Silverstone, Barbara, and Helen Hyman. 2nd ed. *You and Your Aging Parent.* New York: Pantheon Books, 1989.

Swisher, Karen, ed. *The Elderly: Opposing Viewpoints.* San Diego: The Greenhaven Press, 1990.

— 4 —

On the Job

TEENS AND THE JOB MARKET

At what age can a young person work outside the home?

It depends on the type of work. At age 18, any person can be employed at any job. However, federal and state child labor laws regulate the types of work that persons under 18 can legally perform.

Young people under age 18 can't be hired for work that is hazardous, such as work in mines, steel mills, quarries, foundries, and butcher shops. Working with explosives, dangerous chemicals, radioactive materials, power-driven machinery, and earth-moving equipment is also off limits for those under 18.

Persons under age 16 almost always are prohibited from working in factories unless the job involves office work. Teens between the ages of 14 and 16 are permitted to work only after school, on weekends, and during vacation and aren't allowed to hold jobs that are dangerous or unhealthy. They can do office and sales work, wait on tables, be shelvers and baggers at retail stores, and hold similar positions.

Minors above age 12 (above age 10 in some states) can have newspaper routes and work as golf caddies, but only during nonschool hours. They can also do yard work, babysit, and perform certain types of nonhazardous farm work. As a rule, children under age 12 can't work outside the home, although special child labor laws in each state permit minors of any age to do stage and screen work.

Child workers climbing on a spinning frame to mend broken threads. Bibb Mill, Macon, Georgia, January 1909. *Source:* Hine/ LC LC-USZ62-23944.

Can a minor work full-time?

In most states, minors between 14 and 16 are prohibited from working more than 40 hours per week. Furthermore, this age group can't work for more than 3 hours on school days (4 hours in some states), and more than 8 hours on nonschool days and during the summer.

Minors between the ages of 14 and 16 also are prohibited from working the "graveyard shift"—between 9:30 P.M. and 7:00 A.M. (In some states they can work these hours if school isn't in session the next day.)

Couldn't a teen just lie about his or her age to be hired for a particular job?

No, because job applicants under age 16 (under age 18 in some states) must present an "employment certificate" or other proof of age in order to be hired.

Who issues employment certificates?

If state law requires them, the superintendent of schools usually is the issuer. To obtain an employment certificate, the minor must be able to produce:

1. A statement from the prospective employer describing the type of work;
2. A statement that the minor's parents don't object to the job;
3. A birth certificate or other proof of age; and
4. A statement, signed by a doctor, that the minor is physically fit for the job.

Employment certificates are called "work permits" in some states.

Is it illegal for a minor to work without an employment certificate?

If they are required, yes. In states that require them, an employer can't hire a young person who is unable to produce one.

Who, then, is regulated by child labor laws—the minor or the employer?

The employer. When a federal or state child labor law is violated, the employer commits the offense.

Can the government punish a minor for working without an employment certificate (or for working underage if a certificate isn't required)?

No.

What kinds of jobs don't require an employment certificate?
They aren't needed for farm work, babysitting, yard work, selling newspapers, and golf caddying.

Can an employment certificate be revoked?
Yes, if the minor's job interferes with school work or adversely affects his or her physical or mental health. The school principal usually is the person with the power to revoke.

Does a minor need a Social Security card to work outside the home?
Yes. A person's Social Security card shows his or her lifetime Social Security number. Employers need their employees' Social Security numbers to make advance Social Security payments and income tax deposits to the federal government in their employees' behalf. Employers are legally required to make these payments; this is why they ask for a person's Social Security number at the time of hiring.

Who issues Social Security cards?
The local Social Security Administration office. To obtain a card, call the closest office and ask to be sent a Social Security card application. Fill it out, have a parent sign it, then send it back it with an original copy of your birth certificate and one of the other forms of identification requested on the application. Your Social Security card will arrive in about two weeks.

Can minors who aren't United States citizens legally work in the United States?
It depends on whether they have the proper legal authorization.

To be eligible for permanent work, whether full-time or part-time, an alien—a person born abroad—must have a work visa issued by the Immigration and Naturalization Service, or "INS." (Work visas are often called "labor certifications.") There are several types of work visas. An alien should consult an immigration expert to determine the best visa category for his or her job level.

It is unlawful for an employer to hire an alien who can't produce a work visa.

Is permission to work always by visa?
Outside the home, yes.

THE MINIMUM WAGE

Are minors legally entitled to the minimum wage?

Yes. At the end of 1993 it was $4.25. The national Fair Labor Standards Act, or "FLSA," requires a specified minimum pay for each hour worked.

Most states have minimum wage laws as well. When an employer is covered by both federal and state minimum wage laws, employees must be paid the higher of the two minimum wages.

Are certain jobs outside the minimum wage laws?

Yes. "Exempt" positions such as executive and professional positions aren't covered. Certain administrative positions are also exempt. The best way to find out whether a job is exempt is to call the local Wage and Hour Division of the Department of Labor.

Do people have to work full-time to receive the minimum wage?

No.

Are tips treated as wages under the minimum wage laws?

In some cases, yes. If a worker normally receives more than $30 per month in tips, the employer may credit the worker's total tips toward his or her pay. However, this "tip credit" can't exceed 40 percent of the minimum wage, multiplied by the number of hours the worker put in during the month.

Can minors draw overtime pay?

No, but it is because most minors can only work up to 40 hours per week.

Under the FLSA, hourly employees must be paid extra for each hour worked over 40 in any week. (The overtime rate is 1½ times the worker's regular hourly rate.) But under state child labor laws, persons under age 16 can't work more than 40 hours per week, and persons under age 18 who attend school can't work more than 3 hours on school days and 8 hours on nonschool days. Because of these limits, minors usually don't earn overtime pay.

SUMMER JOBS

Can teens work full-time during the summer?

Yes, but only up to 40 hours per week under federal and state child labor laws, which means that teens can't draw overtime pay. Although the FLSA's minimum wage and overtime rules don't apply to certain seasonal work such as jobs at resorts, summer camps, and swimming pools, the 40-hour-per-week limit nevertheless does.

For more about part-time and summer jobs, see "Teens, Parents, and Money" in Chapter Three.

THE OBLIGATIONS AND BENEFITS OF EMPLOYMENT

What do employee and employer "owe" one another?

Every employee has a duty to work hard, be loyal, follow the employer's rules and directions, and work for the employer and no one else while on the job. In return, the employer must pay the employee for performing his or her job, and refrain from discriminating against the employee because of race, color, nationality, gender, age, or religion with respect to pay, promotions, and working conditions. These duties and obligations apply across the board—to teens as well as adults.

What are "fringe benefits"? Are minors entitled to them?

A fringe benefit is any benefit other than pay that an employee receives for working. Examples of fringe benefits are paid holidays, paid or unpaid vacation time, maternity and sick leave, and pensions.

If an employer provides fringe benefits to adult workers, minors are entitled to them also. But employers usually restrict fringe benefits to full-time nonseasonal employees, so most minors don't qualify for them.

What is a pension? Can a minor be in a pension plan?

A pension is a system for putting money aside to provide employees with a steady income after retiring. The main retirement program for most workers is the federal Social Security program. In fact, Social Security is the *only* pension program that many workers ever participate in, since employers aren't required to have their own plans.

Company pension plans are governed by complex federal laws. Under a company plan, either the employer makes a yearly contribution to the employee's pension account or the employee makes a yearly contribution and the employer matches it. The accounts are invested and reinvested over the years. Unless the employee quits, he or she doesn't receive any payments from the pension plan until retiring.

Nothing prohibits an employer from including minors in a pension plan. But if the plan's eligibility is based on age and length of service (as often happens), the employer doesn't have to let employees participate until they reach age 25 and work at least 1,000 hours in 12 months. This means that although the law really doesn't prohibit minors from participating, the terms of the plan rarely permit it.

Is health insurance a fringe benefit? Are employers required to provide health insurance for their employees?

Health insurance is indeed a fringe benefit, and a very important one. It pays an employee's medical expenses (or a large part of them) and often pays the medical expenses of the employee's family. An illness or injury doesn't have to be job related to be covered by employer-provided health insurance.

Although employers aren't required to provide health insurance for their workers, many believe that federal law should require employers to cover at least their full-time employees.

What is workers' compensation?

It is a payment that "compensates" an employee for medical expenses and time off caused by a job-related injury or illness. In this respect it differs from employer-provided health insurance.

The amount of wage compensation normally is a percentage of the disabled person's regular pay. If a job-related injury results in the loss of a body part such as a hand or foot, the employee usually receives a lump sum based on a payment schedule. The more serious the loss, the greater the lump sum.

Workers' compensation is "no-fault," which means that an employee can qualify for it regardless of who was at fault for the injury or illness. The problem—the "disability"—just has to be job related.

Employers are required to provide workers' compensation in most states. Depending on the state, workers' compensation payments are made by an insurance company, the employer, or the state where the employee works.

Are minors entitled to workers' compensation benefits?

Minors as well as adults can receive workers' compensation. Extra benefits are often payable if the injured person is a minor who was employed in violation of a child labor law.

What should a minor do if he or she is injured on the job?

Report the accident to the employer right away. In turn, the employer must report it to the state workers' compensation board. All employers are required by law to post reporting and filing requirements at an easy-to-find location at work.

IF YOU LOSE YOUR JOB

Can an employer fire an employee for "no good reason"? Does it depend on whether the employee is a minor?

As a rule, if an employer hasn't "contracted" with a person to work for a certain length of time or for a specific purpose, that person is an "employee-at-will." Employees-at-will can be fired any time and for any reason that doesn't violate a "public policy"—or for no reason at all.

These rules apply to employees of all ages. However, minors are almost always hired as employees-at-will, which means they usually can be fired for what may look like "no good reason."

Does the law ever prohibit an employer from firing an employee-at-will?

Yes. Title VII of the Civil Rights Act of 1964 prohibits employers from firing any employee because of race, color, gender, age, national origin, or religion. Furthermore, the Americans with Disabilities Act prohibits discrimination in hiring and firing on the basis of disability, and the National Labor Relations Act prohibits employers from firing any employee for either joining a union or refusing to be in one. Also, an employee can't be fired for refusing to perform an unlawful act at work or for filing a workers' compensation claim.

Discrimination at the jobsite is discussed later in this chapter.

If a minor gets fired, can he or she collect "unemployment"?

In some cases, yes. Unemployment compensation is a weekly payment that is meant to hold people over until they find another job. Unemployment compensation is a matter of federal law, although the states actually administer the system.

Some unemployed persons simply don't qualify. To be eligible, an applicant must have held a job a specific number of weeks before being let go. In addition, the employee cannot have quit or have been fired for misconduct.

Minors aren't prohibited from receiving unemployment compensation, but part-time employees and persons under age 14 don't qualify. (Part-time work includes work after school and during summer vacation.) For this reason, minors who are still in school usually can't collect it.

Each state has an unemployment office with detailed information available about how the system works.

INCOME TAXES

Do minors have to pay income tax?

Yes. Everyone who has an income may have to pay income tax, even babies. A person's income may take the form of wages, income from a corporate stock, or a debt that has just been forgiven.

Income taxes are imposed by the federal government and most of the states. Annual federal and state tax returns and any unpaid taxes for the prior year are due from every taxpayer on April 15.

To ensure that income taxes are paid, both the federal government and the states require employers to "withhold" certain amounts from their employees' pay. The employer then pays the "withholding amount" to the government. The payment serves as an advance deposit against income taxes owed by the employee for the year.

Employers must withhold Social Security (FICA) taxes and federal unemployment (FUTA) taxes in addition to state and local income taxes. These withholding amounts are paid to the federal government.

Does this mean a minor's pay is subject to withholding?

Unfortunately, yes.

What happens if the taxes withheld during the year turn out to be more than the total taxes owed?

The taxpayer shows the amount of the overpayment on his or her annual tax return. If the "taxing entity"—either the federal or the state government—agrees with the taxpayer, the excess is refunded.

Are FICA and FUTA withholdings ever refundable, either in whole or in part?

No.

Is babysitting money taxable? How about money earned delivering newspapers?

Although earnings from babysitting and paper routes are types of income that are taxable under Federal and State tax laws, most teens don't earn enough from these pursuits to have to pay taxes on the money they take in. Teens should let their parents know when their earnings from babysitting, delivering newspapers, and similar part-time jobs have exceeded $400 in any single year.

PRIVACY

Can a minor be required to submit to a drug or urine test as a condition of employment?

Yes. An employer can require all job applicants to be tested for drugs. The test results are always confidential. But employers can't legally test employees for human immunodeficiency virus/acquired immunodeficiency syndrome (HIV/AIDS)—either potential or current employees.

Can an employer legally require an employee to be searched?

Yes. Employers sometimes search employees or their personal belongings to prevent theft, seek evidence of suspected theft, or prevent drugs and weapons from coming onto company property. On-the-job searches usually are legal. There isn't much employees can do about them, provided they aren't too "invasive."

Minors as well as adults can be searched.

Can an employer legally enforce rules relating to employees' clothes or hairstyles?

Yes. It is almost always legal for an employer to forbid a particular style of dress or hairstyle, provided the rule doesn't discriminate on the basis of gender. For more about related issues see Chapter Six, "Your Personal Appearance."

DISCRIMINATION IN EMPLOYMENT

What, if anything, prevents an employer from discriminating against employees and job applicants?

Important federal legislation, including Title VII of the Civil Rights Act of 1964 and the Americans with Disabilities Act, or "ADA." These laws make it illegal for employers to discriminate at work on the basis of race, color, religion, gender, age, national origin, or disability.

Title VII and the ADA apply to hiring, firing, promotions, pay, and benefits.

Title VII and the ADA don't require employers to hire people who aren't qualified for a particular position or keep people who can't handle the work. Nor do these laws prohibit employers from basing differences in pay on job performance or length of service. Differences in pay based on these reasons actually are examples of *lawful* discrimination.

For Title VII to be violated, must the employer have intended to discriminate against the job applicant or employee?

No. For example, if an employer requires all applicants to take a test to determine who has a particular job skill and members of a racial minority consistently perform worse than others, a court may declare the test discriminatory because it has the effect of screening out a Title VII "protected class." The impact of the test would be illegal, even if it appeared fair on its face.

In this situation the employer must prove that a job-related purpose justifies the test—that the skills being tested for are needed for the successful operation of the business. In addition, the employer must show that no other testing method would have a less discriminatory impact. If this can't be proved—if the employer can't carry its "burden of proof"—the test must be either revamped or discontinued.

Is it illegal to discriminate against young persons on the basis of age?

No. Title VII doesn't prohibit discrimination against persons under age 40. The reason is that young people don't have a history of being unfairly discriminated against—in contrast to women, the elderly, and racial and ethnic minorities. However, some state laws prohibit discrimination against age groups that aren't covered by Title VII.

What racial groups are protected by Title VII?

All racial groups, including blacks, Asians, Hispanics, and American Indians. So are whites.

What is "reverse discrimination"? Is it legal?

Reverse discrimination occurs when an employer gives an unfair advantage to a class of people who historically have been discriminated against—blacks or women, for example. It occurs when a person is hired for a job or promoted because of minority status and not because he or she is the best candidate or has the best job record.

Reverse discrimination is illegal under Title VII when it illegally favors a Title VII "protected class." For more about discrimination issues see Chapter Thirteen, "Age, Sex, and Race Discrimination."

What, then, is "affirmative action"?

Affirmative action occurs when an employer hires or promotes an employee in a manner that *legally* favors a Title VII protected class. For example, it would be legal for an employer to recruit black candidates to *compete* for a particular job, or set hiring goals to place women in positions in which they have been underrepresented.

Can a woman be discriminated against because she is pregnant? Because she is pregnant and unmarried?

The answer to both questions is no. A 1978 amendment to Title VII makes it illegal to discriminate at the workplace on the basis of pregnancy, childbirth, or a related medical condition such as abortion.

These rules apply to minors as well as adults.

Can a pregnant teen take maternity leave?

Many states now require that women employees be allowed to take maternity leave without risking their jobs. California, for example, requires employers to give four months of maternity leave to full-time female employees. Because federal law doesn't require this, maternity leave basically remains a matter of state law. But federal law does require that if an employer allows employees to take time off for illness, it must allow time off to women for pregnancy. Maternity leave usually is without pay.

These rules apply to women of all ages, but because they apply to only full-time employees, they don't benefit many pregnant teens.

Can teenage fathers take paternity leave?

It depends on the circumstances. In 1993 Congress passed the National Family Leave Act, which allows fathers to take leaves of absense from work when they have newborn children or family medical emergencies. The father of the newborn doesn't have to be married to the child's mother. However, he must be a full-time worker and must have been on the job at least 12 months. Because of these limits, many working teenage fathers fail to qualify; this means they risk losing their job if they take time off.

What is sexual harassment?

It is any unwelcome sexual advance, a request for a sexual favor, or any other words or actions of a sexual type that interfere with work. Sexual harassment is illegal sex discrimination under Title VII.

Consider this clear example. In a 1987 Colorado case, a court found that a woman had been illegally harassed by a job supervisor after he reached across her lap when they were in a company car, rubbed her thigh, and said, ''I think you're going to make it here.'' Not long after, another supervisor at the same job approached the woman, patted her on the buttocks, and said, ''I'm going to get you yet.''

If an employer knows or has reason to know that sexual harassment of an employee is going on and doesn't do anything about it, both the person causing the sexual harassment and the employer can be found responsible.

Consider another example. In a 1991 California case a woman who was being bothered by a male co-worker received a note from him that read:

> I cried over you last night and I'm totally drained today. I have never been in such constant term oil [sic]. Thank you for talking with me. I could not stand to feel your hatred for another day.

After the woman complained, the co-worker was transferred out of town. But a few months later he was transferred back to the local office and began harassing her again. Finally the woman brought sexual harassment charges against her employer (which happened to be the Internal Revenue Service), as well as the co-worker.

If a young person believes he or she has been discriminated against at work or in applying for a job, what can be done?

Sometimes the matter can be resolved by talking to the hiring person, the supervisor, or another individual in charge. If this doesn't help, the ''complainant'' may file a charge against the employer with the local Equal Employment Opportunity Commission or state civil rights office.

Many cases are settled at this level. If no settlement is reached, the complainant at that point is granted the right to sue the employer in court.

This area of law is complex, and it constantly changes. If a person, regardless of age, believes he or she has been illegally discriminated against in connection with work, it is best to discuss the matter with a parent, who may want to contact a lawyer versed in employment law. This can be expensive, so most communities have legal service organizations that provide help with discrimination and civil rights cases at low cost.

What does a complainant have to prove in order to win a Title VII job discrimination case?

These four things:

1. That the complainant belongs to a "protected class"—an ethnic minority, for example.
2. That the complainant applied for and was qualified for a position that the employer wanted to fill, or for a promotion.
3. That despite these qualifications, the complainant was denied the position or the promotion.
4. That after the person was rejected, the employer continued to seek applications, and didn't change the job qualifications.

JOB SAFETY

Are employers required to provide a safe place to work?

Yes, although this wasn't always the case. Under the federal Occupational Safety and Health Act or "OSHA," and also under state law, employers must maintain a workplace that is safe and healthy for employees.

What should a person do if working conditions on the job appear unsafe?

Workers exposed to health or safety hazards have the right under OSHA to ask the employer to correct the problem, or to report it to the closest OSHA office. Workers also have the right to talk privately to OSHA inspectors about what appear to be health and safety hazards. Under federal law, it is illegal for an employer to punish or discriminate against any worker who exercises these rights.

FOR FURTHER READING

Cahn, Rhoda, and William Cahn. *No Time for School, No Time for Play: The Story of Child Labor in America.* New York: Julian Messner, 1972.

Doggett, Clinton L., and Lois T. Doggett. *The Equal Employment Opportunity Commission.* New York: Chelsea House Publishers, 1990.

Greenwood, Mary. *Hiring, Supervising, and Firing Employees.* Wilmette, Illinois: Callaghan, 1987.

Hunt, James W. *The Law of the Workplace: The Rights of Employers and Employees.* Washington, D.C.: Bureau of National Affairs, 1988.

Joseph, Joel D. *The Handbook of Employees' Rights.* Washington, D.C.: National Press, 1984.

Lee, Mary Price. *Money and Kids: How To Earn It, Save It, and Spend It.* Philadelphia: The Westminster Press, 1978.

Madison, Richard. *The Greencard Book: A Guide to Permanent Residence Through Employment in the United States.* New York: Bantam Books, 1983.

Outten, Wayne N., and Noah A. Kinigstein. *The Rights of Employees: The Basic ACLU Guide.* New York: Bantam Books, 1983.

Sherman, Marlene T. *Health Strategies for Working Women: A Guide for the 1990s.* Los Altos, California: Crisp Publications, 1991.

— 5 —

On Your Own

EMANCIPATION

Can minors legally live beyond their parents' control?
In certain cases, yes. Minors can be legally "emancipated" from their parents under the laws of most states.

What exactly is "emancipation"?
It is an act or course of conduct that terminates the right of parents over a minor child, and also terminates the child's right to be taken care of.

Parents usually seek emancipation. If it occurs, often it is because a judge confirms or denies its existence as part of a larger issue in a court case. But a court won't declare an emancipation simply because a minor can't stand his or her folks, or because they can't stand their child. It only happens if a minor already has been living apart from his or her parents and is clearly self-sufficient—if the minor's emancipation already has been "implied."

Consider the following situation. An Iowa doctor went to court to recover payment from the father of a teenage girl after having given her extensive medical treatment. The young woman had previously left home, with her father's permission, to live and work in another town. She supported herself and paid her bills until she contracted typhoid fever.

The young woman's father argued that his daughter had been emancipated, so he shouldn't have to pay her medical bills. After reviewing the facts of the case, the Iowa court said there was no emancipation. Its ruling meant the young woman's father continued to be responsible for her medical costs.

This case was decided in 1890, and the daughter was only 14 years old when she left home, but it demonstrates what emancipation really means.

If parents throw a teen out of the house, is his or her emancipation automatic?

Not in the vast majority of cases, because the teen usually won't have the income or maturity to live independently. Emancipation usually doesn't happen unless it's clear that the child is living an independent life and will be able to do so in the future. If this can't be shown, the child remains the parents' responsibility and continues to be under their authority.

If a minor runs away from home, is he or she emancipated?

Not usually. Parents are responsible for their minor children, including runaways. But if parents allow a runaway child to live independently for a long time and the child develops a reliable means of support or completely abandons the parents, a court may decide that emancipation has been implied.

These days, why might parents seek to establish emancipation?

Often it will be in relation to a child support order in a divorce settlement. For example, in one case a divorced mother went to court to collect past due child support payments from her former husband. After their daughter was age 15 she briefly lived with her mother. Sometimes she lived with friends, worked odd jobs, and was even jailed on two separate occasions. Neither parent knew where she was, although both had tried to help her by offering special schooling and psychiatric care.

The mother wanted past due support payments because she had legal custody of the runaway daughter. The court refused, stating that the daughter was legally emancipated because she had completely abandoned them both.

For more about divorce and child support see Chapter Seven, "If Your Parents Divorce."

What factors will a court use to decide whether a minor is emancipated?

Some important ones are:

1. Whether the minor still lives at home;
2. Whether the minor pays room and board at home;
3. Whether the minor has a job, and whether the minor is allowed to spend his or her earnings without parental interference;
4. Whether the minor owns a car or house;
5. Whether the minor pays his or her own debts; and
6. Whether the minor is being claimed as a dependent on his or her parents' tax return.

If a minor is emancipated, does he or she gain all the rights of adults?
Not usually. Traditionally, emancipation didn't enable a minor to manage or convey property, bring a lawsuit, or consent to medical care—the emancipated minor was still too young to engage in these adult activities. In recent years, however, the laws of many states have given teens these rights when emancipation can be established by the parents or is evident in the minor's actions and lifestyle.

When a minor marries, is he or she instantly emancipated?
Yes, provided the marriage is legal. In most states a person under age 18 must obtain parental consent and must be at least age 16 in order to marry.

Does enlisting in the armed forces constitute automatic emancipation?
Yes. Serving in the armed forces is said to be inconsistent with the idea of parental control. To enlist in any branch of the armed forces except the Army, a high school diploma currently is needed.

If a minor is emancipated, is he or she still required to obey the state's school attendance laws?
Yes, except in cases in which marriage was the basis for emancipation.

Once a minor is emancipated, are the parents relieved of liability for the child's negligent or reckless acts?
Not in every case. In California, for example, parents are responsible for a minor's negligent or reckless acts while driving, even if emancipation has occurred. For more about the responsibility of parents for their

children's negligence while driving, see Chapter One, "Behind the Wheel."

Can a minor be emancipated and still live at home?

The answer to this question is unclear. If a minor pays room and board and has an independent source of income, a court may declare an emancipation. It always depends on the nature of the particular case.

HAVING YOUR OWN APARTMENT

Can a teenager legally rent an apartment?

Teens may enter into contracts, and this includes lease and rental contracts. But many landlords refuse to rent to them—they don't want teens as tenants.

Although minors can walk away from or "disaffirm" contracts they enter into, this probably isn't the reason why landlords refuse to rent to them. Many landlords figure that teens who want their own apartments must be troublemakers, "party animals," or drug dealers—otherwise they wouldn't be living away from home.

Age discrimination against a minor who wants to rent an apartment isn't against the law, although refusing to rent to someone on the basis of race, color, gender, religion, nationality, or handicap clearly is. Some state constitutions or state laws prohibit landlords from renting to "adults only" because such policies discourage families from living together. To date, however, no state prohibits landlords from refusing to rent to teens.

For more about teens and contracts see Chapter Sixteen, "Entering into Contracts."

SERVING YOUR COUNTRY

Do men still have to register for the armed forces? Do women have to register?

With narrow exceptions, all men who are United States citizens and all foreign born males living in the United States and its territories must register for the draft within 30 days before and 30 days after their eighteenth birthday. Women aren't required to register but may enlist.

What is the procedure for registering for the draft?

Each registrant must complete and return a Selective Service draft registration form, available at any post office. Registrants receive notice within 90 days that the Selective Service has received it.

Does everyone who registers for the draft end up in the armed forces?

No. The last year anyone was drafted in the United States was 1973. No one can be drafted unless Congress and the President determine that inducting persons into the armed forces is necessary because of war or other national emergency.

Can people volunteer for the armed forces?

They can if they are age 18, and persons under 18 may enlist if they have parental consent.

What is a conscientious objector?

It is a person who holds a sincere religious, moral, or ethical belief that opposes war. If the person's objection is only to participating in combat, he or she is assigned noncombat military duties if called to serve. If the person's objection is to participating in all military service, he or she is ordered to perform civilian work relating to the national interest.

THE RIGHT TO VOTE

What is the legal voting age?

For national elections it is age 18, and for state and local elections it usually is age 18 as well.

HOLDING PUBLIC OFFICE

Can a minor run for public office?

Whether a minor can run for or hold public office depends on state law. State constitutions typically require, for example, that a person be at least age 24 to hold a seat in the state legislature. City laws (called "ordinances") often require a person to be at least age 21 to sit on the city council. In addition, state laws usually require that a person be a certain age, usually 35, to be installed as a judge.

FOR FURTHER READING

Serving Your Country

Gordon, Susan. *Your Career in the Military.* New York: Arco Publishing, 1983.

Johnson, R. Charles. *Draft, Registration, and the Law.* Occidental: Nolo Press, 1985.

Moran, Tom. *The U.S. Army.* Minneapolis: Lerner Publications, 1990.

The Right to Vote/Holding Public Office

Archer, Jules. *Winners and Losers: How Elections Work in America.* New York: Harcourt Brace Jovanovich, 1984.

Eichner, James A., and Linda M. Shields. *Local Government.* New York: Franklin Watts, 1983.

Samuels, Cynthia K. *It's a Free Country! A Young Person's Guide to Politics and Elections.* New York: Atheneum, 1988.

—6—

Your Personal Appearance

AT HOME

Do parents have a right to decide how their children can dress and style their hair?
Yes. Although most parents give their children plenty of leeway when it comes to personal appearance, they do have the right to forbid particular types of clothes and hairstyles. Parents can forbid a teen to shave his or her head, use hair dye, or wear torn jeans or revealing tops. They can also forbid tattooing and any kind of body piercing.

What happens if a minor ignores his or her parents' requirements in matters of personal appearance?
Nothing in the law prevents the parents from punishing the minor. However, as discussed in Chapter Ten, "Your Right to Be Healthy and Safe from Abuse," parents may never punish children in a manner that amounts to abuse or neglect. If they do, the state can take them to court.

AT SCHOOL

Can a public school legally enforce a dress code?
Yes, unless the provisions of the dress code truly don't promote discipline or good health, or don't serve some other worthwhile purpose. The same is true of rules relating to hairstyle.

In the last 20 years the issue of whether high school dress codes are legal has been argued in the courts countless times. Some states place the "burden of proof" on the *student* to show that the rules don't serve any useful purpose. In these states the students must prove that the rules are "arbitrary"—that they don't make any sense. Others place the burden of proof on the *school* to show that the regulation is related to a source of discipline problems or poor academic performance. The first type of case is difficult for students to win. The second type is tough for the school to win and is therefore more favorable to student rights.

In a case decided in 1984, students at an Alabama high school challenged a rule prohibiting males who participated in sports from wearing beards, sideburns, and long mustaches. The Alabama court ruled that the rule was a reasonable way to further personal hygiene and compel uniformity among the athletes. Since the students couldn't prove that the rule was arbitrary, they lost.

An Illinois court was faced with the same type of rule in 1974, but in this case the rule applied to the entire student body. Here the students won because the school couldn't prove that hairstyles bore any sensible relation to the students' behavior or academic performance.

For a discussion about clothes as a personal or political expression at school see Chapter Two, "At School."

AT WORK

Can an employer require employees to follow a dress code?

Yes, provided the regulations have a sensible business purpose. Courts always hesitate to interfere with business policies relating to dress and hairstyle unless the policies are shown to discriminate on the basis of either gender or race.

A New York court ruled in 1981 that an airline could legally prohibit employees of both sexes from wearing their hair in "corn-rows." The court sided with the airline after it argued that having its employees project a conservative image was a sensible business policy. Likewise, an airline—or a McDonald's—can legally require all employees who work with the public to wear the company uniform.

What if a certain provision in a company dress code only applies to women?

In most cases it discriminates illegally. The Illinois supreme court ruled in 1979 that a bank illegally discriminated on the basis of gender when it tried to enforce a rule requiring all the women to wear the same color, but permitted the men to wear any color of suit, jacket, shirt, or tie. Rules requiring women employees to wear makeup or making women flight attendants stay below a certain body weight also discriminate illegally, unless the employer can prove the rule serves a very important business purpose.

IN PUBLIC

Can a restaurant legally refuse to serve persons who aren't dressed in a certain manner?

In most states a business can require a particular type of dress only if the rule doesn't discriminate on the basis of gender. In 1977 a California man brought a sex discrimination suit against a restaurant with a formal dress code after it refused to seat him for dinner. The man was wearing a polyester leisure suit—and no tie. He argued that all the women in the restaurant were at least as casually dressed as he. The California supreme court ruled in his favor, stating that the restaurant's "no tie, no service" rule discriminated on the basis of gender in violation of the California constitution.

Are "no shoes, no shirt, no service" policies legal?

Yes, because a rule at a business establishment forbidding bare feet and bare chests promotes cleanliness, which is considered good business policy. In addition, such rules promote a positive business image and don't discriminate on the basis of gender. (Topless women would be subject to the rule as well.)

Can a store or restaurant legally keep out "longhairs" or "biker types"?

Under federal law, yes, because the rule doesn't discriminate on the basis of gender, color, religion, national origin, or handicap. A state or local law would have to protect the customer in this type of situation. For more about discrimination see Chapter Thirteen, "Age, Sex, and Race Discrimination."

Is public nudity legal?

Not in very many places. States, cities, counties, and other legal subdivisions may legally forbid public nudity at places such as beaches and parks as both a health measure and a means of upholding community standards of morality. However, California and Florida do have a few nude and topless beaches.

FOR FURTHER READING

Anderson, R. Roy. "Tattooing Should Be Regulated." *New England Journal of Medicine,* January 16, 1992:207.

"Black Students Complain of Georgia School Dress Code." *Jet,* October 18, 1993:24.

"Boots Make a Statement: Is It Fashion or Politics?" *New York Times,* November 5, 1992:A7.

Children's Television Workshop, and Sara St. Antoine. *Dress Code Mess.* New York: Bantam Books, 1992.

"Continental Retracts Rules on Makeup Use." *New York Times,* May 16, 1991:A9.

Davis, Patricia, and Deneen L. Brown. "Fairfax Buckles Down on Heavy Metal Belts." *Washington Post,* December 11, 1992:C1.

Lacey, Marc. "No Sporting Chance; Danger Lurks for Fans as Gangs Adopt Pro Attire." *Los Angeles Times,* March 20, 1991:B1.

Mattera, Joanne. "Breaking the Code." *Glamour,* January 1990:56.

Timnick, Lois, and Bernice Hirabayashi. "Cracking the Dress Code." *Los Angeles Times,* March 28, 1993:J1.

—7—

If Your Parents Divorce

CUSTODY

If a minor's parents plan to divorce, who decides where the minor will live after the divorce is final?

Usually the parents—they determine who will have "custody" of the child.[1] If they can't decide on their own, the court decides for them. Its decision must be in "the best interests of the child," a term often applied in relation to legal matters involving young people.

Married parents have "physical" and "legal" custody of their minor children. Physical custody means the parents are responsible for their children's immediate personal needs such as food, clothing, and shelter; legal custody means they are responsible, legally and financially, for their children's safety, education, and actions with respect to others. When parents divorce, one parent—the "custodial parent"—usually has both physical and legal custody of the children.

How do divorce courts decide which parent should have custody?

They consider the parents' love and affection for the child; each parent's concerns for the child's physical, mental, and financial needs; and the parents' physical, mental, and moral fitness.

Custody decisions can be a close call. In a 1982 Virginia case, a judge awarded custody of twins to a father even though both parents were fit. The judge thought the father's home would be better because the children had been living with him for over three years, and, because he had remarried, they wouldn't have to stay with a babysitter while he was at work.

Does a young person have a right to a lawyer at his or her parents' divorce?

About one-third of the states permit their courts to appoint a special representative for a child when parents disagree on custody. (Half of these states require the representative to be an attorney.) The representative helps the child to express which parent he or she wants to live with and can collect information for the judge to use in deciding custody. The parents pay for the representative in most of these states, although the state or county will pay if they can't afford it.

Does a child of divorcing parents have a right to choose which parent he or she wants to live with?

Not usually. Even so, divorce courts in about half the states are required to take the child's preference into account. The older and more mature the child, the more weight his or her preference is likely to receive, especially if the child can give a good reason for preferring one parent to the other.

In Ohio, children ages 12 and older can choose which parent they want to live with—its courts will respect the child's preference unless living with the chosen parent wouldn't be in the child's best interests. Georgia's divorce courts have been taking the child's preference into account for decades.

Isn't it true that the mother usually wins custody in a divorce?

Yes. In years past, courts almost always resolved custody disputes in favor of the mother. These decisions were based on the notion that mothers are better able to care for children day in and day out, especially when the children are quite young. (On the other hand, teenage boys often lived with their fathers.) Although this "maternal preference" is no longer part of most states' divorce laws, courts still tend to award child custody to mothers (in other than joint custody situations). For more about the maternal preference, see Chapter Nine, "Marrying and Having Children."

What is "joint custody"?

It is a type of custody arrangement in which the parents continue to share physical and legal custody—they both remain lawfully responsible for their children's care. In these situations the child might spend weekdays with one parent and weekends with the other, or live with one parent during the school year and stay with the other during summer vacation. Both parents continue to make important decisions about their child's education, religion, and marriage status. Joint custody arrangements are almost always more flexible than traditional custody arrangements.

Experts believe young people are better able to handle the trauma of divorce if their parents choose joint custody. Many also contend that joint custody cuts down on parental kidnapping (discussed later in this chapter).

Can parents continue to have legal custody over a person who is over the age of majority?

No, because that is the age at which a young person can live independently. However, under the terms of a support decree, parents can be legally required to support a child who is beyond the age of majority (Child support is discussed later in this chapter.) In addition, some states allow minors to be legally emancipated when their parents divorce if a minor is self-supporting. For more about the age of majority see Chapter Three, "At Home," and for more about emancipation see Chapter Five, "On Your Own."

Can a young person "divorce" his or her parents—bring a lawsuit to terminate their parental rights?

In 1992 a Florida judge permitted a young boy to go to court to do just this. The boy had been in foster care, and life at the foster home was stable. His foster parents wanted to adopt him, so he filed a lawsuit to terminate parental rights in order to clear the way for adoption proceedings. He won. This case is important because it is the first time a court has permitted a young person to *personally* seek a termination of parental rights. As Chapter Three explains, the *state* normally seeks to terminate parental rights.

Does a child of divorced parents have a legal right to visit the parent he or she isn't living with?

Not exactly. Visitation rights usually belong to the noncustodial parent, not the child. Courts grant visitation to the noncustodial parent unless it wouldn't be in the child's best interests.

What happens if a child doesn't want to see the noncustodial parent?

In most situations the child can be required to, particularly if the at-home parent has turned the child against the other parent. In a 1983 Pennsylvania case a court permitted a father to visit his 11-year-old daughter against her wishes after the court declared that the mother had been "poisoning her daughter's mind against her father."

Will a court forbid a noncustodial parent to visit a minor child because that parent is "living with someone"?

Not for that reason alone. Courts will forbid a parent to have contact with a child only if spending time together wouldn't be in the child's best interests. These days, very few judges would limit visitation rights solely because the noncustodial parent lives with someone outside marriage.

If it appears that the noncustodial parent might not return the child at the end of a visit, the court has the power to suspend a parent's visitation rights or revoke them altogether. Courts will also suspend or revoke visitation rights if the noncustodial parent physically injures the child or threatens to. If the noncustodial parent abused a child during marriage, his or her visits usually are both short and supervised.

Many states regard sexual promiscuity of the noncustodial parent as grounds for denying visitation.

In custody determinations, does a young person have the right to continue living with his or her siblings?

No, but courts try to keep brothers and sisters together unless there is an important reason not to. It is widely believed that, absent an unusual situation, keeping siblings together is in the best interests of everyone.

CHILD SUPPORT

Are both parents legally required to support their minor children after a divorce?

Yes, unless the parental rights of one or both parents have been terminated in a separate court case. For more about terminating parental rights see Chapter Three, "At Home."

What is child support?

It is an amount of money that the noncustodial parent is required to pay to fulfill his or her legal support obligations. Usually these payments are made to the custodial parent. Child support must cover food, clothing, shelter, medical expenses, and education.

Who decides how much child support the noncustodial parent must pay?

Usually the court. The actual amount depends on how much each parent earns, the family's standard of living, and any child's unique physical, educational, and psychological needs. Parents can agree on the amount, but if they do, the amount has to be court approved.

If the court refuses to grant visitation rights to the noncustodial parent, is that parent relieved of his or her child support obligations?

No. Child support must be paid by the noncustodial parent whether or not visitation rights are granted.

Aren't most children worse off financially after their parents divorce?

Studies show that they are. The purpose of child support is to allow the children to enjoy the same standard of living that they enjoyed before the divorce, but even so, support is often inadequate. A study in the mid-1980s found that after a couple divorces, the average woman's spending money declines by 73 percent, but the average man's spending money increases by 42 percent.[2] Since most children live with their mothers after a divorce, their standard of living also drops. An earlier study argues that support awards are too low to pay even half the costs of child rearing.[3]

Does the noncustodial parent have to pay child support if the custodial parent works outside the home?

Yes, although in some cases the amount the custodial parent earns will reduce the amount of the noncustodial parent's support payments.

Can child support continue after a child reaches the age of majority?

Yes. As part of many divorce settlements between parents, one may be required to pay child support until each child reaches age 21 and may have to pay for each child's college education. In 1989 an Illinois court required a father who earned $77,000 annually to pay $11,000 of the $13,000 cost for his son to attend a four-year private college.

Can a custodial parent take a noncustodial parent to court to enforce a child support order?
Yes. In addition, state child welfare agencies always pursue "deadbeat parents."

Can a young person take a parent to court to recover child support?
Only if he or she is above the age of majority and continues to be entitled to support (such as tuition for a college education) under the parents' child support order.

Are there any special ways to track down deadbeat parents in order to enforce current or overdue support obligations?
Yes. Special laws help parents collect child support from noncustodial deadbeat parents who live within the state's boundaries. In addition, the federal government assists state welfare agencies to locate absent, nonpaying parents in other states.

What's the difference between child support and alimony?
Alimony, or "maintenance," is a payment from one former spouse to the other that reduces the spouse's personal financial hardships after a divorce. A divorced spouse doesn't need legal custody of minor children to receive alimony payments. Divorced women who have never worked outside the home during a lengthy marriage often are awarded monthly or annual alimony. These payments always are separate and distinct from child support.

GRANDPARENTS AND STEPPARENTS

Do grandparents have a legal right to visit their grandchildren after the parents divorce?
Whether grandparents may see their grandchildren used to be decided by the custodial parent. Now 48 states have laws allowing divorce courts to permit grandparent visitation in various circumstances, including whether the child lived with the grandparent before the divorce. In every case the court's decision to allow visitation is guided by the best interests of the child.

Do stepparents have any parental rights over a stepchild?
Not unless they've agreed to assume certain parental obligations. Ac-

cepting legal responsibility for a stepchild gives a stepparent legal rights similar to parental rights. The extent of those rights would depend on the responsibilities assumed.

Do former stepparents have any legal rights?

Sometimes. Courts occasionally grant visitation rights to former stepparents after finding that visitation would be in the child's best interests.

Do stepparents have any obligations with respect to a stepchild?

Again, only if the stepparent has personally agreed to take on parental obligations. A typical example of assumed obligations might be an agreement to provide for or educate a young stepson or stepdaughter.

OTHER ISSUES RELATING TO DIVORCE

What's the difference between a divorce and a legal separation?

A divorce legally dissolves the marriage. A legal separation doesn't dissolve all marriage ties, but it publicly declares that the couple no longer live together as husband and wife. It also declares that they no longer will be responsible for each other's debts.

What is "child snatching"?

Child snatching, sometimes called "child kidnapping," occurs when a noncustodial parent unlawfully takes a child from the custodial parent or the custodial parent's home. Children are often snatched to exact a promise from the custodial parent to accept less child support, or to attempt to change custody or visitation rights through an out-of-state court.

Child snatching is a crime in most states, which means that parents who are guilty of child snatching can be punished under state law. In addition, federal law requires state courts to enforce out-of-state custody orders. This means that if a child is taken across state lines in violation of a custody order, he or she must, by law, be returned to the custodial parent, regardless of how far away that parent happens to live.

If a young person thinks his or her parents should get a divorce, what can he or she do?

From a legal standpoint, nothing. However, the child should consider discussing the family situation with a trusted relative or minister.

NOTES

1. In 1990 there were 2,448,000 marriages in the United States and 1,175,000 divorces.
2. Weitzman, Lenore J. *The Divorce Revolution: The Unexpected Social and Economic Consequences for Women and Children in America* (New York: The Free Press, 1985).
3. Weitzman, Lenore J., and Ruth B. Dixon, "Child Custody Awards: Legal Standards with Empirical Patterns for Child Custody, Support and Visitation After Divorce," 12 *University of California Davis Law Review* 473, 497–499 (1979).

FOR FURTHER READING

In General

Berger, Stuart M. *Divorce Without Victims: Helping Children Through Divorce with a Minimum of Pain and Trauma.* New York: New American Library, 1986.

Fayerweather Street School and Eric R. Rofes, ed. *The Kids' Book of Divorce: By, For, and About Kids.* New York: Random House, 1982.

Gardner, Richard A. *The Boys and Girls Book About Divorce.* New York: Jason Aronson, 1983.

Glass, Stuart M. *A Divorce Dictionary: A Book for You and Your Children.* Boston: Little, Brown, 1980.

Kimbrough, Cassie. *Where Are My Children?* New York: Kensington Publishing, 1991.

McGuire, Paula. *Putting It Together: Teenagers Talk About Family Breakup.* New York: Delacorte Press, 1987.

Rosenberg, Maxine B. *Living with a Single Parent.* New York: Bradbury Press, 1992.

Sussman, Alan, and Martin Guggenheim. *The Basic ACLU Guide to the Rights of Parents.* New York: Avon Books, 1980.

Custody and Support

Conine, Jon. *Fathers' Rights: The Sourcebook for Dealing with the Child Support System.* New York: Walker, 1989.

Terkel, Susan Neiberg. *Understanding Child Custody*. New York: Franklin Watts, 1991.

Stepfamilies

Bailey, Marilyn. *The Facts About Stepfamilies*. New York: Crestwood House, 1990.

Rosenberg, Maxine B. *Talking About Stepfamilies*. New York: Bradbury Press, 1990.

—8—

Your Sexual Life

Do teens have a legal right to engage in all types of sexual activity?

No—the laws don't go this far. States legally regulate, or attempt to regulate, the sexual conduct of minors. Some forbid teens under a certain age to have sexual intercourse, or at least homosexual intercourse. Others attempt to regulate teen sex through statutory rape laws, which are discussed later in this chapter.

A law that regulates teenage sex is a type of law that is intended to preserve community standards of morality. The same type of law still makes it illegal in a few states for consenting but unmarried adults to have sex and for married adults to perform certain sexual acts such as oral sex. Overall, these laws don't violate the privacy protections of the Constitution.

BIRTH CONTROL

Are contraceptives legal?

Both nonprescription and prescription contraceptives are legal in the United States. At one time the laws of most states restricted the sale of contraceptives, although only Connecticut prohibited them altogether. These laws were challenged by individuals who wanted to use them and by doctors who wanted to prescribe them for their patients.

In 1951 the Supreme Court finally ruled that states interfere with special privacy rights protected by the Constitution when they pass laws banning the sale or use of contraceptives. It is now clear that states may not interfere excessively with an individual's personal decisions about reproduction.

Can teens legally use contraceptives?

Yes. The early contraceptive cases dealt with the right of married couples to make decisions about childbearing, but later cases established that all sexually active people have this right.

Do teens have a right to obtain contraceptives without parental consent?

Teens don't need parental consent to purchase nonprescription contraceptives such as foams, jellies, sponges, and condoms, and stores don't have to notify a teen's parents about such purchases. But prescription contraceptives such as birth control pills, diaphragms, interuterine devices (IUDs) and Norplant (a new long-term contraceptive method) raise special legal issues.

As a rule, minors need parental consent for medical treatment, including the use of prescription drugs. But every state now permits minors to obtain prescription as well as nonprescription contraceptives without the consent of a parent. To date, 24 states and Washington, D.C., specifically permit minors to receive prescription contraceptives without parental consent, and 26 states have no restrictions at all on these purchases. No state requires doctors to notify the parents when a teenage child receives a contraceptive prescription.

Courts have set aside state laws requiring federally funded family planning clinics to notify parents when a minor receives a prescription for contraceptives. These decisions are based on the notion that clinics providing federally funded family planning services are legally required to maintain client confidentiality. Even so, a teen who goes to a family planning clinic should always ask a staff person whether the clinic keeps its records confidential.

Do teens have a right to family planning counseling and services from federally funded family planning agencies?

Yes. The purpose of these "Title X clinics" is to make family planning available to all eligible persons at little or no cost. (Planned Parenthood is a Title X clinic.) Although eligibility is based on a person's income and financial resources, Title X clinics consider a teen's financial resources separate from the resources of the parents, which means teens almost always qualify for Title X family planning. Young people are especially dependent on Title X clinics for contraceptives—they represent one-third of the clinics' caseloads.[1]

Strict confidentiality rules apply to all Title X agencies.

Does a teen have a right to be sterilized without parental consent?

Few states actually have laws requiring minors to obtain parental consent for a sterilization. When state law doesn't deal with sterilizations directly, laws allowing minors to obtain contraceptives without parental consent probably don't apply, because a sterilization usually is irreversible and therefore very serious. A doctor would undoubtedly require parental consent. Florida, Maryland, North Carolina, and Virginia specifically exclude sterilizations from the list of medical services that don't require parental approval.

See Chapter Ten, "Your Right to Be Healthy and Safe from Abuse," for more about situations in which young people can arrange for their own medical care.

Would an older teen be entitled to federal funding for a sterilization?

No. Although federal funds can be used to perform sterilizations on adults in some cases, no funds are available for persons under age 21.

Does a young person have a right to sex education classes in public school?

No, even though many states now require them above a certain grade level. When sex education is included in the curriculum, parents sometimes argue that public schools violate their constitutional right to control their children's religious upbringing. Although parents have never won these cases in court, most states allow parents to stop a child from attending sex education classes if the requirements of the class can be fulfilled in some other meaningful way.

ABORTION RIGHTS

Are abortions legal?

Abortions have been legal in the United States since 1973, when the Supreme Court decided the famous and controversial case of *Roe v. Wade*.

The Supreme Court ruled in *Roe v. Wade* that the decision to have an abortion is another type of personal decision that the Constitution protects from *excessive* state interference. *Roe v. Wade* stated that before a fetus is able to survive outside the womb—before a fetus is "viable"—a woman has the private right to choose an abortion. Viability is estimated to occur 12 to 13 weeks after conception.

But states can pass laws restricting abortions of viable fetuses in certain cases. With respect to the second 12 weeks of pregnancy—the second "trimester"—states may restrict abortions in cases in which the procedure is likely to endanger the woman's life or health. In the third trimester, states may legally forbid abortions. These restrictions don't unconstitutionally interfere with a woman's personal privacy.

Does a teenage woman have a legal right to an abortion?

Yes. Although *Roe v. Wade* dealt with an adult woman's right to an abortion, later Supreme Court decisions have stated that this right extends to teens. This special privacy right applies to all women—adult or teenager, married or single.

Can a teen legally obtain an abortion without parental consent?

In some states, yes. The Supreme Court has ruled that states may not give parents absolute veto power over a daughter's decision to have an abortion. But it also has ruled that a state may legally require a teen to obtain consent from a judge. This alternative, known as "judicial bypass," means that states may permit a teen to obtain consent for an abortion from a judge instead of notifying or otherwise involving a parent. (In other words, the *parents* are *bypassed.*)

To complicate the issue, however, the Supreme Court has also ruled that states may require a doctor to notify one or both parents of their minor daughter's plans to have an abortion. What these Supreme Court decisions add up to is that the law of consent with respect to teen abortions remains unclear.

See Table 3 for a summary of state laws relating to parental consent for an abortion in the 50 states and the District of Columbia.

What must a teenage woman prove to obtain a judge's consent for an abortion?

She must establish that she has the "legal ability" to consent. This means the young woman must prove she has the maturity and knowledge to make an independent decision about an abortion after having consulted her doctor, and that it would be in her best interest to have the abortion without parental consent. If the teen can show this, the judge must give consent. Some of the factors a judge would consider in reaching a decision are the teen's emotional and intellectual development, outside interests, and life experiences.

Must a pregnant teen obtain the consent of her sex partner to obtain an abortion?

No—otherwise her constitutional right to privacy in the area of childbearing would be violated. If consent from the sex partner were required, the Supreme Court's ruling in *Roe v. Wade* would have little meaning.

Can a young woman's parents legally force her to have an abortion she doesn't want?

No, and neither can the state. All women have a constitutional right to decide about having children without excessive interference from anyone.

If a teen can't afford to pay for an abortion, is she entitled to one at public expense?

The answer to this question is complex, and troublesome to many. The federal government and a number of states have restricted the use of public money such as Medicaid for abortions. (Medicaid is a federal program that funds health care for poor people.) Some states even prohibit the use of public funds for abortions needed to save the life of the mother.

In 1991 the Supreme Court upheld a federal rule prohibiting family planning clinics supported by Title X money from providing information about abortions. In early 1993, President Clinton had this rule repealed. However, in late 1993 the United States Senate voted to uphold the 16-year ban on funding for abortions with Medicaid money.

Teens have a right to *state-funded* abortions in some states, and many state supreme courts have ruled that state laws prohibiting the use of state funds for abortions and abortion counseling violate their state constitutions. What these rulings mean is that if state money is used to provide public medical care for poor women, abortion services can't be denied.

Table 3
State Laws Relating to a Minor's Right to Consent to an Abortion, 1992

STATE	LAW
Alabama	Parental Consent Required
Alaska	No Law Found
Arizona	No Law Found[1]
Arkansas	Parental Notice Required[2]
California	No Law Found[1]
Colorado	No Law Found
Connecticut	Minor May Consent[3]
Delaware	No Law Found[4]
D.C.	Minor May Consent
Florida	No Law Found1
Georgia	Parental Notice Required
Hawaii	No Law Found[4]
Idaho	Parental Notice Required[2,5]
Illinois	No Law Found[6]
Indiana	Parental Consent Required
Iowa	No Law Found
Kansas	No Law Found
Kentucky	No Law Found[1]
Louisiana	Parental Consent Required
Maine	Minor May Consent[7]
Maryland	No Law Found[8]
Massachusetts	Parental Consent Required[9]
Michigan	Parental Consent Required
Minnesota	Parental Notice Required[2]
Mississippi	No Law Found[1]
Missouri	Parental Consent Required
Montana	No Law Found
Nebraska	Parental Notice Required
Nevada	No Law Found[6]
New Hampshire	No Law Found
New Jersey	No Law Found
New Mexico	No Law Found
New York	No Law Found
North Carolina	No Law Found[4]
North Dakota	Parental Consent Required[9]
Ohio	Parental Notice Required
Oklahoma	No Law Found
Oregon	No Law Found
Pennsylvania	No Law Found1
Rhode Island	Parental Consent Required
South Carolina	Parental Consent Required[10]
South Dakota	No Law Found

Table 3 (continued)

STATE	LAW
Tennessee	No Law Found[1]
Texas	No Law Found[4]
Utah	Parental Notice Required[2,5]
Vermont	No Law Found
Virginia	No Law Found[11]
Washington	No Law Found[12]
West Virginia	Parental Notice Required[13]
Wisconsin	Minor May Consent[14]
Wyoming	Parental Consent Required

1. Enforcement of a law requiring parental consent or judicial bypass is enjoined at this time.
2. Both parents must be notified unless one parent is not readily available. In Minnesota a "diligent effort" must be made to locate both parents; in Arkansas a "reasonably diligent effort" must be made.
3. Minor under 16 must receive intensive counseling from physician or other qualified professional, who must discuss the possibility of involving the minor's parents.
4. The law authorizing a minor to consent to prenatal care and delivery services excludes abortion. However, this imposes a blanket prohibition on abortions without parental consent and therefore appears to be unconstitutional under Supreme Court decisions.
5. Physician may notify parents. In Maryland the law prohibits disclosure of information about an abortion.
6. Enforcement of a law requiring parental notice or judicial bypass is enjoined by the courts.
7. Minor must have the consent of a parent or other adult family member, use the judicial bypass, or be counseled by the attending physician or a counselor, who can be a psychiatrist, psychologist, social worker, ordained clergy, physician's assistant, nurse practitioner, guidance counselor, or nurse.
8. The law requires notification of one parent with no judicial bypass. However, a physician may waive notification if the minor does not live with a parent; if the doctor determines that the minor is mature enough to give informed consent or that notification may lead to physical or emotional abuse of the minor or otherwise be contrary to her best interests; or if reasonable effort to give notice was unsuccessful. The statute is not being enforced.
9. Both parents must consent. If the parents are divorced, only the custodial parent must consent. In Massachusetts the same is true if one parent is "unavailable."
10. Consent may be given by a grandparent.
11. The state attorney general says the history of the state law authorizing a minor to consent to services in connection with birth control, pregnancy, and family planning indicates that the law is intended to encompass abortion.
12. Mature minor is authorized to consent under state case law.
13. Notification or use of the judicial bypass can be waived if a second physician determines that the minor is mature enough to give consent or that notice would not be in her best interests.
14. Abortion provider must strongly encourage the minor "to consult" her parents, another family member, or an appropriate person. Every provider must have a policy on parental involvement that includes information on the availability of services to assist the minor involving her parents.

Source: Reproduced with the permission of The Alan Guttmacher Institute from Patricia Donovan, *Our Daughter's Decisions: The Conflict in State Law on Abortion and Other Issues,* 1992.

SEXUALLY TRANSMITTED DISEASES

Does a minor have a right to counseling and treatment without parental consent for sexually transmitted diseases such as herpes, gonorrhea, syphilis, and human immunodeficiency virus/acquired immunodeficiency syndrome (HIV/AIDS)? [2]

Yes. Even though doctors usually are required by law to obtain parental consent before treating young people, every state except South Carolina makes an exception for sexually transmitted diseases, or "STDs." Laws permitting minors to consent to treatment for STDs appear to cover treatment for HIV/AIDS. Even so, 11 states expressly authorize a minor to consent privately to HIV/AIDS treatment.

Minors can usually obtain these services at very low cost or no cost at Title X clinics.

RAPE

How is rape defined?

Rape is sexual intercourse that is forced on a person against his or her will. In some states the legal definition of rape is any forced contact of a man's penis with a woman's vagina. In others, both men and women are able to rape or be raped, and the act of rape includes forced oral sex, forced anal sex, and forcing objects into sexual openings of a person's body. Rape is always a crime, and the punishment for it is severe.

What is "date rape"?

It is forced sexual intercourse or any other forced sexual act that occurs in a social situation or between a dating couple. Date rape carries the same legal conseqences as rape that occurs in a nonsocial setting.

Must a rape victim forcibly resist the aggressor in order for rape legally to occur?

No. If the circumstances are such that resisting might place the victim in even greater danger—as almost always is the case—no proof of resistance is needed.

Is rape difficult to prove?

It can be. Some state laws distinguish between "simple rape" and "aggravated rape." With simple rape there is little or no evidence of struggle or violence, but with aggravated rape the rapist uses a weapon, threatens injury, or is violent. Simple rape often is more difficult to prove than aggravated rape because many still believe that with simple rape the victim is partly to blame.

What is statutory rape?

It is sexual intercourse with a woman who is below a certain age. In every state there is an age below which a woman can't legally consent to have sex—even though she may in fact have given her consent, either expressly or by implication. The age usually is between 14 and 18 years, depending on the state. Statutory rape is also illegal.

To be charged with statutory rape, does the man involved have to be above a certain age?

In many states, yes. It usually is between the ages of 15 and 18, depending on state law.

Does this mean that if a teenage couple has sex, the man can be charged with statutory rape?

In some states, yes.

Why isn't the woman also charged with statutory rape? Isn't the law unfair if it only punishes the male partner?

Statutory rape laws that punish only the male aren't considered unfair and aren't unconstitutional. Courts have ruled that states have a legitimate interest in preventing young women from becoming pregnant or contracting sexually transmitted diseases—and from being "taken advantage of."

Is it statutory rape for a woman over age 18 to have sexual intercourse with a young man under, say, age 14?

Not usually. Courts have ruled that women who have sexual intercourse at a very young age are at much greater risk than young teenage men. A teenage woman may become pregnant, for example, or have to go through an abortion. These experiences can be traumatic for many women, but particularly young teens.

NOTES

1. From tabulations by the Alan Guttmacher Institute of data from the 1988 *National Survey of Family Growth,* conducted by the National Center for Health Statistics, U.S. Department of Health and Human Services.

2. HIV is the virus that causes AIDS. It can be transmitted through sexual contact.

FOR FURTHER READING

In General

Boston Children's Hospital. *What Teenagers Want to Know About Sex: Questions and Answers.* Boston: Little, Brown, 1988.

Hyde, Margaret O. *Teen Sex.* Philadelphia: The Westminster Press, 1988.

Johnson, Earvin "Magic." *What You Can Do to Avoid AIDS.* New York: Times Books, 1992.

Nourse, Alan E. *Birth Control.* New York: Franklin Watts, 1988.

Wachter, Oralee, et al. *Sex, Drugs, and AIDS.* New York: Bantam Books, 1987.

Abortion

Emmens, Carol A. *The Abortion Controversy,* rev. ed. New York: Julian Messner, 1991.

Terkel, Susan Neiberg. *Abortion: Facing the Issues.* New York: Franklin Watts, 1988.

Rape

Bode, Janet. *Rape: Preventing It, Coping with the Legal, Medical, and Emotional Aftermath.* New York: Franklin Watts, 1979.

Braswell, Linda. *Quest for Respect: A Healing Guide for Survivors of Rape.* 2nd ed. Ventura, California: Pathfinder Publishing, 1989.

Date Rape

Parrot, Andrea. *Coping with Date Rape and Acquaintance Rape.* New York: The Rosen Publishing Group, 1988.

Warshaw, Robin. *I Never Called It Rape: The Ms. Report on Recognizing, Fighting, and Surviving Date and Acquaintance Rape.* New York: Harper and Row Publishers, 1988.

—9—

Marrying and Having Children

PARENTAL CONSENT FOR MARRIAGE

At what age can a young person marry without parental consent?

At the age of majority, which in most states is age 18. The minimum age for marrying *with* parental consent is age 16 in most states, although a few, including Delaware, Florida, and Georgia, permit 16-year-old minors who are pregnant or have a child to marry without parental consent. Some states allow judges to give consent for 16-year-olds to marry.

For a marriage to be legal, both marriage partners must be old enough to marry or must have obtained the required consent.

See Table 4 for ages at which minors can legally marry in the 50 states and the District of Columbia, and see Chapter Three, "At Home," for more about legal rights at the age of majority.

Early marriages tend to be unstable. Studies show that the earlier a woman marries, the greater the chance she has of divorcing or separating within 5 years. And women who marry as teens are twice as likely to separate as those who marry after age 22.[1]

What happens if a minor marries without the required parental consent?

Some states say there is no marriage. Others take the position that the marriage can be set aside in court but is valid until this actually happens.

Table 4
Marriage Consent Laws for Minors Under Age 18, by State, 1993

STATE	LAW
Alabama	Parental Consent Required
Alaska	Parental Consent
Arizona	Parental Consent Required
Arkansas	Parental Consent Required
California	Parental Consent Required
Colorado	Parental Consent Required
Connecticut	Parental Consent Required
Delaware	Minor May Decide[1]
D.C.	Parental Consent Required
Florida	Minor May Decide[1]
Georgia	Minor May Decide[1]
Hawaii	Parental Consent Required
Idaho	Parental Consent Required
Illinois	Parental Consent Required
Indiana	Parental Consent Required
Iowa	Parental Consent Required
Kansas	Parental Consent Required
Kentucky	Minor May Decide[2]
Louisiana	Minor May Decide[3]
Maine	Parental Consent Required
Maryland	Minor May Decide[1]
Massachusetts	Parental Consent Required
Michigan	Parental Consent Required
Minnesota	Minor May Decide
Mississippi	Minor May Decide[4]
Missouri	Parental Consent Required
Montana	Parental Consent Required
Nebraska	Minor May Decide[5]
Nevada	Parental Consent Required
New Hampshire	Parental Consent Required
New Jersey	Parental Consent Required
New Mexico	Parental Consent Required
New York	Parental Consent Required
North Carolina	Parental Consent Required
North Dakota	Parental Consent Required
Ohio	Parental Consent Required
Oklahoma	Minor May Decide[6]
Oregon	Minor May Decide
Pennsylvania	Parental Consent Required
Rhode Island	Parental Consent Required
South Carolina	Parental Consent Required

Table 4 (continued)

STATE	LAW
South Dakota	Parental Consent Required
Tennessee	Parental Consent Required
Texas	Minor May Decide[7]
Utah	Parental Consent Required
Vermont	Parental Consent Required
Virginia	Parental Consent Required
Washington	Parental Consent Required
West Virginia	Parental Consent Required
Wisconsin	Parental Consent Required
Wyoming	Parental Consent Required

1. Minor who is pregnant or has a child may marry without parental consent; in Florida, a judge must authorize a marriage in such circumstances; in Maryland the minor must be at least 16.
2. A pregnant minor may marry without parental consent, but with court approval.
3. A judge may authorize the marriage of a minor of any age without parental consent when there is a compelling reason.
4. Females 15 or older and males 17 or older may marry without parental consent; however, parents must be notified if either party is under age 21.
5. Minor must be 17 or older.
6. Minor may marry without parental consent if she has given birth to an illegitimate child or is pregnant and the marriage has been authorized by court order.
7. Minor 16 to 18 may petition a court for permission to marry but must be represented by a court-appointed guardian to speak for or against the petition, and the parents must be notified. The court may authorize the marriage if it determines it is in the minor's best interests.

Source: Reproduced with the permission of The Alan Guttmacher Institute from Patricia Donovan, *Our Daughter's Decisions: The Conflict in State Law on Abortion and Other Issues,* 1992.

If teens who are too young to marry in their home state are married in a state where they are old enough to marry without parental consent, is the marriage legal?

The marriage usually is legal in the state where it was performed. As to the legality of the marriage at home, some states rely on the rule that if a marriage is legal where it was performed, it is legal everywhere. Others refuse to honor an out-of-state marriage that wouldn't have been legal if performed in-state.

In one case a 15-year-old New York girl married a 20-year-old Virginia resident in Georgia. They separated a few years later. The woman sued to have the marriage set aside or "annulled" in New York. The court said the marriage was valid in Georgia, and it recognized the marriage under the laws of New York because it didn't involve polygamy (having more than one wife).

If a teen marriage is illegal, does it automatically become legal if the couple is still together when both partners have reached the age of majority?
In most states, yes.

OTHER TEEN MARRIAGE ISSUES

Does marriage emancipate a minor?
Yes. When minors are emancipated, their parents no longer have any legal power over them and are no longer required to support them. For more about emancipation see Chapter Five, "On Your Own."

Are interracial marriages legal?
Yes. A law restricting marriage between members of different races would be a clear violation of the federal Constitution.

The Supreme Court first ruled on this issue as late as 1966. Two residents of Virginia, a black woman and a white man, were married in Washington, D.C., in 1958. When they moved back to Virginia in the same year they were charged with violating Virginia's ban on interracial marriages. The couple pleaded guilty to the charges and were sentenced to 1 year in jail, although the judge suspended their sentences on the condition that they leave Virginia and not return for 25 years. On appeal, the Supreme Court declared Virginia's ban on interracial marriages unconstitutional.

Can a married teen legally buy alcoholic beverages if the drinking age in a particular state is 21?
No. State laws prohibiting the sale of alcoholic beverages to persons under age 21 apply to everyone.

Can a married couple be prohibited from obtaining public welfare benefits because they happen to be teens?
No, provided they are truly independent of their parents.

Can the parents of a married teen carry the teen on their car insurance policy?
Only if the auto that the teen drives is owned by the parents and is

garaged at their residence. Insurance companies have special rules relating to coverage for married children of policyholders. A sales agent for the insurance company should be consulted when this issue comes up.

THE RIGHTS OF TEENAGE PARENTS

Do teenage parents always have the right to make independent decisions about raising their children?

Yes, except when a family court decides that they really can't handle such decisions. The parent-child relationship is protected by the federal Constitution, and states may not excessively interfere with the way parents raise their children. This right extends to teenage parents and their offspring.[2] For example, a state may not require a parent to abandon custody of a child just because the parent hasn't reached the age of majority.

As with adult parents, a child can be removed from a teenage parent's home only if the child has been neglected, mistreated, abused, or abandoned, and *then* only after a full due process hearing. For more about these and related matters, including due process, see Chapter Ten, "Your Right to Be Healthy and Safe from Abuse."

What legal responsibilities do teenagers have as parents?

The same responsibilities as adult parents. In every state, teenage parents must provide their offspring with adequate care, nurturing, and support. These responsibilities exist whether or not the child is born outside marriage, and they continue to exist until the child reaches the age of majority, even if a court forbids a parent to visit his or her child.

Can teenage parents consent to medical care for their child?

Twenty-eight states and the District of Columbia now have laws authorizing parents under age 18 to consent to their children's medical care. No state requires the involvement of a teen's parents in such matters.

Does a teen have legal rights with respect to a child born outside marriage?

Yes. The Constitution gives parents of all ages the right of custody over their minor children. This right always includes children born outside marriage and children of teenage parents.[3]

When the parents of a child born outside marriage are involved in a dispute over child custody, will a family court always award custody to the mother?

No. Courts in many states still regard the mother as the natural guardian of a minor child, particularly a very young child. (This is called the "maternal preference.") But a mother's right to custody of a child born outside marriage isn't absolute—it may have to yield to the child's best interests.

As a practical matter, family courts are most likely to award custody to the parent who has been *caring for* the child since that parent knows the child best. If the parents are unmarried teens, the mother almost always is the caregiver, because teenage fathers rarely live with their children. What this means is that unless a teenage father can convince a court that the mother can't take care of the child *and* that he can, the mother usually will be awarded custody.

Even so, a teenage father who wants to take day-to-day responsibility for his child certainly can obtain custody. In a disputed case, if a family court determines that awarding custody to the father is in the child's best interests, it will do so, even if the parents have never lived under the same roof.

Can custody of a child ever be changed?

Most family courts hesitate to modify custody arrangements once they have been established. To modify them, the circumstances in the child's home must have changed dramatically and the court must be convinced that a new home clearly would be in the child's best interests. If this can be shown, the court might award custody to the child's father, a grandparent, or another relative.

As discussed in Chapters Three and Ten, every state has the power to remove neglected, mistreated, or abandoned children from their homes, either temporarily or permanently. Matters such as these are handled in child protection proceedings in family court.

If a teenage mother has physical custody of a child born outside marriage, is the father legally entitled to visit the child?

Yes, unless the family court believes that contact with the child isn't in the child's best interests. A teenage father has the right to be involved with his offspring unless he has been proved unfit or has forfeited his parental rights.

Can a teenage mother voluntarily place her child for adoption?

Yes. The District of Columbia and every state except Michigan, Minnesota, Pennsylvania, and Rhode Island authorize teenage mothers to consent to a child's adoption. These four states require the involvement of the mother's parents in the adoption decision.

Can a teenage father stop the mother of his child from placing their child for adoption?

There is no simple answer to this question. Some states require the consent of both teenage parents to place a child for adoption unless the father can't be found or hasn't provided for the child financially. Some require the father's consent only if his "paternity" has been established. Some provide that an unmarried father isn't entitled to be notified of the adoption at all, and others say the father can be notified, but it isn't legally necessary. Some legal scholars believe that a state law which fails to require notification to the father is an unconstitutional denial of "due process of law." For more about due process, see Chapter Two.

Can parental rights ever be terminated without a court hearing?

No. Terminating parental rights without a full due process hearing in family court would be a clear violation of the Constitution.

FINANCIAL HELP FOR YOUNG FAMILIES

Do teenage parents have the right to receive financial assistance at public expense?

There is no constitutional right to public financial assistance. Even so, the federal government and many state and county governments do provide a modest level of help to needy families. Young families who meet the financial qualifications for assistance aren't turned down just because of the parents' ages.

The largest public assistance program for parents is a jointly funded federal/state program called Aid to Families with Dependent Children, or "AFDC." It provides assistance to needy children when one parent is incapacitated or lives someplace else. AFDC seeks to compensate families partially for the support that the missing parent should otherwise be contributing. A typical AFDC family consists of a mother and at least one young child.

How does a family qualify for AFDC?

First, there must be a needy, dependent child in the house. A child is "needy" if the household income and other family resources are beneath a certain dollar amount. (Both amounts are very low.) Second, one parent must have left home, died, or become incapacitated although still living at home. If a family qualifies for AFDC, the recipients are automatically covered by Medicaid, another jointly funded federal/state program that provides medical care for victims of poverty.

AFDC recipients are regularly visited by AFDC caseworkers. If the recipient refuses to allow the caseworker in the house, she (or he) may have current benefits terminated. In addition, certain AFDC recipients must participate in a special work program called JOBS, which requires the participant to seek employment or participate in a job training program. If the recipient doesn't participate, AFDC benefits can be terminated altogether.

AFDC recipients are required to cooperate with AFDC program administrators to obtain support from the absent parent, usually by supplying the parent's name and address (unless giving such information could place the AFDC recipient in danger). Recipients must also help AFDC administrators establish the paternity of any child born outside marriage.

Can a teenage parent qualify for food stamps?

If a teenage parent qualifies for AFDC because he or she has physical custody of a child, there is a good chance that both the parent and child will qualify for the federal Food Stamp Program. Food stamps are coupons issued to households and used to purchase food items in grocery stores (but not in restaurants). As with AFDC, the food stamp applicant's income and resources must be under a specific dollar amount to qualify.

Besides the Food Stamp Program, a special federal program, called the WIC program, provides low-income pregnant women and their children with extra food such as eggs, milk, infant formula, fruit juice, cereal, and cheese.

NOTES

1. T. C. Martin and L. L. Bumpass, "Recent Trends in Marital Disruption," *Demography,* 1989;26:37.

2. In 1988, of the 3,909,510 babies born in the United States, 488,941 were born to women under 20 years old. Source: United States Department of Health and Human Services, National Center for Health Statistics.

3. Of the 488,941 babies born to women under age 20 in 1988, 322,400 were born to unmarried women. Source: United States Department of Health and Human Services, National Center for Health Statistics.

FOR FURTHER READING

Teen Marriages

Ayer, Eleanor. *Everything You Need to Know About Teen Marriage.* New York: The Rosen Publishing Group, 1990.
Lindsay, Jeanne Warren. *Teenage Marriage: Coping with Reality.* Buena Park, California: Morning Glory Press, 1984.

Teens with Children

Bode, Janet. *Kids Having Kids: The Unwed Teenage Parent.* New York: Franklin Watts, 1980.
Comfort, Randy Lee, and Constance D. Williams. *The Child Care Catalog: A Handbook of Resources and Information on Child Care.* Littleton, Colorado: Libraries Unlimited, 1985.
Ewy, Donna, and Rodger Ewy. *Teen Pregnancy: The Challenges We Faced, the Choices We Made.* New York: New American Library, 1984.
Lindsay, Jeanne Warren. *The Challenge of Toddlers: Parenting Your Child from One to Three.* Buena Park, California: Morning Glory Press, 1989.
Lindsay, Jeanne Warren, and Sharon Rodine. *Teen Pregnancy Challenge, Book One: Strategies for Change.* Buena Park, California: Morning Glory Press, 1989.
Lindsay, Jeanne Warren, and Sharon Rodine. *Teen Pregnancy Challenge, Book Two: Programs for Kids.* Buena Park, California: Morning Glory Press, 1989.
Owens, Carolyn Pearl, and Linda Roggow. *Pregnant and Single: Help for the Tough Choices.* Grand Rapids, Michigan: Pyranee Books, 1990.
Richards, Arlene Kramer, and Willis, Irene. *What to Do If You or Someone You Know Is Under 18 and Pregnant.* New York: Lothrop, Lee and Shepard Books, 1983.

Poverty and Welfare

Davis, Bertha. *Poverty in America: What We Do About It.* New York: Franklin Watts, 1991.
Weiss, Ann E. *Welfare: Helping Hand or Trap?* Hillside, New Jersey: Enslow Publishers, 1990.

— 10 —

Your Right to Be Healthy
and Safe from Abuse

ABUSE AND NEGLECT

What is child abuse?

The definition varies somewhat from state to state, but usually it is any serious physical injury to a minor that is caused by a parent or person caring for the minor. It always includes child sexual abuse and child sexual molestation, and in some states it includes psychological abuse. Child abuse can also occur when a parent or other responsible person lets someone abuse a child.

What are some examples of child abuse?

Serious physical injuries are naturally the easiest to imagine, but bones don't have to be broken and weapons don't have to be used for abuse to occur. Severe spankings, beatings, and whippings may constitute child abuse even if no cuts or bruises result. An adult who intentionally burns a minor with a lighted cigarette or deliberately pushes a minor down a flight of stairs has committed child abuse.

Here are some grim facts about child abuse:

1. In 1986, the medical profession treated 300,000 physically abused minors, another 140,000 sexually abused minors, and 700,000 minors who were neglected or maltreated.[1]
2. Since 1980, reports of child abuse have quadrupled.
3. An estimated 2.4 million cases of suspected child abuse, child sexual abuse, and child neglect are reported to state child protective agencies each year.

4. Abused and neglected young people often suffer drops in IQ and an increase in learning disabilities, depression, and drug use.

5. Parental abuse of alcohol and other drugs is a major factor contributing to child abuse and early death. Nearly 10 million minors are affected in some way by the substance abuse of their parents.

6. More than three children die every day in this country as a result of abuse and neglect.[2]

How does child neglect differ from child abuse?

Child neglect is less precisely defined than child abuse, but usually it is described as a lapse of care by a parent or other responsible person. Child neglect occurs when parents don't do something for a child that the law requires them to do. The clearest examples are failures to provide a minor child with adequate food, clothing, shelter, or supervision.

How are child abuse and child neglect cases reported?

The easiest way to report a suspected case is to call the state or local child protective agency. The address and phone number of each state child protective agency are listed in Table 5. Crisis intervention groups and medical clinics such as Planned Parenthood can also be called—they have reporting information at their fingertips.

In addition, most communities have 24-hour child abuse and child neglect telephone hotlines (sometimes called "helplines"). The numbers to call usually are listed in the front of the local phone book. Important national hotline numbers, including those of national child abuse hotlines, are listed in Table 6. Calls to hotlines are always confidential.

If a young person is being abused by a parent, a housekeeper, a coworker, a date, a neighbor, a parent's boyfriend or girlfriend, a brother or sister—*anyone*—the young person or anyone else may report it. The abuser doesn't have to be a parent for the state to be concerned about stopping it and preventing it from happening again.

Can a minor report an abusing parent?

Anyone can make a report. For the sake of the victim, the abuser, and the abuser's family, all physical and sexual abuse cases should be reported, as should all neglect cases. The more detailed the report, the better the chance that the child protective agency will respond promptly.

Are reports of abuse to child protective services offices confidential?

Always.

Table 5
State Child Protective Services Offices (Call the office in your state to report cases of abuse or neglect. Someone will tell you whom to contact locally.)

ALABAMA
Family & Children Services Division
Human Resources Dept
50 N Ripley Street
Montgomery AL 36130-1801
205-242-9500

ALASKA
Family & Youth Services Division
PO Box 110630
Juneau AK 99811-0630
907-465-3191

ARIZONA
Child Support Enforcement Division
Economic Security Dept
PO Box 6123
Phoenix AZ 85005
602-252-0236

ARKANSAS
Children & Family Services Division
Human Services Dept
PO Box 1437
Little Rock AR 72203
501-682-8772

CALIFORNIA
Adult & Family Services Division
Social Services Dept
744 P Street
Sacramento CA 95814
916-657-2596

COLORADO
Child Welfare Services Division
Social Services Dept
1575 Sherman Street
Denver CO 80203-1714
303-866-3672

CONNECTICUT
Children & Youth Services Dept
170 Sigourney Street
Hartford CT 06105
203-566-3536

DELAWARE
Child Protective Services Division
Services for Children, Youth,
& Their Families
1825 Faulkland Road
Wilmington DE 19805
302-633-2650

DISTRICT OF COLUMBIA
Family Services Administration
Human Services Dept
801 N Capital Street NE
Washington DC 20002
202-727-5947

FLORIDA
Children, Youth & Families Program
Health & Rehabilitative Services Dept
1317 Winewood Blvd.
Tallahassee FL 32399-0700
904-488-8762

GEORGIA
Family & Children's Services Division
Human Resources Dept
47 Trinity Avenue SW
Atlanta GA 30334-1202
404-894-6386

HAWAII
Family & Children's Services Division
Human Services Dept
1390 Miller Street
Honolulu HI 96809
808-586-5680

IDAHO
Family & Children's Services Division
Health & Welfare Dept
450 West State Street
Boise ID 83720
206-334-5700

ILLINOIS
Children & Family Services Dept
406 E Monroe Street
Springfield IL 63701-1496
217-785-2509

Table 5 (continued)

INDIANA
Family & Children's Division
Family & Social Services
Administration
402 W Washington Street
Indianapolis IN 46204
317-232-4705

IOWA
Adult, Children & Family Services
Division
Human Services Dept
Hoover State Office Building
Des Moines IA 50319
515-261-5521

KANSAS
Young & Adult Services
300 SW Oakley, Biddle Bldg.
Topeka KS 66606
913-296-3284

KENTUCKY
Family Services Division
Social Services Dept
275 E Main Street
Frankfort KY 40621
502-564-6852

LOUISIANA
Social Services Dept
PO Box 3776
Baton Rouge LA 70621
504-342-0286

MAINE
Child & Family Services Bureau
Human Services Dept
State House, Station 11
Augusta ME 04333
207-287-5060

MARYLAND
Child Protective Services
Human Resources Department
Saratoga State Center
311 W Saratoga Street
Baltimore MD 21201
410-461-0268

MASSACHUSETTS
Children's Office
10 West Street, 5th Floor
Boston MA 02111
617-727-8900

MICHIGAN
Children & Family Services Bureau
Social Services Dept
235 S Grand Avenue, Box 30037
Lansing MI 48909
517-335-6158

MINNESOTA
Children's Services Division
Human Services Dept
444 Lafayette Road
St. Paul MN 55155
612-296-5890

MISSISSIPPI
Family & Children's Services Division
Human Services Dept
PO Box 352
Jackson MS 39205-0352
601-354-6662

MISSOURI
Youth Services Division
Social Services Dept
221 W High Street
PO Box 1527
Jefferson City MO 65102
314-751-3324

MONTANA
Family Services Dept
Box 8005
Helena MT 59604
406-444-5900

NEBRASKA
Center for Children & Youth
Social Services Dept
PO Box 95026
Lincoln NE 68509
402-471-3305

Table 5 (continued)

NEVADA
Children & Family Services Division
Human Resources Dept
Room 600, 505 E King Street
Carson City NV 89710
702-687-5962

NEW HAMPSHIRE
Children & Youth Services Division
Health & Human Services Dept
Hazen Drive
Concord NH 03301
603-271-4451

NEW JERSEY
Youth & Family Services Division
CN 717, Capitol Circle
Trenton NJ 08625-6920
609-292-6920

NEW MEXICO
Children's Bureau
Human Services Dept
PO Box 2348
Santa Fe NM 87504-8439
505-827-8439

NEW YORK
Family & Children's Services Division
Social Services Dept
40 N Pearl Street
Albany NY 12243
518-474-9428

NORTH CAROLINA
Youth Advocacy & Involvement Office
121 W Jones Street
Raleigh NC 27611
919-733-9296

NORTH DAKOTA
Children & Family Services Division
Human Services Dept
600 E Boulevard
Bismarck ND 58505
701-224-2316

OHIO
Family, Children & Adult Services
Division
Human Services Dept
30 East Broad Street, 32nd Floor
Columbus OH 43266-0432
614-466-2206

OKLAHOMA
Children & Youth Services Division
Human Services Dept
PO Box 25352
Oklahoma City OK 73125
405-521-4088

OREGON
Children's Services Division
196 Commercial Street SE
Salem OR 97310
503-378-4374

PENNSYLVANIA
Children & Families Dept
Public Welfare Dept
Box 2675
Harrisburg PA 17105
717-787-4756

RHODE ISLAND
Children & Their Families Dept
810 Mount Pleasant Avenue
Providence RI 02906-1935
401-457-4708

SOUTH CAROLINA
Child Protective and Preventive Services
Social Services Department
1535 Confederate Avenue
Columbia SC 29201
803-734-5670

SOUTH DAKOTA
Child Support Enforcement Office
Social Services Dept
700 Governors Drive
Pierre SD 57501
605-773-3641

Table 5 (continued)

TENNESSEE
Family Assistance
Human Services Dept
400 Deaderick Street
Nashville TN 37248-0001
615-741-5463

UTAH
Health & Social Services
210 State Capitol
Salt Lake City UT 84114
801-538-1000

TEXAS
Protective and Regulatory Services
7901 Cameron Road, Bldg 3
Austin TX 78753
512-834-0034
800-252-5400 (hotline)

VERMONT
Social & Rehabilitation Services Dept
Human Services Agency
103 S Main Street, State Complex
Waterbury VT 05671-0204
802-241-2101

VIRGINIA
Child Welfare Services Bureau
Social Services Dept
8007 Discovery Drive
Richmond VA 23229-8699
804-662-9081

WASHINGTON
Children & Family Services Division
Social & Health Services Dept
MS OB-44
Olympia WA 98504
206-586-2688

WEST VIRGINIA
Health & Human Resources Dept
State Capitol Complex, Bldg. 3
Charleston WV 25305
304-558-0684

WISCONSIN
Youth & Families Bureau
Health & Social Services Dept
PO Box 7850
Madison WI 53707
608-266-5838

WYOMING
Family Services Dept
Hathaway Building, 3rd Floor
Cheyenne WY 82002
307-777-5831

Can one parent report the other parent?
Yes.

If a person fails to report a case of child abuse or neglect, has that person broken the law?
In some situations, yes. Doctors and nurses, including school nurses, are required by law to report suspected cases because they often are the first to discover the evidence. Some states also require social workers, grade school and high school teachers, and other professionals who are responsible for children to report suspected abuse and neglect. These people are sometimes called ''mandatory reporters.''

Table 6
National Toll-free Hotline Numbers

ABUSE
Parents Anonymous
1-800-352-0386 (California)
1-800-421-0353 (elsewhere)

National Child Abuse Hotline
1-800-4-A-CHILD

DRUG ABUSE
National Institute on Drug Abuse
1-800-662-HELP

National Cocaine Hotline
1-800-COCAINE

"Just Say No Clubs" Hotline (Drug Abuse)
"Just Say No" International
1-800-258-2766

ALCOHOLISM
National Council on Alcoholism and Drug Dependence Hotline
1-800-622-2255

Mothers Against Drunk Driving (MADD)
1-800-438-6233

CIVIL RIGHTS
Civil Rights Complaint Hotline
1-800-368-1019

HEALTH CARE
National Health Information Center
Department of Health & Human Services
301-565-4167 (Maryland)
1-800-336-4797 (elsewhere)

SEXUALLY TRANSMITTED
DISEASES (STDs)
National STD Hotline
1-800-227-8922

CDC National AIDS Hotline
U.S. Public Health Service
1-800-342-2437
SIDA (Spanish line) 1-800-344-7432

AIDS Drug Information
National Institute of Allergies and Infectious Diseases
1-800-874-2572
TTY (hearing impaired) 1-800-243-7012

PREGNANCY
Pro-Choice
Abortion Hotline
1-800-770-9100

Right-to-Life
Birthright, Inc.
1-800-848-LOVE

RUNAWAYS
National Runaway Switchboard
1-800-621-4000
TTY (hearing impaired) 1-800-621-0394

Runaway Hotline
1-800-231-6946

The questions and answers that follow assume the suspected abuser is a parent. However, for a child protective agency to act, the abuser or neglectful person needn't be a parent. He or she can be a teacher, housekeeper, relative, sibling, or any person in a position of responsibility over the minor.

How does a child protective agency act on a report of abuse or neglect?

If the problem is occurring at home, the agency first conducts a home investigation. Usually a team of social workers visits the minor's home, and they often arrive unannounced. The social workers interview the parents, the minor, other suspected abusers, and often the neighbors. Sometimes they also decide to interview the minor's doctor and teachers.

If evidence of abuse or neglect turns up, the lawyer for the child protective agency may file a "petition" in state family court for authority to take custody of the minor or protect the minor in some other way. Filing a petition officially begins the case, which is a "civil" action as opposed to a "criminal action." In most states these cases are called "child protection proceedings."

For more about the difference between civil and criminal actions see Chapter Seventeen, "Taking Matters to Court."

Does the overall investigation procedure differ in emergency situations?

Yes. If the young person is in serious danger and there's no time for a home study, he or she can be removed immediately. In these cases the family court must hold a hearing as soon as possible after the removal to decide how to proceed with the case. If it turns out that removing the minor wasn't necessary, the minor must be returned home right away.

Is a petition filed in family court after every investigation?

No, a petition won't be filed if the investigation doesn't reveal evidence of abuse or neglect. But even if evidence of abuse or neglect exists, the agency may decide against filing a petition if the parents agree to participate in parenting classes, counseling, or some other suggested rehabilitation program. Meanwhile a social worker from the child protective agency makes periodic visits to the family to make certain the home situation is stable. If the parents don't make the effort to attend the special classes, counseling, or rehab program, often the agency will decide to go ahead and file the petition.

Does the minor remain at home between the time of the investigation and the hearing date?

It depends on the circumstances. If the abuse or neglect appears especially serious or if allowing the minor to stay home is likely to be a bad idea for some other reason, the judge may order the minor to stay with a relative or perhaps a family friend. Other possibilities are placing the minor in temporary foster care or with a volunteer family. (Foster care is discussed at the end of this chapter.)

What actually happens in a family court hearing?

Investigators, social workers, and medical witnesses present their evidence to the family court judge. These individuals might be cross-examined by the parents' attorney, who will attempt to protect the parents' interests and reputation as parents. Documents, medical records, and studies might be offered, and the judge often asks the witnesses additional questions. Usually no one is in the courtroom except witnesses, social workers, relatives and persons with a stake in the outcome, although family court hearings are rarely closed to the general public.

Will the minor testify in the hearing?

It depends on his or her age and maturity, and on the nature of the case. Small children seldom testify, but teens often do.

Although an abused or neglected minor usually is the most important witness at an abuse or neglect hearing, minors often find court intimidating. Even though there's never anything to be afraid of, many minors fear their testimony will infuriate their parents, and sometimes it does. For these reasons, family court judges sometimes permit a minor's testimony to be taken outside the courtroom and away from the parents. Testimony might be videotaped or tape-recorded, or taken inside the judge's office.

Can a minor be forced to testify?

Yes, if the judge determines that the minor is "competent" to do so. See Chapter Seventeen for additional information about the testimony of minors.

Will the court always remove a minor from the home in proven abuse and neglect situations?

No. If the problem isn't expected to continue and allowing the minor to stay home appears to be the preferred arrangement, a family court won't authorize a removal. Instead, a social worker will monitor the family and try to help it better understand its problems. In-home counseling often is an enormous help to troubled families.

If parents are suspected of abuse or neglect, will a lawyer be appointed to represent their interests if they can't afford one?

Yes, in both civil and criminal cases. Although parents don't have a constitutional right to a lawyer in child protection proceedings, most states now authorize a court-appointed attorney in such cases for poor parents.

Is the minor entitled to a court-appointed lawyer as well?

In most states, yes. The minor's lawyer represents the minor in child protection proceedings, and no one else. The lawyer is legally required to look after the child's best interests and no one else's.

Does this mean the minor's lawyer and the parents' lawyer will be different people?

Yes, because the parents' position in the case might be contrary to the child's. They might, for example, claim that neither has ever laid a hand on the child, despite the child's obvious cuts and bruises. For this reason, family courts usually appoint another lawyer to represent the minor's separate legal concerns.

Can a young person insist that his or her lawyer take a certain position in an abuse or neglect case—in defense of a parent, for example?

No. The minor's lawyer (often called the guardian ad litem) must act in the best interests of the minor even if the minor doesn't agree with the way the case is being handled.

Who pays for the minor's lawyer?

Usually the state.

Does the family court go after the abuser?

No. A family court's basic purpose is to protect a minor from abuse or neglect. But as this is being arranged, the state prosecuting attorney will decide whether to charge the suspected party with criminal abuse or neglect, or perhaps even battery or attempted homicide.

Whether the state decides to make a criminal charge against a parent depends on a variety of factors such as whether the parent abused or neglected any children in the past or whether the minor will be cared for if the parent goes to jail. It may also depend on the parent's overall attitude.

Another factor in the decision is this: the prosecutor knows that *criminal* abuse and neglect are harder to prove than *civil* abuse and neglect. For a person to be convicted on criminal charges, the prosecutor must prove "beyond a reasonable doubt" that the person committed the act. But for a family court to intervene, the facts of the case only have to show it was "more likely than not" that abuse or neglect occurred. (These levels of proof are called "burdens of proof.") If the prosecuting attorney doesn't believe the state's higher burden of proof can be met, he or she won't file criminal charges and the case will only go to family court.

Criminal abuse trials are discussed in detail in the next section.

SEXUAL ABUSE

How does the law define sexual abuse?

Sexual abuse is any forced sexual contact. The sexual contact can be oral sex and includes attempted or actual penetration of a minor's vagina or anus. It might also be an adult's handling of a minor's genitals or a request for a minor to handle an adult's genitals.

Sometimes sexual abuse doesn't have to involve physical contact. It is illegal for a minor to be forced to look at an adult's genitals or be forced to undress or expose himself or herself.

Is sexual abuse always a crime?

Yes. Persons who sexually abuse or sexually molest minors or adults can be charged with criminal sexual abuse. Most states impose a maximum of between ten and twenty years' imprisonment for sexual intercourse with a child, although the sentence isn't as lengthy when the offense is sexual touching. When the victim is an adolescent, the maximum sentence for forced sex usually is ten years, although some states provide penalties as low as one to two years.

Many believe that criminal prosecution in child sexual abuse cases can cause more emotional damage to a minor than the abuse itself, especially when a parent is the abuser. Even so, a criminal prosecution is a symbol that society will protect minors and that their rights and welfare are respected.[3]

Can a parent be criminally charged with child sexual abuse?

Anyone can be charged with child sexual abuse, including a parent.

If a parent is charged with suspected child sexual abuse, can the other parent also be charged?

In certain cases, yes. Usually it depends on whether the nonparticipating parent knew the child was being sexually abused but didn't do anything to stop it.

Can a teen be charged with criminal sexual abuse for having sex with another teen?

Here it depends on whether the sex is forced. (An obvious example of teen sexual abuse would be date rape.) Penalties for sexual abuse vary depending on the age difference between the perpetrator and the other minor. Slight age differences often result in light sentences, in part to abolish criminal liability for consenting sex between teens. For more about teens and sex, see Chapter Eight, "Your Sexual Life."

How can a sexually abused minor obtain immediate help?

By contacting the state child protective agency or the police. Child sexual abuse is a form of child abuse, so the state child protective agency can always intervene. As in physical abuse and neglect cases, it can act in emergencies, then bring child protection proceedings after intervening. At a later date the state prosecuting attorney will decide whether to criminally prosecute the suspected abuser.

What would a criminal physical or sexual abuse or neglect trial be like?

In all honesty, it wouldn't be fun. Prior to trial the minor would be required to repeat the details of the incident to several different police officers, doctors, social workers, counselors, and probably the suspect's attorney. The trial would probably be open to the public. The minor might be required to take the stand, and there would be plenty of legal jargon used during the investigation and trial that the minor wouldn't comprehend.

No civil hearing or criminal trial on a physical or sexual abuse matter is pleasant for the individuals involved. The law can require or "subpoena" all key persons to participate. However, the social workers, counselors, lawyers, and others involved in the case are always extremely caring and supportive of the minor.

Is criminal physical and sexual abuse tough to prove in court?

Not necessarily. Child abuse used to be difficult to prove because courts didn't trust the testimony of minors, even when the minor was a teen and the only eyewitness to the abuse. But these days a minor's testimony is permitted and often required in both civil and criminal physical sexual abuse cases unless the minor is a young child.

A special issue in criminal sexual abuse cases is "hearsay," which is a person's statement about what someone else said. Hearsay statements usually aren't permitted in court. In abuse cases, the rule against hearsay could prevent another person, such as a school nurse, from stating what the minor confided about the sexual abuse—instead, the court would require the minor to testify on his or her own.[4] This can be an obstacle if the minor is afraid to testify against a parent.

In many states, the hearsay rule is loosened in child sexual abuse and rape cases, but only if the witness's hearsay statements appear particularly reliable. In a 1988 Connecticut child custody case a court permitted a psychologist to testify that a minor spontaneously confided that her father had caused her genital injuries. The court ruled that although the psychologist's testimony was hearsay, it was reliable, and as a result, the father's visitation rights were drastically restricted.

On the other hand, in a 1987 Georgia case a mother wasn't permitted to testify about talk spoken by her son in his sleep regarding a certain act of anal sex by another person. Not surprisingly, the court ruled that her testimony was unreliable hearsay.

Testimony by a minor in court is discussed earlier in this chapter and also Chapter Seventeen.

MEDICAL CARE

If parents don't provide a minor child with adequate medical care, what can happen?

The state child protective agency can intervene, because failing to provide medical care is a form of neglect. The state can also intervene if parents remove their child from a doctor's care before treatment is complete.

Family courts consider both the seriousness of the problem and the risks and benefits of treatment when deciding whether to order medical help. They also consider whether the child wants to go through with the procedure.

Does a minor's life have to be in danger before a family court will order treatment?

No, but it can be difficult to predict whether a court will order it if the child's life isn't hanging in the balance. In 1972 a Pennsylvania court refused to order a spinal operation for a young boy because neither he nor the parents wanted to go through with it, even though his condition was very serious. But in the same year an Iowa court approved simple tonsillectomies for three siblings over the religious objections of the parents.

Can parents prevent a minor child from receiving medical treatment for religious reasons, even if the minor wants it?

Yes, but only if the refusal to obtain treatment doesn't seriously endanger the minor's health or otherwise amount to neglect. Cases like this raise a freedom of religion issue under the First Amendment's Free Exercise Clause, so courts hesitate to order treatment unless the minor's condition is very serious.

For more about First Amendment rights, including the First Amendment's Free Exercise Clause, see Chapter Two, "At School."

Can a minor arrange for his or her own medical care?

As a rule, minors can't enter into agreements for medical care and can't provide legal consent for their own treatment. But there are two exceptions. First, a minor, particularly a teen, can do so if the parents refuse. This wrinkle in the law also applies to other "necessaries"—to a minor's separate arrangements for food, shelter, and clothing.

Second, older, married, pregnant, and "emancipated" minors and those who are parents or runaways can give consent to routine treatment.[5] (Emancipation gives a minor most of the privileges and responsibilities of adulthood, as Chapter Five explains.) In addition, most states now have laws permitting minors to consent to treatment for alcoholism, drug abuse, and sexually transmitted diseases (STDs) including human immunodeficiency virus/acquired immunodeficiency syndrome (HIV/AIDS).[6]

Wouldn't a doctor still hesitate to treat a minor absent parental consent?

Probably. Although the exceptions discussed earlier mean that a doctor can't be sued for "battery" if he or she treats a minor without parental consent in the situations described, many won't take the risk. (Battery is any touching of another person without first obtaining consent from the person who is legally allowed to give it.)

What, then, should a teen do if he or she needs medical care and the parents won't cooperate?

Call the state child protective agency, or at least a teacher, minister, or adult friend or relative. The addresses and phone numbers of child protective agencies in each state are listed in Table 5.

Can a minor sign up for publicly funded medical care such as Medicaid if he or she doesn't live at home?

In most states it depends on whether the minor is still under the control of his or her parents, or, on the other hand, whether the minor is emancipated.

In a 1977 case, New York's highest court decided that because a teenage woman had emancipated herself, she could legally apply for publicly funded medical services. The young woman had left home to avoid her father's control. The state medical welfare agency argued in court that it shouldn't have to pay for her care because her father had enough income to support her and hadn't thrown her out of the house. However, the New York court ruled that the woman's "implied" emancipation relieved her father of his parental responsibilities. She was therefore entitled to public medical assistance.

OTHER ISSUES RELATING TO ABUSE AND NEGLECT

Can a minor be taken from the custody of a parent because the parent is "living with someone"?

Not for that reason alone. A California appeals court ruled in 1967 that a mother wasn't unfit to parent just because she and her children were living with a man she wasn't married to. The judge's decision, rendered against the county agency seeking custody of the woman's two children, said that she and her boyfriend were "satisfying the children's need for family love, security and physical well-being." The decision noted that "many homes, however blessed by marital vows, fall short of an ideal environment for children." Courts across the country have reached the same conclusion in similar cases.

Can a minor be taken from the custody of his or her parents because their home is dirty and messy?

Again, not for that reason alone. A home that strikes someone as dirty or messy doesn't necessarily indicate that the parents are neglectful—some parents just place more importance on a clean house than others. However, a home that is so filthy that it becomes a health hazard could well be the basis for neglect proceedings.

Can a minor be taken from the custody of his or her parents because one of them has been convicted of a crime?

In some states the fact that a parent has been convicted of a serious crime can be grounds for child protection proceedings, and so can a parent's habitual drug or alcohol use.

Can a state take custody of a minor because a parent who is living in the home is gay or lesbian?

In most states a custodial parent's homosexuality can't support a claim of child neglect in and of itself. But family courts will consider a parent's active homosexual conduct when deciding whether the parent is fit to raise children. To learn about situations in which parental rights can be terminated altogether, see Chapter Three, "At Home."

MENTAL HEALTH ISSUES

Can a teen see a psychiatrist or psychologist without parental consent?

Although twenty states and the District of Columbia now permit minors to consent to outpatient mental health treatment (instead of requiring the consent of their parents), it is very difficult for a young person to obtain mental health counseling without parental approval. Many public and private mental health agencies refuse to meet with a teen more than once without notice to a parent. (Psychiatrists and psychologists in private practice rarely confront this issue because teens usually can't afford to see them.)

A state or county mental health association is the best place to contact for information about confidential mental health counseling and treatment.

Can parents admit a minor to a mental hospital without the minor's consent?

Parents have the legal power to consent to a minor's mental health treatment in a private hospital.

Can parents admit a minor child to a public mental hospital without a court hearing?

A full due process hearing in court isn't required, but some sort of review hearing must take place to see whether admitting the minor is necessary or whether the parents are simply shoving a difficult minor aside. Usually these reviews are conducted by a doctor who hasn't treated the minor in the past. For information about the meaning of due process, see Chapter Two.

FOSTER CARE

What is foster care?

It is a living arrangement for young people whose parents are unable to provide proper care. In foster care, "foster parents" take minors into their homes and are responsible for their day-to-day care and supervision. Foster care is meant to last for a limited period, although sometimes foster care arrangements last many months, and sometimes years.

A foster child usually is placed in a foster home at the direction of a family court, although parents can place a child in a foster home voluntarily. The state agency authorized to place children in foster care retains legal custody over the foster child, licenses foster homes, and supervises the foster parents.

Can a teen be a foster "child"?

Yes.

Why might a family court judge order a minor into foster care?

The reason might be the parents' financial difficulties or perhaps a parent's bad health or emotional problems. It might be that the parents have abused, neglected, or abandoned the child or that one of them is in prison. There are dozens of reasons for placing young people in foster care.

Do minors in foster care have any legal rights?

Young people in foster homes always have the right to receive adequate care, including food, clothing, shelter, education, and medical treatment, all at state expense. Foster children with special needs are legally entitled to receive special medical or psychiatric care and also rehabilitation training.

Foster children also have the right to be protected from abuse and neglect at the hands of their foster parents. If a young person is abused while in foster care, the state must remove the child. In addition, in most states a foster child (assisted by an adult) can go to court to recover money damages against the foster care agency for its failure to supervise the foster parents properly. For more about recovering damages in court see Chapter Seventeen, "Taking Matters to Court."

Do minors in need of foster care have a right to choose their foster parents?

No, the decision is made by the state foster care agency after the family court orders the minor into a foster home. However, many agencies actively seek relatives who might be willing to serve as foster parents.

Do the natural parents retain any authority over a child in foster care?

In most states, yes. Although the family court transfers legal custody to the foster care agency, it often permits the natural parents to continue to make major decisions relating to their child, including decisions about his or her medical care, schooling, and religion.

Do foster children have a legal right to see their natural parents while in foster care?

In most cases, yes, and the parents usually have a right to see their child. There is a strong belief that foster children need to maintain contact with their parents; as a result, foster care agencies now authorize regular visits by them except in extreme cases.

Do foster children have a legal right to be reunited with their families after being in a foster home?

Yes. Federal law requires that states develop case plans to help reunite foster children with their natural families as soon as possible, provided it is in the child's best interests. States must determine within eighteen months of placement whether the child should be returned home, placed for adoption, or put in a more permanent foster home. This law was passed after studies proved that children remain in foster care either too long or for no good reason.

Can foster parents legally prevent a foster child from being returned to his or her natural parents?

The laws of some states now allow foster parents to challenge a foster child's return to his or her natural parents in either family court or at a hearing before the foster care agency. Usually the foster parents may only object to a foster child's removal if the child has been with them for a long time—three to eighteen months, depending on the state.

Do foster parents have a legal right to adopt a foster child?

In many states, yes, provided the parental rights of the natural parents actually have been terminated. Although foster parents used to be forbidden to adopt a foster child, in recent years such adoptions have gained favor with legislatures, courts, and child protective agencies.

Can a minor adopt his or her foster parents?

No, but if foster parents want to adopt a foster child, many states require the child's consent to the adoption if the child has reached a certain age. The consent age falls between ages 10 and 14, again depending on the state.

For a discussion of whether a minor can divorce his or her parents in favor of foster parents or others, see the discussion in Chapter Seven.

Do foster parents receive payment for taking a foster child?

In most cases, yes. The state makes regular payments to foster parents to assist with the cost of care.

NOTES

1. A. Sedlak, *Study of National Incidence and Prevalence of Child Abuse and Neglect.* Bethesda: Westat, Inc., 1987.

2. U.S. Department of Health and Human Services, *Children Today* 1992;21:2.

3. Finkelhor, David. *Sexually Victimized Children.* New York: The Free Press, 1979.

4. The hearsay rule protects the criminal suspect's constitutional right to confront his or her accuser and the constitutional right to cross-examine.

5. More than 500,000 young people run away annually. Unfortunately, consent by minors in many medical and clinical settings, particularly for runaways, often is not accepted. Council on Scientific Affairs. "Health Care Needs of Homeless and Runaway Youths" *Journal of the American Medical Association* 1989; 262:1358–1361.

6. Few patient populations are more vulnerable than runaway adolescents. Sexual abuse and physical victimization, substance abuse, pregnancy, and HIV/ AIDS leave runaways in serious need of good medical care and psychological support. *New York Times* October 8, 1989:A1. Runaway teens are at very high risk for contacting HIV/AIDS, as 5.3 percent of runaways in New York City and 8.2 percent of those in San Francisco are HIV infected, through either sexual activity or intravenous drug use. Stricof, R. L., et al., "HIV Seroprevalence in a Facility for Runaway and Homeless Adolescents" *American Journal of Public Health* 1991; 181:50–53. "Prevalence of Sexually Transmitted Diseases (STDs) and HIV in a Homeless Youth Medical Clinic in San Francisco."

Abstracts of the Sixth International Conference on AIDS. Abstract 231. San Francisco, June 23, 1990.

FOR FURTHER READING

Physical Abuse and Neglect

Berger, Gilda. *Violence and the Family.* New York: Franklin Watts, 1990.

Erickson, Edsel L., et al. *Child Abuse and Neglect: A Guide for Educators and Community Leaders.* 2nd ed. Holmes Beach, Florida: Learning Publications, 1984.

Kyte, Kathy S. *Play It Safe: The Kids' Guide to Personal Safety and Crime Prevention.* New York: Alfred A. Knopf, 1983.

Whittemore, Gerard. *Street Wisdom for Women: A Handbook for Urban Survival.* Boston: Quinlan Press, 1986.

Sexual Abuse

Benedict, Helen. *Safe, Strong and Streetwise: The Teenager's Guide to Sexual Assault.* Boston: Joy Street Books, 1986.

Crewdson, John. *By Silence Betrayed: Sexual Abuse of Children in America.* Boston: Little, Brown, 1988.

Kempe, Ruth S., and C. Henry Kempe. *The Common Secret: Sexual Abuse of Children and Adolescents.* San Francisco: W. H. Freeman, 1984.

Kosof, Anna. *Incest: Families in Crisis.* New York: Franklin Watts, 1985.

Los Angeles Commission on Assaults Against Women and the National Council of Jewish Women. *Surviving Sexual Assault.* New York: Congdon and Weed, 1983.

Mental Health

Arthur, Lindsay G., et al. *Involuntary Civil Commitment.* Washington, D.C.: American Bar Association Commission on the Mentally Disabled, 1988.

Gordon, James S. *Stress Management.* New York: Chelsea Street Publishers, 1990.

Greenberg, Harvey R. *Hanging In: What You Should Know About Psychotherapy.* New York: Four Winds Press, 1982.

Maloney, Michael, and Rachel Kranz. *Straight Talk About Anxiety and Depression.* New York: Facts on File, 1991.

Newman, Susan. *Don't be S.A.D.: A Teenage Guide to Handling Stress, Anxiety and Depression.* Englewood Cliffs, New Jersey: Julian Messner, 1991.

Redding, Richard E. *Due Process Protections for Juveniles in Civil Commitment Proceedings.* Washington, D.C.: American Bar Association, 1991.

Foster Care

Armstrong, Louise. *Solomon Says: A Speakout on Foster Care.* New York: Pocket Books, 1989.
Horowitz, Robert M. *The Rights of Foster Parents.* Washington, D.C.: National Legal Resource Center for Child Advocacy and Protection, 1989.
Hyde, Margaret O. *Foster Care and Adoption.* New York: Franklin Watts, 1982.
Lubben, Twyla M. *Christina's World.* Grand Rapids, Michigan: Zondervan Books, 1985.

— 11 —

Alcohol and Drugs

THE LEGAL DRINKING AGE

At what age can young people legally buy alcoholic beverages?
In most states it is age 21. Many states lowered the legal drinking age to 18 in the early 1970s when the legal age for voting in national elections was lowered from 21 to 18. But in recent years many of the same states have raised the drinking age back to 21, mainly because of concern over teens who drink and drive.

Businesses may not sell alcohol to underage persons; this is why teens and young adults often are "carded" when they attempt to buy it.

At what age can a person legally possess or consume alcohol?
In most states it is the same age at which a minor can legally buy it.

Does this mean that possessing alcohol when under the legal age is a crime?
Yes, although it is a misdemeanor. When a minor purchases, possesses, or consumes alcohol, he or she commits a delinquent act. In most states the case will go to juvenile court.

Can a minor legally drink alcohol at home?
In some states it isn't illegal if the minor has parental permission, although in recent years many states have repealed this twist in their drinking laws.

Whether a law prohibits young people from drinking at home, it prohibits minors from giving alcohol to others. In other words, teens who can't legally buy alcohol can't have parties for other underage drinkers. In a 1989 New Jersey case, a 19-year-old, home for Christmas, threw a "kegger" at his parents' house when they weren't around. About 150 young people came. Many were 16 or 17 years old, and most of them were drinking when the police arrived. They charged the underage host with distributing alcohol to minors.

If a minor marries or is legally emancipated, is he or she still subject to state laws prohibiting persons under a particular age from purchasing and drinking alcohol?

Yes. Everyone is subject to state laws regulating the purchase and consumption of alcohol, regardless of marital or legal status.

If a minor is caught drinking under age or buying alcohol with false or altered ID, what can happen?

In most states the minor will be arrested, sent to juvenile court, and placed on probation.

If a minor legally purchases alcohol across state lines and brings it into a state that prohibits the possession or consumption of alcohol until age 21, has the minor broken the law?

Yes. State laws regulating the sale, possession, and consumption of alcohol apply to everyone within its borders, regardless of where the alcohol was purchased and regardless of whether it was purchased legally.

Can minors work in bars?

Not usually. Most states prohibit minors from working in lounges, bars, night clubs, restaurants, and other establishments that serve alcoholic beverages. Some states and cities permit minors to bus tables in restaurants that serve meals in addition to alcohol.

DRINKING AND DRIVING

Is drinking and driving a crime?

Yes. The police can arrest a person for committing the crime of driving while intoxicated, or "DWI." In 1989, a total of 19,256 drinking or drunk drivers were involved in fatal traffic accidents, and of this number, 3,778 were under age 21.[1]

Drunk driving arrests usually are "warrantless" because drunk drivers are an immediate danger to other drivers and pedestrians. For more about arrests and warrants, see Chapter Twelve.

The police don't arrest people for committing minor traffic offenses such as exceeding the speed limit, parking illegally, or driving at night with one headlight—they simply issue a citation, which requires the offender to pay a fine. But they do arrest for serious offenses such as DWI and reckless driving. For more about arrests see Chapter Twelve, "Teens and Crime."

How do the police know that a driver is legally intoxicated?

In most states a driver is legally intoxicated if his or her blood alcohol content, or "BAC," is above 0.10. Most people are unable to operate a vehicle properly when their blood alcohol content is above this level.[2] In some states the legal BAC is even stricter. Maine and Vermont, for example, have a BAC of 0.08.

The most common form of BAC testing is a breath test that the police administer by having the DWI suspect blow deeply into a breathalyzer machine. (Sometimes the machine is called a "drunkometer.") The test usually is given at the station—and is given to both teens and adults.

However, the police always require DWI suspects to take a series of "field sobriety tests" at the arrest scene. The suspect might be required to attempt walking steadily along a straight line, recite the ABCs, stand on one leg, or do certain other acts that might indicate legal intoxication.

In most states a DWI suspect, whether a minor or an adult, doesn't have the right to consult an attorney before taking a breathalyzer test. If the suspect asks to see an attorney about the test, the police won't wait for the attorney if he or she doesn't show up in short order.

What happens if a person refuses to take a breathalyzer test?

In most states his or her driver's license or learner's permit is automatically suspended. The length of the suspension can be up to 12 months.

Can a person be convicted of DWI if his or her BAC is less than 0.10 (or is less than the state's actual BAC limit)?

In most states, yes, if there is other reliable evidence of drunkenness such as slurred speech, stumbling, or alcohol breath.

If a minor is arrested for drunk driving, does the case go to adult court?

No, it goes to juvenile court.

If a minor accused of DWI can't afford a lawyer to fight the charge, will the court appoint one?

Yes, particularly if the offense is punishable by residential treatment.

Can an adult be jailed for a DWI conviction?

Yes. This often happens.

Is it against the law to have open alcoholic beverages in a car, even if none of the passengers is drinking or drunk?

Yes.

Can the police stop cars at random to determine whether the driver is legally intoxicated?

Not usually. As a rule, a car stop is allowed only if the officer has a good reason to believe the driver is committing a traffic offense or some other criminal act. For example, a driver can only be pulled over if the officer sees the car speeding or drifting in and out of a lane of traffic. If the officer believes the driver is intoxicated after asking some questions, observing the driver's movements, and perhaps detecting alcohol on his or her breath, an arrest can be made.

Are drunk driving roadblocks legal?

Sometimes, even though the police can't otherwise stop drivers who don't appear to be breaking the law. Many believe "sobriety checkpoints" violate the search and seizure protections of the Fourth Amendment for this reason.

In 1985, roadblocks in New Hampshire were declared illegal because in a six-month period 175 DWI arrests were made using traditional police methods, but during the same period only 18 drivers were arrested for DWI out of 1,680 cars stopped at 47 roadblocks. Other courts have ruled that drunk driving roadblocks are legal if they don't delay the driver too long and the police officers are well supervised in the field.

ILLEGAL DRUGS

Which drugs are illegal?

There are dozens. The laws of each state list the drugs that always are illegal within its borders (such as cocaine or heroin) and illegal unless prescribed by a doctor. Various federal laws also prohibit the possession of dozens of types of drugs.

The law often refers to illegal drugs as "controlled substances." (An older term is "contraband.") Heroin, cocaine, LSD, and marijuana are just a few.

Is possession of an illegal drug always a crime?

In fact, no. State and federal laws only prohibit persons from "knowingly or intentionally" possessing illegal drugs. Being innocently in possession of a controlled substance usually isn't sufficient to support a criminal conviction—although a court would have to be thoroughly convinced that the suspect didn't intend to possess the drugs. For example, if a person receives a package in the mail that contains drugs, the person can only be convicted of illegal possession if it is shown that he or she knew the drugs would be delivered and intended to take possession of them.

Of course, it isn't illegal for a person to possess certain drugs if they have been prescribed by a doctor for that person's illness or injury.

Are *selling* illegal drugs and *possessing* illegal drugs separate criminal acts?

Yes. Selling illegal drugs is more serious. In a single incident, a suspect can be charged with both.

Is *giving* drugs to another person a criminal act?

Yes. The "sale" of a controlled substance includes giving a drug to someone—it's not necessary to receive something in exchange. This means cash doesn't have to change hands for an illegal drug sale to occur.

Does the seriousness of a drug offense depend on the quantity of drugs the suspect possesses or sells?

Yes. In many states possessing a small quantity of marijuana is a misdemeanor but possessing large amounts of any illegal drug is a felony. Trafficking in large amounts of drugs always is a serious offense, particularly when the drugs cross state lines.

Can the police personally search a minor for drugs?

The police can search anyone who has been placed under arrest. Furthermore, they can stop and frisk anyone for both drugs and weapons.[3]

If the police find drugs on a minor, will the drugs always be used as evidence?

Not if the police search is illegal—in which case the drug evidence would be "suppressed."

Rules relating to personal searches, including stop and frisks, are discussed in Chapter Twelve, "Teens and Crime."

If a minor is arrested for a drug offense, does the case go to juvenile court?

In most cases, yes. If the minor's parents can't afford an attorney to represent their child, the minor has a right to be assigned one at public expense.

In 1989, juvenile courts in the United States disposed of 78,000 drug cases.[4] The juvenile justice system is explained in Chapter Twelve.

How do juvenile courts handle drug cases?

Cases involving the possession or sale of drugs are often easier to prove than other criminal offenses because the "elements" of the offense are straightforward. As a result, guilty pleas are common in juvenile court drug cases and formal hearings on drug charges are infrequent.

This makes a minor's sentencing the focus of the case. As explained in Chapter Twelve, juvenile delinquents are entitled to "treatment" after being convicted, because the legal philosophy behind juvenile courts is to rehabilitate rather than punish. Because of this philosophy, a minor who is guilty of (or pleads guilty to) a drug offense almost always is ordered to participate in a drug rehabilitation program. Participation may be required during the minor's probation or may occur during his or her institutional treatment.

In a drug-related offense, does a minor ever go to adult court?

Yes. If the offense involved a particularly large quantity of drugs, if the minor's "accomplices" were adults, or if the minor has been convicted of a drug offense in the past, in many states an adult court will take "jurisdiction."

Can school officials personally search a minor for drugs? Can they search a minor's locker, desk, gym bag, or purse?

Yes.

Can the police come onto school property to arrest a minor for possessing or selling drugs?

Yes, provided the police have "probable cause" for the arrest. Possessing or selling drugs on school grounds is a criminal act.

Drug possession on campus also violates school rules and usually results in long-term suspension or expulsion, whether or not the student is arrested.

Important rules about school searches are discussed in Chapter Two.

Can a minor obtain drug treatment without parental consent?

In most states, yes, despite the fact that under state law the minor might not be able to give consent to routine medical treatment. For more about situations in which a minor may legally consent to medical care, see Chapter Ten, "Your Right to Be Healthy and Safe from Abuse."

NOTES

1. U.S. Federal Highway Administration, *Selected Highway Statistics and Charts,* annual.

2. BAC is a means of expressing, in terms of a percentage, the ratio of alcohol normally in the blood to the amount in the blood at the time of the test, based on the alcohol in a person's breath.

3. In a recent study, almost 2,000 out of 18,000 eighth graders said they had tried marijuana. Drug use is increasing among grade school students but decreasing among high schoolers. *The New York Times,* April 14, 1993:A1.

4. U.S. National Center for Juvenile Justice, Pittsburgh, PA, *Juvenile Court Statistics,* annual.

FOR FURTHER READING

In General

Bartimole, Carmella R., and John E. Bartimole. *Teenage Alcoholism and Substance Abuse: Causes, Consequences and Cures.* Hollywood, Florida: Frederick Fell Publishers, 1987.

Ketcham, Katherine, and Ginny Lyford Gustafson. *Living on the Edge: A Guide to Intervention for Families with Drug and Alcohol Problems.* New York: Bantam Books, 1989.

Newman, Susan. *It Won't Happen to Me: True Stories of Teen Alcohol and Drug Abuse.* New York: Perigee Books, 1987.

Ryan, Elizabeth. *Straight Talk About Drugs and Alcohol*. New York: Facts on File, 1989.

Sloan, Irving. *Alcohol and Drug Abuse and the Law*. Dobbs Ferry, New York: Oceana Publications, 1980.

Alcohol

Hjelmeland, Andy. *Drinking and Driving*. New York: Crestwood Press, 1990.

Kinney, Jean, and Given Leaton. *Loosening the Grip: A Handbook of Alcohol Information*. 3rd ed. St. Louis: Times Mirror/Mosby College Publishing, 1987.

Ward, Brian R. *Alcohol Abuse*. New York: Franklin Watts, 1987.

Drugs

Berger, Gilda. *Addiction*. New York: Franklin Watts, 1992.

Bernards, Neil. *War on Drugs: Opposing Viewpoints*. San Diego: Greenhaven Press, 1990.

Hughes, Barbara. *Drug-Related Diseases*. New York: Franklin Watts, 1987.

Jackson, Michael, and Bruce Jackson. *Doing Drugs: Teenagers Talk About the Most Serious Problem Afflicting Them Today*. New York: St. Martins/Marek, 1983.

McMillan, Daniel. *Winning the Battle Against Drugs: Rehabilitation Programs*. New York: Franklin Watts, 1991.

Otteson, Orlo, et al. *Kids and Drugs: A Parent's Guide*. New York: CFS Publishing, 1983.

Pownall, Mark. *Understanding Drugs: Inhalants*. New York: Franklin Watts, 1987.

Shulman, Jeffrey. *Drugs and Crime*. Frederick, Maryland: Twenty-First Century Books, 1991.

Terkel, Susan Neiberg. *Should Drugs Be Legalized?* New York: Franklin Watts, 1990.

Woods, Geraldine, and Harold Woods. *Cocaine*. New York: Franklin Watts, 1985.

— 12 —

Teens and Crime

ARRESTS

What exactly is an arrest?

It is an action in which a police officer takes away a person's freedom in some significant way. A person can be arrested when an officer has a good reason to believe the person has committed a crime or is in the process of committing one.

A police officer doesn't have to say "you're under arrest" for an arrest to occur—a command such as "Stand still" or "Come along" usually is enough. A good test for an arrest is whether the suspect realizes or should realize he or she really isn't free to walk away.

If a person isn't sure whether he or she has been arrested, it is always appropriate to ask the officer, "Am I under arrest?"

Can minors be arrested?

Yes, although strictly speaking, minors aren't "arrested"—they are "taken into custody." This distinction in the law emphasizes the fact that the juvenile court system exists to protect and rehabilitate minors rather than punish them. In this chapter, however, the terms "arrested" and "taken into custody" mean the same. Many terms in this chapter are also defined in the Glossary at the back of the book.

What can adults be arrested for?

Adults can be arrested if they commit or are suspected of committing "felonies" or "misdemeanors," the two broad categories of crimes. Felonies are more serious than misdemeanors. Joyriding, for example, is a misdemeanor in most states, but stealing a car without any intent to return it is a felony. As a rule, felonies are punishable by at least one year in prison.

What can minors be arrested for?

For almost all the same reasons as adults. In addition, minors who need supervision, special care, or medical treatment or who are runaways can also be arrested.

Whom do the police represent?

They represent the state or a political subdivision within a state, such as a city or county. States grant authority to their political subdivisions to enforce state laws and pass laws of their own. Police officers have the job of enforcing the law, and one of their most important enforcement tools is the power to arrest.

What makes a particular act a crime?

An act is a crime only if a public law says it is. If an act isn't prohibited by a federal, state, or local law, the police can't arrest for it and the state prosecuting attorney can't bring criminal charges against a person suspected of committing it.

Do the police have to be absolutely certain that a person committed a crime before the person can be arrested?

No. To arrest an adult, a police officer only needs "probable cause" to believe that a crime was committed and the person committed it.

To understand the meaning of "probable cause," consider the following situation. Two people are exchanging money, and one has a brother who is a known drug dealer. With only this evidence, a police officer can't arrest either of them for attempting a drug deal. The evidence isn't sufficient to establish "probable cause" to suspect they are trafficking in illegal drugs—they could be exchanging money for a perfectly legal reason.

Does "probable cause" apply when minors are arrested?

No, a looser rule applies. In every state a minor can be arrested if a police officer has "reasonable cause" or "reasonable suspicion" to believe a crime was committed and the minor is the one who committed it. From a legal standpoint, reasonable cause and reasonable suspicion are easier to establish than probable cause. This means it is somewhat easier for the police to place minors under arrest.

THE *MIRANDA* WARNING

What actually happens when a person is arrested?

To begin with, a police officer confronts an individual and asks some questions about a particular incident. Then the officer will request the person's name and address and probably ask to see some identification. It is always best to cooperate on these preliminary matters.

If the officer has probable cause to believe the person being questioned has committed a crime—or has reasonable cause to believe it in the case of minors—he or she usually will state that the suspect is under arrest and then recite the suspect's "*Miranda* rights." That is, the officer will advise the suspect of the following:

1. That the suspect may legally refuse to answer any police questions;

2. That the suspect may call a lawyer or be assigned one at public expense;

3. That the suspect may stop answering police questions at any time, or wait until a lawyer arrives before answering any additional questions; and

4. That anything the suspect says may be used by the state prosecuting attorney to establish the suspect's guilt.

Miranda v. Arizona, a famous Supreme Court case, established that every criminal suspect has these rights—hence the term "*Miranda* rights." A police officer's recitation of a suspect's *Miranda* rights is referred to all over the country as the "*Miranda* warning."

Are minors entitled to the *Miranda* warning?

Yes.

What happens if a police officer doesn't recite the *Miranda* warning at the time of an arrest?

The law treats any statements made by the suspect as having been made in violation of his or her Fifth Amendment right to remain silent. The suspect's statements are treated as involuntary, and therefore illegal, even though he or she actually may have made them freely and willingly. When statements such as these are illegal under the law, they may not be used as evidence to convict a suspect of a crime.

Ernesto Miranda in a lineup, Phoenix, Arizona, March 13, 1963. Miranda is on the far left, wearing glasses. *Source:* Archives Division, Department of Library, Archives and Public Records, State of Arizona, Phoenix. Can you figure out why this is an illegal lineup?

In a recent case a teen's juvenile court conviction for criminal sexual abuse was set aside after an appeals court determined that he had been arrested and questioned without receiving the *Miranda* warning. A police officer went to the teen's house and asked him to step out to the squad car for a chat. After two hours of questioning, the young man admitted he had committed the offense.

When the officer got out of the squad car, the youth asked whether he was under arrest. The officer said he wasn't. The appeals court disagreed, saying he had been placed under arrest as soon as he got into the squad car. Because the officer failed to recite the *Miranda* warning at that moment, the youth's damaging admissions couldn't be used against him.

What happens if a suspect decides to confess to a crime after being "Mirandized"?

The confession can be used to convict. The suspect is assumed to have given up freely, or "waived," the right to remain silent.

Once a person waives the right to remain silent, can he or she withdraw the waiver and refuse to answer any more questions?

Yes. At any point, a criminal suspect may decide to quit talking—and may at that point request a lawyer.

If a person receives the *Miranda* warning and later confesses to a crime, will the confession always be treated as voluntary?

No. A court can declare a confession illegal if it was given when the suspect was under too much pressure from the police during questioning, whether or not the *Miranda* warning was recited.

Is a police officer required to recite the *Miranda* warning in connection with casual questioning?

No. Neither probable cause nor reasonable suspicion is required for an officer to ask questions about a particular event, and the officer needn't recite the *Miranda* warning before asking them. But if probable cause develops during the questioning—or, in the case of minors, if reasonable suspicion develops—the officer must recite the *Miranda* warning before continuing.

WHEN MINORS ARE ARRESTED

What should a minor do if taken into custody by the police?

First, when the police officer asks for a name and address, the minor should give it. Second, the minor should ask to telephone his or her parents in private, but shouldn't answer any questions or volunteer any information until a parent arrives and parent and child have discussed the situation with a lawyer.

Does a minor have a legal right to call his or her parents after being taken into custody?

Yes, although it's important to know that in some states the police aren't required to advise minors of this right.

Can a minor forfeit or "waive" his or her Fifth Amendment right to remain silent?

Yes, but the law makes it difficult. If an adult waives the right to remain silent and then confesses to a crime, the waiver is presumed valid. However, if a minor chooses to confess, the state prosecuting attorney must prove that the minor's waiver and confession truly were voluntary. This shifting of the "burden of proof" occurs because minors are considered particulary vulnerable to police pressure, especially at the police station, and therefore less likely to remain silent.

The legality of a minor's waiver depends on a number of factors, including the minor's age, maturity, and past involvement with the police. It may also depend on whether the minor's parents or lawyer were present when the waiver and confession were made.

Consider a recent New Mexico waiver case in which a 17-year-old's juvenile court conviction for firing a deadly weapon was upheld as voluntary. Two police officers were called to investigate gunshots. When they approached the car of a young suspect to ask some questions, one of them spotted some beer and a rifle on the car seat. The suspect immediately stated, without pressure from either officer, that he had fired a shot into a residence.

As the other officer prepared to recite the *Miranda* warning, the young man said he had fired a shot but didn't know if he'd hit anything. The second officer said, "Stop, let me read you your rights," but the suspect said he knew what his rights were. Under these circumstances, the court ruled that the youth's admission was voluntary; this meant it could legally be used as evidence against him in juvenile court.

If a minor calls his or her parents but confesses to a crime before they arrive, is the confession valid?

It depends on whether the confession was the result of additional police questioning. Once a minor asks to talk to a parent or lawyer, the police must stop asking questions. If they continue and the minor confesses to a crime, the confession usually is treated as involuntary and is therefore illegal. But if the minor's confession is clearly voluntary, it can be used in court.

SEARCHES AND SEIZURES

Once the *Miranda* warning is recited, are the police permitted to search their suspect?

Yes. In the usual case, one police officer will conduct an on-the-spot personal search and another will search the scene, including any vehicles involved. Each of these searches is a "search incident to an arrest." The police will always question their suspect both during and after a search incident to an arrest unless the suspect has exercised his or her Fifth Amendment right to remain silent.

Can a minor be searched?

Yes.

What is a search warrant? Does a search incident to an arrest require a search warrant?

A search warrant is a court order authorizing a search of a person, place (such as a bedroom or locker), or object (such as a purse or backpack). A request to the court for a search warrant must be based upon "probable cause" that specific items actually will turn up and must clearly describe the person, place, or object to be searched.

Under the Constitution, every search requires a warrant. "Warrantless" searches are legal only if they fall under one of the few legal exceptions to the warrant requirement. A search incident to an arrest is a type of search that usually can be conducted without a warrant; another is a search required in an emergency situation, such as a car search.

Why isn't a search warrant required for a search incident to an arrest?

For this simple reason. If an officer needed a search warrant before making an on-the-spot search of a suspect or his or her surroundings, evidence of a crime could be hidden or disposed of while the officer was in court obtaining the warrant.

Do special rules apply to car searches?

Yes. If a car is involved in an incident for which an arrest is made, certain areas of the car can be searched immediately and without a warrant. The police can search any bags and containers within the suspect's reach inside the car, and also the glove compartment. The trunk usually can't be searched until the police obtain a warrant, although to prevent the contents of the trunk from being removed, the police may seize or "impound" the car until a warrant is obtained.

What is a "stop-and-frisk" search?

A "stop and frisk" is a limited search that a police officer may conduct if he or she thinks a dangerous situation exists. The purpose of stop and frisks, which are also called "pat-downs," is to search for weapons.

"Reasonable cause" to believe that danger is lurking, and not full "probable cause," is needed for a stop and frisk. If the police detect a hard object such as a weapon during a stop and frisk, they can then arrest the suspect, recite the *Miranda* warning, and proceed with a full personal search.

In 1993, the Supreme Court ruled that if the police detect something that "feels like drugs" during a stop and frisk, they can make an arrest and then fully search their suspect.

Can minors can be subjected to stop-and-frisk searches?

Yes.

Are police searches ever illegal?

Yes, in two situations. If a personal search other than a search incident to an arrest or a stop and frisk is made without full probable cause, the search is illegal. In addition, a search can be illegal if a warrant is required but the police don't obtain one. It is important to note that in either case the "fruits" of the illegal search can't be used to convict the suspect in court.

Locker searches at school are governed by different, somewhat looser rules. For information about searches on school grounds, see Chapter Two, "At School."

Can a minor consent to an otherwise unlawful personal search?

It depends. Like a minor's waiver of the right to remain silent, the legality of the consent depends on the minor's age, maturity, and past contacts with the police. Courts tend to rule that a minor can't legally consent to a search that would be illegal (because conducted without a warrant or conducted in connection with an unlawful arrest) except for the consent.

Can parents consent to a warrantless police search of a teen's room or car?

Courts in some states have ruled that parents legally control their minor children's property, so they have the power to forfeit a child's right to be free from searches without a warrant. Other states have ruled that parents who have no involvement in a suspected criminal act can't consent to a warrantless search of a child's "space."

In yet other states, whether a parent can consent to a warrantless search of a minor's room or other property depends on whether the minor should be able expect an extra level of privacy with respect to the area to be searched. In these states, parents can lawfully permit the police to look at items on a child's desk or chest of drawers, but a closet or purse couldn't be searched without a warrant. If the police find illegal drugs inside a closet or purse, they can't be used as evidence against the minor in court.

INTAKE

What happens to a criminal suspect at the police station?

Unless the suspect has exercised his or her right to remain silent, the police will ask more questions. Their purpose will always be to obtain a confession and discover the names of any "accomplices."

The police have the power to detain a suspect even if they don't have enough evidence for criminal charges at that point. When they do have sufficient evidence, they usually will "book" the suspect. (Sometimes the police let suspects go in simple misdemeanor cases, especially if the "misdemeanant" didn't injure anyone.)

If the police book a minor, will the case always end up in juvenile court?

No. After booking, the police and one or more juvenile probation officers (and possibly a social worker) meet to discuss how the case should be handled. This stage is called "intake." The intake participants may decide to place the minor on probation, send the minor to counseling, dismiss the case altogether, or determine that the minor should be charged with a delinquent act.

Intake officials consider many factors in deciding how to handle a case, including the seriousness of the offense, the minor's school record and home life, and previous delinquent acts. ''Attitude'' is also a consideration. A young person's attitude usually is conveyed by his or her actions or language at intake, but it can also be shown by clothing, and even hairstyle.

Does the minor participate in the intake meeting?

Yes. Intake officials always interview the minor, although the minor does have the right to remain silent. The parents also participate.

Can a minor be represented by a lawyer at intake?

In many cases the minor won't yet have a lawyer. But a lawyer normally doesn't participate, because the purpose of intake is to decide whether to handle the minor's case outside juvenile court—without judges and lawyers. But a minor's lawyer can always advise what kinds of information the minor should reveal at intake, and what to keep quiet about.

What is diversion?

It is a special way of handling a minor's case outside the juvenile court system. Under a diversion program, intake officials decide to ''divert'' a minor to a private agency that arranges for special services such as counseling, rehabilitation, or foster care. The agency might also assist the minor in finding a job or adjusting better at home or in school.

Diversion programs operate with the consent of the juvenile court, the state prosecuting attorney, and the court's probation officials. To a great extent, their success depends on the minor's voluntary participation because the agencies coordinating them don't have any enforcement powers. This sometimes reduces their success.

Across the country, about 50 percent of all cases against minors are removed from the juvenile courts at intake.

If the intake officials determine that a minor should be charged with a delinquent act, when are formal charges made?

At the minor's ''advisory hearing,'' which usually is the minor's first encounter with the juvenile court judge. At this hearing, which is short, the judge states the charges, explains that the minor has the right to an attorney at public expense, and asks the minor whether he or she wants to plead guilty or innocent. In addition, a trial date is set.

In some states the advisory hearing is called the ''initial appearance.''

Does a minor have a right to a lawyer in juvenile court?
Yes, at every stage.

Is a minor always free to plead not guilty?
Yes. A plea of not guilty means there will be a trial, or "formal hearing."

Is a minor always free to plead guilty?
Yes. In fact, a minor's lawyer often recommends that he or she do so in return for a milder sentence. But a juvenile court won't accept a guilty plea unless the minor fully understands its consequences, including the fact that there won't be a formal hearing to present evidence.

Guilty pleas are common in juvenile court.

PRETRIAL DETENTION

If a minor isn't diverted out of juvenile court at intake, is detention next?
It can be. The police usually release the minor to a parent or relative after intake, but the minor can legally be held until the advisory hearing. Furthermore, the judge may legally order "pretrial detention" until the hearing if the minor is dangerous, in need of protection, or likely to leave the state. Detention until the formal hearing may be in a foster home, a juvenile facility, or shelter care.

A minor's pretrial detention hearing usually takes place at the same time as the advisory hearing. In many states, minors can't be detained more than 72 hours without a pretrial detention hearing, and in some states they can't be detained more than 24 hours.

Is there a minimum age for pretrial detention?
Detention below a specified age is prohibited in about 15 states. The minimum age varies from New York, which prohibits detention below age 10, to Illinois, which prohibits detention below age 16.

Do most juvenile suspects receive pretrial detention?
No. Most are released to a parent or relative.

Can a minor be represented by a lawyer at his or her detention hearing?

Yes. The constitutional right to be represented by a lawyer in criminal cases applies to minors in all juvenile court hearings.

Does a minor have any legal rights while in detention?
Yes. The juvenile "detainee" has a right to be free of all special restrictions—except, of course, the right to leave. This means he or she has a right to adequate clothing, bedding, sanitary conditions, educational facilities, and medical care, and also access to a library.

Is a detention facility the same as a jail?
No, only adults go to jail. Minors cannot legally be incarcerated with adults. Physical and sexual abuse of juveniles illegally detained in adult jails isn't uncommon.

In a 1974 Kentucky case a 16-year-old youth was taken into custody for a curfew violation. The police refused to allow him to call his parents, and he was immediately placed in an adult jail although under Kentucky law he should have been released. The boy remained in jail for five days.

A federal appeals court stepped in, ruling that in refusing to permit the boy to call a parent and keeping him in jail before trial with the general population, the police inflicted "cruel and unusual punishment" on him in violation of the Constitution.

JUVENILE COURT HEARINGS

What types of cases do juvenile courts handle?
They handle criminal offenses committed by minors. In every state these offenses are called "delinquent acts." Sometimes a state's juvenile court is referred to as its family court or children's court.

Juvenile court is always separate from adult court. A minor's age at the time of his or her offense determines which of the two courts receives the case. In some states, including New York, juvenile court "jurisdiction" only extends to minors up to age 16.

What is a "juvenile delinquent"?
A juvenile delinquent is a person, usually under age 18, who is proved to have broken a criminal law.

In some states a minor who is charged with murder, rape, kidnapping, or other serious crime can be tried in adult court. If convicted of one of these offenses in adult court, the minor will be a "criminal" rather than a "juvenile delinquent."

How does a minor's case actually get to the juvenile court judge?

If the juvenile court's intake process doesn't divert the minor out of the system, the state prosecuting attorney files a "petition" against the minor. This formal document describes the specific charges against the juvenile suspect and the facts supporting them.

How does a minor discover the contents of the petition?

The minor and his or her parents are entitled to a copy of it. In some states if the petition doesn't clearly spell out the possible consequences of a finding of guilt, a juvenile court conviction on the charges can be "reversed."

Can a minor handle his or her juvenile court case without a lawyer?

Yes, but as in waiving the right to remain silent, the minor must have a clear understanding of the consequences of waiving the right to a lawyer. For a juvenile court judge to accept such a waiver, the minor must fully comprehend the charges in the petition and also the possible punishment. In addition, he or she must understand that a lawyer will be assigned free of charge if his or her parents can't afford one. Finally, the minor must understand the difficulties involved in going ahead without a lawyer, especially the challenges involved in presenting evidence to the court at the formal hearing.

Some juvenile courts prohibit a minor from waiving the right to a lawyer unless one has already been involved in the case and has explained to the minor the consequences of the waiver.

Do minors have a right to a jury at a formal hearing?

Not usually. Under the Constitution, the right to a jury trial applies only to adults. But some states, including Alaska, Colorado, Michigan, Texas, Wyoming, and New Mexico, do allow jury trials in juvenile court.

If a minor doesn't plead guilty to a delinquency charge, can he or she present witnesses and evidence at the formal hearing?

Yes, usually through his or her lawyer. These are constitutional rights, guaranteed by the Due Process Clause of the Fourteenth Amendment. Minors also have the constitutional right to question or "cross-examine" those who testify against them. For more about court procedure including cross-examination, see Chapter Seventeen, "Taking Matters to Court."

A judge in juvenile court, Litchfield, Minnesota. Photo: Dennis Wolf. Reprinted with permission.

May the minor choose to remain silent during the formal hearing?

Yes. Minors can't be required to testify against themselves.

Nothing prevents a minor from testifying in his or her own behalf. However, taking the stand often hurts rather than helps a minor's case because it gives the state prosecuting attorney a chance to cross-examine—it gives the state the opportunity to ask probing questions about the minor's earlier "direct" testimony. The perils of cross-examination are the reason why lawyers often advise both criminal defendants and minors charged with delinquent acts not to testify at all.

Can a minor be convicted in juvenile court on a confession alone?

It depends on the state. In many, a minor's out-of-court confession is insufficient to convict unless it is supported by additional "hard" evidence, because a minor is considered more likely than an adult to give a false confession. In other states, a minor's confession is sufficient if supported by the testimony of another person involved in the crime—if it is supported by the testimony of an accomplice. In still others, even an accomplice's testimony isn't enough to convict a minor. Instead, the confession must be supported by the testimony of an independent, innocent witness.

What must the state prove in order to convict a minor of a delinquent act?

It must prove the minor's guilt "beyond a reasonable doubt." This is the state's "burden of proof."

Proving guilt beyond a reasonable doubt is the burden of proof required in all criminal cases, including juvenile court cases. This is a higher burden than in noncriminal or "civil" cases—which means that convicting a minor in a juvenile court trial sometimes can be difficult. For more about burdens of proof, see Chapter Seventeen, "Taking Matters to Court."

What happens if the minor is found guilty?

He or she is then considered a juvenile delinquent. At that point the judge has a right to sentence the minor to "treatment" or some form of juvenile probation.

May a minor claim insanity as a defense to a delinquent act?

In some states, yes. In others, the insanity defense has no bearing on whether the minor is guilty of a delinquent act—it is only important in deciding how to handle the minor's case after the court has declared the minor a delinquent.

Proving the insanity defense is complicated and difficult. To establish insanity under the Constitution, it must be shown that the offender was insane when the offense was committed and couldn't have understood the nature of the act because of the insanity. In cases in which the offender actually understood what he or she was doing, it must be shown that insanity prevented the defendant from realizing the act was wrong.

Can a minor appeal a juvenile court conviction?

There is no federal constitutional right to appeal any court decision. However, most state constitutions or state laws guarantee this right to both adults and delinquents.

If a minor has the right to appeal a decision of delinquency, does the minor have the right to a lawyer free of charge for the appeal?

Yes.

MINORS IN ADULT COURT

Can a minor be tried as an adult?

Yes. Every state permits minors above a certain age to be tried in adult court for a handful of particularly serious offenses. In Connecticut, for example, a minor can be transferred to adult court if he or she is charged with murder, rape, or another serious felony *and* has committed a serious felony in the past. To try a minor as an adult in Illinois, the minor must be at least age 13, the offense must be very serious, and the juvenile court judge must have determined that it wouldn't be in the best interests of either the minor or the community to try the case in juvenile court.

In most states a minor can be transferred to adult court between the ages of 14 and 16, provided the minor has committed an offense such as murder or attempted murder, aggravated robbery, arson, burglary, and sometimes possession of explosives and killing by auto if under the influence of drugs. (The types of offenses vary from state to state.) About 15 states set the age at 16 for any crime and at age 14 for a short list of particularly serious crimes.

Even if the required conditions have been met, a minor's transfer to adult court isn't automatic. State laws permit rather than require minors to be transferred to adult court, although a few require transfer to adult court for certain offenses regardless of age.

To determine the circumstances in which a minor in a given state can be tried as an adult, check the state's criminal laws at any public library. For more about finding the law, see Chapter Eighteen.

Who finally decides if a minor should be tried as an adult?

Usually the juvenile court judge. In some states an adult court judge decides whether the seriousness of the offense requires that the case be decided in adult court. In a few, the prosecuting attorney decides.

What factors are important in determining whether the minor actually goes to adult court?

In addition to the legal age requirement, the key factors are the seriousness of the offense, the amount of evidence supporting the charges, the maturity of the minor, whether his or her accomplices are adults, and whether the minor is likely to respond to discipline or treatment from the juvenile court.

If the prosecuting attorney wants a transfer to adult court, is the minor entitled to a hearing on the issue?

Yes—due process of law requires it.

In most cases it is the prosecuting attorney who will seek an adult court trial. He or she must therefore establish the factors described. However, if state law requires that cases involving particularly serious offenses *originate* in adult court, the burden is on the minor's attorney to prove to the adult court judge that adult court is inappropriate—that juvenile court is the best "forum" for the case. In other words, the burden of proof "shifts" to the minor's attorney.

Can a minor be sentenced to death in adult court?

The answer to this question isn't clear. To date, sentencing a minor to death hasn't been found to constitute "cruel and unusual punishment" in violation of the federal Constitution. However, some state constitutions or laws forbid capital punishment for minors.

As of the end of 1989, only six persons under the age of 20 were on death row.[1]

SENTENCING

How are juvenile delinquents sentenced?

Sentencing occurs at a "disposition hearing." But unlike sentencings in adult court, juvenile court dispositions have traditionally focused on treatment and rehabilitation rather than punishment. This is an important concept to keep in mind when learning about teen rights and the criminal justice system.[2]

When is the disposition hearing?

Usually within a few months of the formal hearing. This lapse of time occurs because school, medical, work, probation, and other records which the judge uses to decide on the minor's form of treatment must be gathered. In many states the disposition hearing must occur within two months of the formal hearing.

Where does the delinquent stay in the meantime?

Usually at home, although if the minor needs special supervision, the court can order detention or place the minor in a foster home.

Is the minor entitled to have a lawyer at the disposition hearing?

In most states, yes. But in fact, the state prosecuting attorney, the attorney for the minor, and a social worker often work out the terms of the disposition and the judge simply agrees. This means the disposition hearing can be quite short.

What type of treatment might a juvenile delinquent receive?

Often the judge orders in-home detention. When this happens, the minor usually must obey a strict curfew and is required to enroll in a treatment program for drugs, alcohol, or other disabilities or behavioral problems. In more serious cases the minor is placed in a foster home or supervised group home or is referred to treatment in an institution.

Sometimes juvenile institutions are referred to as "training schools," "industrial schools," or "juvenile correction facilities," and these days, many aren't unlike prisons. School instruction is given in them, however, and delinquents who are sentenced to them have a right to be personally safe.

When a minor is institutionalized, an important goal is to reunite the minor with his or her family as soon as possible.

Can a minor be required to pay a fine, make restitution, or perform community service for a delinquent act?

Yes, and the juvenile court can also require a minor to repair property he or she has damaged. These measures are part of today's more punishment-oriented approach to treating juvenile delinquents and also part of the growing concern for the rights of crime victims.

But a minor can't be convicted in juvenile court just because he or she can't pay a fine. In a recent case a minor who stole a cap, a knife, and a wrench was convicted in juvenile court of petty theft. The judge would have dropped the case if the youth had been able to come up with $62.50 to pay restitution. The appeals court set aside the boy's sentence, ruling that a minor can't be convicted simply because he or she is poor, or "indigent."

Does a delinquent ever leave court without receiving any form of treatment or punishment?

Yes, if the judge believes this course of action is appropriate.

Can a minor be sentenced to death in juvenile court?

No. But if a minor is transferred to adult court and tried for a capital offense, the death penalty is possible in most states. To date, the Supreme Court has ruled that sentencing a minor to death isn't necessarily "cruel and unusual punishment" in violation of the federal Constitution.

PROBATION

What is probation?

It is a type of disposition in which a juvenile delinquent is kept under the supervision of the juvenile court but isn't institutionalized. Probation is a common alternative to confinement in a treatment facility.

Probation always restricts the delinquent's personal freedom in some major way. A strict curfew may be imposed and the delinquent may have to maintain good grades in school. If the delinquent's offense involved a car, his or her driver's license may be revoked. A probation officer keeps strict tabs on the delinquent, with regular meetings and also phone calls.

How long does probation last?

It varies, but many states limit it to two years. In certain states probation can't extend into a delinquent's majority (usually age 18), but in others it can extend up to age 21.

If a juvenile delinquent violates the terms of his or her probation, is there a right to a hearing before probation is revoked?

Yes. Adults have been granted this right by the Supreme Court and in most states it has been extended to minors. Juvenile delinquents don't have a constitutional right to an attorney at a probation revocation hearing, but again, certain states have laws guaranteeing this right.

What must the state prove to revoke probation?

That the delinquent violated at least one condition of the judge's probation order and that there was no good reason for the violation.

What happens if the judge revokes probation?

The judge has the power to send the delinquent to a treatment facility, group home, or foster home, although he or she can also decide simply to place the minor back on probation.

TREATMENT IN AN INSTITUTION

Does an institutionalized delinquent always have a right to treatment?

Yes. As a matter of constitutional law, a delinquent in a treatment facility is entitled to counseling, educational and social services, and treatment for special medical problems. The form of treatment might be classes to correct a learning disability, a behavioral or emotional problem, or a physical impairment.

How long does institutional treatment last?

Most states practice "indeterminate sentencing," which means the judge can send the delinquent to a treatment facility for as long as needed. In indeterminate sentencing, the social welfare agency supervising the treatment releases the delinquent once it believes treatment is complete.

Can a delinquent be ordered to a treatment facility for a certain period of time, such as one year?

Not usually. The agency supervising the treatment, and not the juvenile court, decides how long the delinquent minor needs to stay. However, there is a modern trend toward institutionalizing delinquents for a minimum number of months for particularly serious offenses, regardless of how much help they need. This is called "specific sentencing" and is another example of today's more punishment-oriented approach to treating juvenile delinquents.

In New York, for example, minors age 14 and 15 who have committed serious felonies against elderly victims may be held for six months to one year in a maximum security facility and kept another six months to one year in residential treatment. (The power of the juvenile court only extends to age 16 in New York State.)

Can the juvenile court give a delinquent minor a longer sentence than an adult court could give for exactly the same offense?

In most states, yes. A delinquent can be kept in a treatment facility until the agency supervising his or her treatment believes the minor is ready to leave.

If equal or better treatment can be obtained for the delinquent outside a treatment facility, is he or she entitled to it?

In many states, yes. Most states require their juvenile courts to consider the "least restrictive alternative" to institutional treatment.

In a 1987 Nevada case, an appeals court set aside a 13-year-old girl's sentence to one year in a treatment facility after she struck a schoolmate. The young woman had never been in juvenile court before, and her church had even suggested its counseling program to the court for her probation. A higher court set aside the girl's sentence, ruling that probation is always proper unless it is against the best interests of either the minor or the state.

Most states will not provide a lawyer free to assist a minor in challenging a sentence to a treatment facility.

Are personnel in treatment facilities prohibited from using corporal punishment?

The Constitution prohibits punishment that is excessive to the point of being "cruel and unusual," so corporal punishment would appear to be unconstitutional in the setting of juvenile detention or a juvenile treatment facility. Beatings, solitary confinement for an extended length of time, and the use of unnecessary psychiatric medications have been declared forms of cruel and unusual punishment.

JUVENILE COURT RECORDS

Is a juvenile delinquent a criminal? Does a juvenile delinquent have a "record"?

The answer to both questions is no. A delinquent isn't a criminal because a conviction in juvenile court isn't a criminal conviction.

Are juvenile court records confidential?

In most states, yes. The purpose of keeping juvenile court records confidential is to promote the rehabilitation of young people. Confidentiality keeps the records out of the hands of school officials, government agencies, future employers, and the general public.

Inactive juvenile court files are either sealed, stamped "confidential," or destroyed. If a file is sealed, a judge's written order is required to open it. States that don't destroy juvenile court records usually permit limited inspection of them by the minor, probation officers, any agency caring for the minor, and persons doing scholarly research.

Some states have laws requiring a delinquent's court file to be destroyed or permanently sealed after the delinquent reaches age 23, or after a specified number of years from the date of the conviction. On the other hand, police records relating to a delinquent's actions usually aren't confidential.

In states in which juvenile court records are confidential, can a minor deny that he or she has a juvenile record?

In many of these states the delinquent may legally deny that delinquency proceedings ever took place. In other states the juvenile court may legally advise outsiders that a particular delinquent has no juvenile record.

If a minor is a witness in an adult criminal trial, can he or she be required to answer questions about past juvenile court convictions?

Yes. Minors can be cross-examined about past delinquent acts as a way to test their credibility as witnesses, particularly if their delinquent acts were both serious and recent.

Can juvenile court records be used against a former delinquent who is on trial in an adult criminal case?

In most states an adult can't be cross-examined about previous delinquent acts. The reason is that delinquent acts aren't considered crimes and should therefore be off-limits. However, many states permit judges to review juvenile records to help in determining what sentence to give a convicted adult.

Can a judge legally exclude the press or public from a juvenile court hearing?

No. Juvenile courts rarely close their courtroom doors. In 1980 the Supreme Court ruled that excluding the press from the courtroom violates the First Amendment's guarantee of freedom of the press unless privacy clearly is needed to ensure a fair trial.

Can the press be prosecuted for publishing the name of a young person charged with a delinquent act?

No. States violate the First Amendment if they pass laws prohibiting the media from publishing information about trials, whether or not a minor is being tried. If such laws could legally be enforced, newspapers could be prosecuted for publishing truthful information.

In a 1982 case, two Virginia newspapers reported the identity of two high school students who were charged with murdering a classmate. The newspapers were prosecuted under a state law that prohibited the print media from publishing the name of any delinquent without prior authorization from the juvenile court. The Supreme Court overturned the conviction, ruling that laws prohibiting the media from printing information about delinquents violate the First Amendment if the purpose of the law is solely to preserve the minor's anonymity.

NOTES

1. Of the 2,250 prisoners on death row in the United States in 1989, 1,120 had completed less than 11 years of school. *Source:* United States Bureau of Justice Statistics, *Capital Punishment,* annual, from *Statistical Abstract of the United States,* 1991.

2. Juvenile courts across the country disposed of 1,189,000 cases in 1989. Disposition of a case means taking action to dismiss the case, placing the juvenile on probation or in a treatment facility, or taking action such as demanding fines, restitution, or community service. *Source:* National Center for Juvenile Justice. Pittsburgh, Penn., *Juvenile Court Statistics,* annual.

FOR FURTHER READING

In General

Blake, Stephen. *Arrested? Now What? A Self-Help Guide to the Criminal Justice System.* Vancouver: Self-Counsel Press, 1986.

Dudley, William, ed. *Crime and Criminals: Opposing Viewpoints.* San Diego: Greenhaven Press, 1989.

Dudley, William, ed. *Police Brutality.* San Diego: D. L. Bender, 1991.

Hyde, Margaret O. *Juvenile Justice and Injustice.* New York: Franklin Watts, 1977.

Jussim, Daniel. *Drug Tests and Polygraphs: Essential Tools or Violations of Privacy?* New York: Julian Messner, 1988.

Kramer, Rita. *At a Tender Age: Violent Youth and Juvenile Justice.* New York: Henry Holt, 1988.

LeVert, Marianne. *Crime.* New York: Facts on File, 1991.

Prescott, Peter S. *The Child Savers: Juvenile Justice Observed.* New York: Random House, 1990.

Rubin, Sol. *Juvenile Offenders and the Juvenile Justice System.* Dobbs Ferry, New York: Oceana Publications, 1986.

Sands, Bill. *My Shadow Ran Fast.* Englewood Cliffs, New Jersey: Prentice-Hall, 1964.

Shaw, Clifford R. *The Jack-Roller: A Delinquent Boy's Own Story.* Chicago: University of Chicago Press, 1966.

Punishment

Hjelmeland, Andy. *Kids in Jail.* Minneapolis: Lerner Publications, 1992.

Landau, Elaine. *Teens and the Death Penalty.* Hillside, New Jersey: Enslow Publishers, 1992.

Owens, Lois Smith, and Vivian Verdell Gordon. *Think About Prisons and the Criminal Justice System.* New York: Walker, 1992.

Rudovsky, David. *The Rights of Prisoners.* Carbondale: Southern Illinois Press, 1988.

Stevens, Leonard A. *The Death Penalty: The Case of Life vs. Death in the United States.* New York: Coward, McCann and Geohegan, 1978.

— 13 —

Age, Race, and Sex Discrimination

AGE DISCRIMINATION

Is age discrimination against minors legal?

In many situations, yes. Society lawfully discriminates against minors on the basis of age every day and in dozens of situations. Young people can't drive, vote, go to school, drink, buy tobacco, marry, or hold certain jobs until they reach a certain age. In criminal matters, they don't have the range of constitutional due process rights in juvenile court that exists for adults in adult court.

Discrimination on the basis of minority or "nonage" is in many ways the opposite side of teen rights.

Federal law prohibits age discrimination in employment, but only with respect to persons between the ages of 40 and 70. But when federal and state age discrimination laws do apply, they prohibit employers from discriminating because of age with respect to pay, conditions of employment, promotions, and fringe benefits. (Age discrimination is sometimes called "ageism.")

For more about laws relating to age discrimination in the workplace see Chapter Four, "On the Job."

RACE DISCRIMINATION

> No state shall make or enforce any law which shall ... deny to any person within its jurisdiction the equal protection of the laws.
>
> —Fourteenth Amendment,
> U.S. Constitution

Is race discrimination illegal?

Yes, when the discrimination is "state-sponsored"—when laws or other government action are the basis for the discrimination.

What are some examples of illegal race discrimination in the past?

Some very obvious ones are:

1. In 1879 the Supreme Court struck down state laws excluding blacks from serving on juries.

2. In 1886 the Supreme Court found illegal discrimination when each of 200 Chinese applicants was denied a permit to operate a laundry in San Francisco even though almost every non-Chinese applicant was granted one.

3. In 1917 the Supreme Court struck down a St. Louis city law prohibiting blacks from living on any city block if at least 50 percent of the residents on the block were white.

4. In 1938 the Supreme Court struck down a scheme in which Missouri provided a state-funded law school for whites but paid for blacks to go to law school out-of-state.

5. In 1954, in the case of *Brown v. Board of Education,* the Supreme Court unanimously rejected the "separate but equal doctrine" in public education. In this decision it ruled that placing black children in separate schools or classes within a school system deprived all children—blacks as well as whites—of an equal education.

All the above cases violated the Equal Protection Clause of the Fourteenth Amendment. In each a racial minority was illegally denied the "equal protection of the laws."

Brown v. Board of Education is a landmark case, not only because it declared "separate but equal" schemes unconstitutional, but because it began the modern "civil rights" movement. Within a short time after *Brown* was decided, the American civil rights movement was reshaping the nation's thinking on countless issues relating to personal rights. Many believe today's feminist and gay rights movements, and even the

Young people on the steps of the Chicago Art Institute. Photo: Hal Martin Fogel. Reprinted with permission.

environmental movement, were rooted in the civil rights concerns that the *Brown* case sparked.

Did the Supreme Court's rejection of "separate but equal" in *Brown v. Board of Education* affect other race issues?

Yes. After *Brown*, the Supreme Court struck down state laws authorizing the separation of races in public parks, restaurants, and bathrooms; at golf courses, beaches, and airports; and in public transportation. The decision reached every corner of American life. Now, no law or public policy can treat people differently in higher education, in public housing, or in public health and welfare services simply because of race. A white person can't be prohibited from marrying a black person, and the armed services are fully integrated. America's second black justice now sits on the Supreme Court. Never again will blacks have to go to the back of the bus.

Is it ever legal to have discriminatory laws?

Yes. State and city governments pass them all the time.

Government has the power to treat different categories of people differently. That's what many laws do, so it is true to say that laws can legally discriminate.

For example, a city can legally require all its homeowners to pay a property tax to finance its public schools, even though certain homeowners don't have children. Such a law would discriminate against childless homeowners and renters. It would be legal, however, because laws that discriminate for reasons other than race, gender, nationality, religion, age or disability only have to be reasonable. A law to raise money for schools clearly would be that.

But a law that discriminates on the basis of race, gender, nationality, religion, or disability must be more than reasonable. The purpose of such a law must be extremely important, and the law must *precisely* fit the government's purpose. Laws that discriminate on the basis of race never pass this test.

Can private persons or private businesses discriminate on the basis of race?

It depends on the circumstances. The Constitution prohibits government bodies from treating people differently because of race, but strictly speaking, private individuals and businesses aren't forbidden to. But if an individual or business is engaged in a government-related function, even remotely, discrimination is prohibited. Furthermore, states, counties, cities, and Congress have passed laws prohibiting race discrimination by private individuals and private businesses in situations that the Constitution doesn't cover. The clearest examples are laws that require restaurants to seat blacks and laws prohibiting private clubs from excluding blacks under their membership policies.

How does student busing relate to race discrimination?

Busing is state-sponsored "desegregation." Public schools must take positive steps to eliminate injustices caused by race discrimination, both past and present. Busing white children to predominantly black schools and black students to predominantly white schools is a state-sponsored way of correcting racial imbalances and racial injustice. Busing is almost always court ordered.

Is discrimination against whites illegal?

Yes, it is another form of race discrimination. *Bakke v. California,* decided in 1978, is the leading case on "reverse discrimination." Here the Supreme Court ruled that public schools can't give special treatment to minorities just because they've been discriminated against in the past.

The *Bakke* case involved a medical school admissions program that set aside 16 of 100 seats for racial and ethnic minorities. One applicant, Alan Bakke, was denied a seat in the freshman class even though he had a better academic record than the average student admitted under the minority program. He was white.

The Supreme Court ruled that the admissions program illegally discriminated against whites and in favor of minorities. The school's interest in having a student body with a variety of races and backgrounds—an interest that the Court praised—didn't justify the existence of the set-aside program. Bakke was admitted because the school couldn't prove he wasn't a victim of "reverse discrimination."

Would the *Bakke* case apply to teens who are applying to college?

Yes, it would.

What can governments do legally to remedy discrimination that occurred in the past?

They can, for example, establish "affirmative action programs" to admit or hire a certain percentage of minorities. Under these programs, minorities who are admitted or hired must be at least as qualified as nonminority persons who are turned down.

For more about reverse discrimination and affirmative action see Chapter Four, "On the Job."

Do laws prohibiting discrimination on the basis of race similarly apply to ethnic minorities such as Native Americans, Hispanics, and Asian Americans?

Yes, and they apply irrespective of the age of the minority individual.

SEX DISCRIMINATION

Is sex discrimination legal?

It used to be legal, across the board. In 1945 the Supreme Court upheld a state law prohibiting any woman from obtaining a bartender's license unless she was the wife or daughter of a man who already had one. This is just one example of past state-sponsored gender discrimination—literally hundreds existed across the nation.

Laws authorizing or permitting sex discrimination began to fall in the 1970s. In 1975 the Supreme Court ruled unconstitutional a Utah law that placed the age of majority at 21 for males but age 18 for females. Utah reasoned that parents should have to support their sons through their college years because a man's education is so important—but because women marry younger, parents should only have to support their daughters to age 18. Similar laws have been struck down.

The Supreme Court has ruled against gender discrimination in other types of cases. Here is a sampling:

1. In 1976 it ruled that Oklahoma couldn't set the legal age for males to buy 3.2 percent beer at age 21 but set it at age 18 for females (3.2 percent beer has less alcohol content than regular beer).

2. In 1979 it struck down a New York law requiring the consent of a child's natural or "birth" mother, but not the birth father, to place a child born outside marriage for adoption.

3. In 1981 it struck down a state law enabling a husband to dispose of property jointly owned with his wife without the wife's consent.

What are some examples of lawful gender discrimination?

Women can legally be kept out of combat, and they can be required to wear tops in public places.

Can public high schools legally put men and women on separate high school sports teams?

Sometimes, although it usually depends on whether the sport is a contact sport. For more about gender bias in high school athletic programs see Chapter Two, "At School."

Can a business fire a woman because she becomes pregnant?
Under a 1993 federal law full-time women employees can now take unpaid pregnancy leave from certain jobs without fear of job loss or demotion. For more about gender issues at work see Chapter Four, "On the Job."

FOR FURTHER READING

Race Discrimination

Bentley, Judith. *Busing: The Continuing Controversy*. New York: Franklin Watts, 1982.

Latham, Frank B. *The Rise and Fall of "Jim Crow," 1865–1964*. New York: Franklin Watts, 1969.

Leone, Bruno. *Racism: Opposing Viewpoints*. 2nd ed. St. Paul, Minnesota: Greenhaven Press, 1986.

McKissack, Patricia, and Frederick McKissack. *Taking a Stand Against Racism and Racial Discrimination*. New York: Franklin Watts, 1990.

Newman, Edwin S., and Daniel S. Moretti. *Civil Liberty and Civil Rights*. 7th ed. Dobbs Ferry, New York: Oceana Publications, 1987.

Pascoe, Elaine. *Racial Prejudice: Issues in American History*. New York: Franklin Watts, 1985.

Sex Discrimination

Hanmer, Trudy J. *Taking a Stand Against Sexism and Sex Discrimination*. New York: Franklin Watts, 1990.

Loeb, Robert H. *Breaking the Sex-Role Barrier*. New York: Franklin Watts, 1977.

Whitney, Sharon. *The Equal Rights Amendment: The History and the Movement*. New York: Franklin Watts, 1984.

Other Discrimination Issues

Meltzer, Milton. *The Hispanic Americans*. New York: Thomas L. Crowell, 1982.

— 14 —

Gay and Lesbian Teens

IS IT LEGAL?

Are homosexual acts illegal?

In many states, yes. States and cities may legally enforce laws prohibiting homosexual activities among persons of all ages.

In 1986, the Supreme Court ruled in the case of *Bowers v. Hardwick* that a Georgia statute prohibiting oral and anal sex (or ''sodomy'') isn't an unconstitutional invasion of privacy when applied to homosexual conduct between adults. This case means that neither consenting adults nor consenting minors have a constitutional right to engage in homosexual acts. This doesn't mean that homosexuality is always illegal—it just means that homosexual conduct is not a privacy right protected by the Constitution.

The *Hardwick* case has been criticized by legal scholars because its reasoning appears contrary to that of earlier Supreme Court cases upholding the right of privacy in matters relating to sex. Many find it inconsistent with a 1969 Supreme Court case recognizing the right of individuals to view pornography in the privacy of their homes. Others find it inconsistent with *Roe v. Wade,* the 1973 Supreme Court case which ruled that the constitutional right to privacy includes a woman's right to have an abortion.

Although states may legally prohibit homosexual acts, about half the states have revoked laws making private homosexual conduct between consenting adults illegal.

If homosexual conduct between consenting adults isn't illegal under the laws of a certain state, would the same conduct be legal between consenting teens?

No. States that have revoked laws prohibiting homosexual acts between adults haven't gone so far as to legalize such acts between minors.

Can a person who has homosexual relations be convicted of statutory rape?

In some states, yes, although in others, statutory rape can only occur with respect to heterosexual sex.

As discussed in Chapter Eight, statutory rape occurs when an adult has sex with a minor. It doesn't matter that both parties may have privately agreed to have sex. In most states only the older sex partner can be charged.

FAMILY MATTERS

Can parents forbid a minor child to engage in homosexual acts?

Yes, consistent with their right to raise and discipline their children. However, a rule forbidding a minor child to engage in sex, whether heterosexual or homosexual, isn't always the easiest rule for parents to enforce.

For more about teen and parental rights at home, see Chapter Three.

Can parents throw a minor out of the house because he or she is homosexual?

No. Parents are responsible for the care and nurturing of their minor children, regardless of a child's sexual orientation or sexual activities. Even so, it is estimated that up to 500,000 homosexual and bisexual youths live on America's streets.

Can parents emancipate a minor just because he or she is homosexual?

No—that wouldn't be a sufficient reason for emancipation in the eyes of the law. To be emancipated, the minor would have to be financially independent and able to live safely and in good health on his or her own. For more about emancipation see Chapter Five, "On Your Own."

Can two men legally marry?

No, and neither can two women. Homosexual marriages aren't recognized in any state. But some cities, including San Francisco, Minneapolis, and Seattle, permit two adults of the same gender who live together to register with the city clerk as "domestic partners." In San Francisco, registering as a domestic partner permits a gay or lesbian city employee and his or her partner to be covered under the city's group health insurance. In addition, registering makes each partner responsible for the other's basic living expenses as well as his or her own.

Can a parent who is lesbian or gay obtain custody of a minor child in a divorce?

Lesbian and gay parents find it difficult to obtain custody of their children when divorcing. As discussed in Chapter Seven, the basis for awarding custody is "the best interests of the child." Many judges believe that awarding custody to a homosexual parent can't in any instance be in a young person's best interests.

Even so, some courts have awarded custody to homosexual parents. Custody of the child has been awarded to the lesbian mother in most of these cases. Divorce courts in approximately 10 states can no longer lawfully deny custody to a parent simply because of sexual orientation.

After divorcing, can a gay or lesbian parent be denied the right to visit his or her child?

Not for that reason alone. In order for a court to deny visitation to a gay or lesbian parent, the straight parent would have to persuade the court that such visits would for some proven reason be against the child's best interests. Visitation could be denied, for example, if the homosexual parent and his or her same-sex partner had a habit of kissing or caressing in the minor's presence.

In some states, gay and lesbian parents have been prohibited from keeping a child overnight and also have been prohibited from taking a child to the home the parent shares with a same-sex partner. But courts in other states have permitted these and similar activities.

AT SCHOOL

Can school administrators prevent a gay and lesbian club or support group from meeting on public school property?

The answer to this question remains unclear. It appears that public high school administrators only may prohibit lesbian and gay rights clubs from meeting at school if clear evidence shows that the meetings would either disrupt school discipline or offend the rights of others.

Clubs and support groups for gay and lesbian students have formed in high schools in Chicago, Los Angeles, Minneapolis, New York, San Francisco, and other cities. For more about the constitutional right of free assembly see Chapter Two, "At School."

In states in which school officials can't prevent gay and lesbian teens from organizing at school, what types of school facilities can the club legally use?

The same facilities that other clubs use, such as meeting rooms, school supplies, access to bulletin boards, and other school benefits and services.

Can schools make gay and lesbian teens stay away from each other at school?

No. That would be a clear violation of the constitutional right of free assembly.

In 1981 a federal appeals court in Rhode Island ruled that a public high school couldn't prohibit a male student from taking another male to the senior prom. However, the court based its decision on the First Amendment right of free speech and not the right of free assembly; it ruled that taking a gay man to the prom was a form of symbolic speech.

For more about symbolic speech under the First Amendment see Chapter Two, "At School."

Can schools forbid gay and lesbian teens to display intimate feelings of affection at school?

Yes. It is clearly within the authority of schools to prohibit all students from kissing, embracing, and caressing on school grounds—both homosexuals and heterosexuals.

What can be done if gay and lesbian teens are harassed by other students at school?

The incident should be reported to school authorities. If the problem persists or if this solution is unwise or even foolish, the best thing to do is discuss the matter with a lawyer associated with a gay or lesbian rights club or a community legal services organization. Legal services attorneys charge little or nothing and are legally required to keep such matters in strict confidence.

The same approach should be followed if a gay or lesbian teen is harassed by a teacher.

IN PUBLIC

Can a person be discriminated against at work because he or she is gay or lesbian?

Most states don't have laws prohibiting discrimination against lesbians and gays in the workplace. Federal law protects racial and ethnic minorities, women, handicapped persons, and the elderly from job discrimination, but not lesbians and gays. However, the federal government may not fire or demote a government employee just because of sexual orientation. A homosexual can be dismissed from federal government work because of sexual orientation only if his or her conduct is inappropriate for the job.

The laws of some states forbid discrimination against state and city employees because of sexual orientation. In addition, some communities now have laws forbidding discrimination on the basis of sexual orientation in restaurants, with respect to membership in social organizations and sports clubs, and in other situations.

Can a landlord legally refuse to rent to gay and lesbian couples?

Yes, unless state or local law forbids discrimination in housing because of sexual orientation. In the absence of such a law, a landlord can legally refuse to rent to anyone for almost any reason. Sometimes landlords even hire tenant-screening services to identify renters they believe might be unacceptable.

Can homosexuals join the armed forces?

There have always been homosexuals in the American military, but most have kept their sexual preference a secret from their commanding officers. When a person joins the armed forces, the person is asked if he or she is homosexual. Over the years, this question hasn't been answered truthfully in every case. Gays and lesbians feel the duty to serve their country no less than heterosexuals.

As this book is being written, efforts are being made in the nation's capital to forbid the armed forces from inquiring about a person's sexual orientation at the time of induction.

FOR FURTHER READING

Alyson, Sasha, ed. *Young, Gay, and Proud.* Boston: Alyson Publications, 1980.

Cohen, Daniel, and Susan Cohen. *When Someone You Know Is Gay.* New York: Dell, 1992.

Hanckel, Frances, and John Cunningham. *A Way of Love, a Way of Life: A Young Person's Introduction to What It Means to Be Gay.* New York: Lothrop, Lee and Shepard Books, 1979.

Rench, Janice. *Understanding Sexual Identity: A Book for Gay Teens and Their Friends.* New York: Lerner, 1990.

Property Rights and Crimes Against Property

EARNINGS

Are minors legally entitled to keep their personal earnings?

Not necessarily. Because parents are entitled to their children's services, they actually have a legal right to their children's income. This issue is discussed at length in Chapter Three, ''At Home.''

Do minors legally own the property that their parents provide for them such as clothes, books, bicycles, electronic equipment, and cars?

Not usually. Although parents ''give'' such property to their children in a definite sense, courts say the parents are the owners. This is because parents have the right to reclaim the property if it is stolen, and they have ''standing'' to bring a court case against someone if the property is damaged or destroyed.

WHAT CAN A MINOR OWN?

Can teens legally own property?

Yes, despite the fact that they may not have a legal claim to their earnings. They can purchase property, inherit it, and receive it by gift. Property actually and legally owned by a minor belongs to the minor exclusively, although a minor can also own property ''jointly'' with someone else. (When a person owns property jointly, at one owner's death all the property often passes to the other joint owner.)

Can a minor have a bank account?

In most states a minor can establish a bank account and make withdrawals without parental consent. But a parent can serve as a "custodian" for a minor's account. This means a parent's name can appear on the account along with the minor's, as a sort of money manager. The parent can make deposits and sign for withdrawals, but only for the minor's benefit.

In addition, federal law permits parents to serve as custodians for property they give to a child directly, except when the property is real estate. (The parent would serve under the authority of the federal Uniform Transfers to Minors Act.) Except for custodian accounts, parents don't have the right to manage their children's property simply because of their adult or parental status.

Can a minor legally sell property?

Minors do have the power to "transfer title" to property. But if a minor sells property—if a minor sells a large item such as a house or business—the minor may later revoke the sale unless his or her "property guardian" received court approval for the transaction.

What is a property guardian's job?

A property guardian is appointed by a court to manage a minor's "estate" and serves until discharged. The guardian must manage the estate with a high degree of care and regularly report or "account" to the court about the estate's status and value. Some transactions that property guardians enter into, such as selling land and purchasing large investments, must be preapproved by the court.

Property guardians are sometimes called "conservators" or "guardians of the estate." As a practical matter, courts only appoint property guardians if the amount of property owned by the minor is worth more than a few thousand dollars. A property guardian is paid from the property being managed (subject to probate court approval) unless the guardian agrees to do the job for free.

In fact, one or both parents usually are the ones who serve, but a relative, friend, or bank can also be appointed. (This often happens when a minor inherits property from a deceased parent.) Guardians are also appointed to manage property for adults who, because of illness or old age, are incapable of managing property on their own.

Does this mean a minor can't legally sell or trade personal items to friends, or even strangers?

No. Such transactions are really too small to involve a court or guardian.

Do parents have a legal right to use property inherited by a child?

Only if the property was inherited by the child and the parents jointly. Parents are powerless to dispose of a minor's interest in property unless they are the minor's custodian or court-appointed property guardian.

Can a minor require a property guardian to enter into a particular transaction?

No. The property guardian manages the property independently.

Can a minor have a property guardian dismissed?

In certain circumstances. Some states provide that minors age 14 years or older may nominate their own property guardian, although the court must approve the choice. In most states a minor is free to choose a new property guardian at age 14, again subject to court approval.

Might a minor have a legal guardian as well as a property guardian?

Yes, and they can be the same person. For more about legal guardians see Chapter Three, "At Home."

Can a minor retrieve his or her estate from the guardian at the age of majority?

Usually. The court revokes the guardianship at that point unless it believes a good reason exists to keep it in place, such as a person's physical or mental disability.

Can a minor legally give property away?

Yes, but like a minor's sale of property, the gift can be revoked. Again, this only applies to large gifts of property—not birthday presents and such.

WHEN PARENTS DIE

If a parent dies, who inherits his or her property?

It depends on whether the parent died leaving a valid will.

Persons above the age of majority may legally decide how their property will pass at death, and wills are the normal way of directing who gets what. Married people often leave their entire estate to a surviving spouse, although they aren't legally required to. If the "decedent" is a child's second parent to die, the estate often passes to the child and his or her brothers and sisters. This would happen whether or not the children are minors.

What happens if a parent dies without a valid will?

The property passes "intestate," which means it passes according to the state's inheritance laws. Under most state "intestacy" laws, if a parent is survived by a spouse and children, the spouse is entitled to one-third to one-half the decedent's estate and the children are entitled to the rest. If there is no surviving spouse, the children share the estate equally. (Contrary to popular belief, if someone dies intestate, his or her property isn't forfeited to the government.)

Do the courts get involved in the distribution of decedents' estates?

In most cases, yes—particularly when the estate is large.

"Probate" is the legal process for determining the validity of a decedent's will (when one exists), collecting the decedent's property, paying all debts, and distributing the estate to the proper persons. Most states have separate "probate courts" that supervise the orderly administration of decedents' estates, whether or not the person died with a will.

Can a spouse or child be disinherited?

Yes, but only under a will and not under the laws of intestacy. In some states, if a spouse attempts to disinherit a spouse in a will, the spouse inherits the amount he or she would have inherited had the decedent died intestate.

Can adopted children inherit from their adoptive parents?

Yes. Children of adoptive parents have the same legal rights as children who are related to their parents by blood. In many states adopted children may also inherit from the parents, aunts and uncles, and other relatives of their adoptive parents.

Can adopted children inherit from their natural parents?

In most states an adopted child may not inherit from a natural or "birth" parent if the birth parent dies intestate because the relationship between child and parent no longer exists under the law. But nothing

When parents are older, special legal issues often arise. Photo: Hal Martin Fogel. Reprinted with permission.

legally prevents a birth parent from leaving property by will to a child who has since been adopted.

Can children born outside marriage inherit from their parents?

In years past, children born outside marriage couldn't inherit from their natural *fathers*. Today they may inherit from both parents. To inherit under state intestacy laws, however, the identity of the father may have to be established in a "paternity" proceeding in court.

In some states an "illegitimate" child can inherit from his or her father only if the father's identity is established before he dies. Paternity can also be established if the child's parents marry one another or if the father legally declares the child is his own.

Are stepchildren entitled to inherit from their stepparents?

Only under a will. Intestacy laws don't apply to the relationship of stepparent and stepchild.

If a minor inherits property, can he or she sell it, spend it—do anything with it whatsoever?

No. Again, because minors are legally incapable of managing their own property (except bank accounts), a probate court often will appoint a property guardian to handle their financial affairs. In an inheritance situation, property guardians often are nominated in the decedent's will.

Property guardianships can be complicated and inconvenient, particularly if the minor owns substantial property. For this reason, parents often create "trusts" during their lifetime to manage property their children stand to inherit. With a trust, money or property is set aside by one or both parents before death. After they die a "trustee" manages it for the minor and distributes it when the minor becomes an adult. The property never needs to pass through probate.

Although trusts are easy to establish, less costly than guardianships, and subject to very little court supervision, a lawyer should draft the trust document. In addition, the trustee should contact a lawyer if problems arise with the trust's management.

WHEN MINORS DIE

Can a minor write a valid will?
No. Only adults can make legally binding wills.

If a person dies before reaching the age of majority, who inherits his or her property?

Because a minor is too young to leave property by will, it must pass intestate, which again means the law dictates who inherits it. Usually a minor's parents (or the surviving parent) inherit the property. If neither is living, the minor's brothers and sisters inherit it in equal shares.

THE PROPERTY OF OTHERS

Is shoplifting the same as theft? What kind of punishment can a minor receive for shoplifting?

Shoplifting is a form of "larceny," the legal term for theft. From a legal standpoint, shoplifting is taking property displayed for sale without paying for it. The mere act of concealing store property inside a coat or purse is shoplifting; this means the shoplifter doesn't have to leave the store to commit the offense.

Teens who are caught shoplifting go to juvenile court. But whether or not the teen is convicted and regardless of whether the court orders probation, the shoplifter usually is required to return the property or make restitution for it.

Is robbery the same as larceny?

Robbery is larceny accompanied by the use of force and is a much more serious crime than simple larceny.

Do teens who steal and rob always go to juvenile court?

Usually, although a mature minor can be tried in adult court in some states if charged with "aggravated robbery," which is robbery using a deadly weapon, and for other serious crimes such as arson, kidnapping, rape, murder, and attempted murder.

Chapter Twelve, "Teens and Crime," gives important information about how courts handle young offenders.

TRESPASSING AND PROPERTY DAMAGE

If a store manager asks a teen to leave the premises, can the teen legally refuse? If the teen refuses, is he or she a trespasser?

A store manager can legally request any customer to leave, but only if the reason for wanting the customer out isn't based on race, color, gender, nationality, religion, or handicap. If the customer refuses to leave after being asked to, he or she is a trespasser and can be arrested.

So trespassing is against the law?

Yes—it is a misdemeanor. A person can be a trespasser if he or she refuses to leave after being asked to, and also if the person wasn't on the property legally in the first place.

If a person causes damage to property or vandalizes it while trespassing, what can the owner do?

Recover money against the trespasser to compensate for the damages, because the property damage is a civil "tort." For more about torts and recovering money in court actions, see Chapter Seventeen.

Legally, what can happen when a minor damages property?

He or she can be sent to juvenile court. Minors can land in juvenile court for throwing rocks through windows, drawing on street signs, defacing bridges and buses, driving across lawns, and breaking through gates and fences. See Chapter Twelve, "Teens and Crime."

Is spray-painting graffiti on walls and buildings illegal?

Drawing on property owned by the government (such as a city or state) is a crime. Drawing on private property is a tort.

Can parents be forced to reimburse a property owner for damage caused by their minor children?

In many cases, yes. They can be held liable in court for the torts of their children, particularly if the parents should have been supervising the child when the damage occurred. This rule applies to legal guardians as well.

FOR FURTHER READING

The Basics About Property

Hughes, Michael F., and David Klein. *How to Use the Various Forms of Ownership*. New York: Charles Scribner's Sons, 1984.

When Parents Die

Bratman, Fred. *Everything You Need to Know When a Parent Dies*. New York: The Rosen Publishing Group, 1991.

Fayerweather Street School, and Eric E. Rofer, ed. *The Kids' Book About Death and Dying.* Boston: Little, Brown, 1985.

Gaffron, Norma. *Dealing with Death.* San Diego: Lucent Books, 1989.

Trespassing and Property Damage

Francis, Dorothy B. *Shoplifting: The Crime Everybody Pays For.* New York: Elsevier/Nelson Books, 1979.

Francis, Dorothy B. *Vandalism: The Crime of Immaturity.* New York: Lodestar Books, 1983.

— 16 —

Entering into Contracts

THE BASICS

What is a contract?

It is simply an agreement in which one party promises to do something in exchange for another party's promise to do something in return. If one party performs but the other doesn't, the first party can take the second party to court for "breach of contract."

People make contracts all the time, and many are so simple that people don't realize when they've entered into them. A customer contracts with a grocery store when the customer brings his or her selections to the check-out. The nature of their contract is simply this: the store will permit the customer to take the items away if the customer pays the amount shown on the register.

Consider another basic contract. When a person buys an airline ticket, the airline is contracting to take the person to a particular destination. The contract actually is written out—the printed information on the front and back of the plane ticket are the contract terms.

A sophisticated type of contract would be a contract for the sale of land or a contract to buy a car.

Do certain types of contracts have to be in writing?

Yes. By law, contracts that can't be performed in less than one year and contracts for the sale of land must be written. But contracts that don't have to be in writing often are—written contracts give the parties a permanent and reliable record of their agreement. And sometimes state laws require various types of contracts to be in writing.

How are contracts enforced if one party refuses to perform?

The party who wants the contract performed often takes the other party to court for "breach of contract." If that party loses money as a result of the other's failure to perform, the court can award money or "damages" to the injured party.

Breach of contract actions in civil court are explained in Chapter Seventeen, "Taking Matters to Court."

Do minors have a legal right to enter into contracts?

Yes, and minors can be legally required to perform contracts they enter into. But in every state minors can "avoid" or "disaffirm" contracts, which means they can use the fact of their minority—their "nonage"—to back out of most of their contracts.

If a minor enters into a contract, does an adult have to co-sign it or agree to be jointly responsible in order for it to be enforceable?

No, but an adult can certainly agree to do so. Co-signing a contract or agreeing to be jointly responsible means the adult can be required to perform the entire contract (such as paying all the money owed), and not just half of it.

DISAFFIRMING CONTRACTS

Why can minors disaffirm contracts?

The reason given is to protect minors against businesspeople who try to take unfair advantage of them in the marketplace. Many people think the rule allowing minors to disaffirm contracts is outdated and actually unfair, for two reasons. First, it can be a hardship on the adults who contract with minors evenhandedly and in good faith; second, most minors are at home in the marketplace and are usually smart about how it operates.

The rule that minors can disaffirm contracts doesn't mean, for example, that a minor can agree to buy a computer, take it home, use it, then refuse to pay. It simply means a minor can agree to buy a computer, take it home, then back out of the contract and return it even if the seller doesn't have a return policy. It means the seller must refund the amount paid—although in some states the seller can reduce the refund by the value of any wear and tear.

If the computer has been damaged or heavily used, many states now require the minor to pay the difference between the original price and its current value. This is called "restitution." Even so, the minor can disaffirm the contract, but adults can't.

Can a minor disaffirm a contract for a car?

It depends on the state. In many, minors can't disaffirm contracts for cars, motorcycles, car insurance, or school loans. Furthermore, minors can't back out of contracts in California and a number of other states once they reach age 16.

Can an adult disaffirm a contract with a minor?

Not if the minor wants to keep it in force. The contract is "binding" on the adult but not the minor, and the minor can require the adult to complete it.

If an adult agrees to be jointly responsible with a minor on a contract, can the adult disaffirm the contract as well?

No. The adult may be required to perform the contract fully, or pay contract "damages."

NECESSARIES

Are there any types of contracts that can't be disaffirmed by minors?

Yes. Contracts for "necessaries" such as food, clothing, lodging, and medical care can't be disaffirmed, assuming the minor is still dependent on his or her parents. Both the minor and the parents can be legally required to pay the entire bill, unless the minor is emancipated. For more about emancipation see Chapter Five, "On Your Own."

A proper education often is considered a "necessary," although what constitutes a "proper" education will always vary from family to family.

If a minor misrepresents his or her age in order to enter into a contract, can the minor later disaffirm it?

In many states, no. Certain states also prohibit minors from avoiding their contract obligations if they engage in business as an adult.

FOR FURTHER READING

Elias, Stephen. *Simple Contracts for Personal Use.* Berkeley, California: Nolo Press, 1986.

Neubert, Christopher, and Jack Withiam, Jr. *How to Handle Your Own Contracts.* New York: Sterling Publishing, 1991.

Privette, Mari W. *Sign Here? Everything You Need to Know About Contracts.* Garden City, New York: Doubleday, 1985.

—17—

Taking Matters to Court

THE VOCABULARY OF A LAWSUIT

What is a lawsuit?

It is a process by which a "plaintiff" takes a "defendant" to court to satisfy a wrong the plaintiff believes the defendant caused.

The legal system has its own vocabulary. Plaintiffs and defendants are "parties" to a lawsuit. Parties don't have to be individuals—they can be businesses, cities, states, the federal government, or a foreign country. A plaintiff's injuries, physical or otherwise, are called "damages." When a plaintiff's relief takes the form of money—it usually does—the money award is called "compensation."

Cases are "civil" in nature when a plaintiff seeks to protect a personal or private right such as property. They are "criminal" in nature when a public entity such as a state or city seeks to protect rights embodied in its public laws.

This chapter is about *civil* cases. For more about the criminal justice system and what happens when young people commit criminal acts see Chapter Twelve, "Teens and Crime."

WHY PEOPLE GO TO COURT

What types of wrongs can a plaintiff seek to recover for?

There are literally dozens, but the main categories are "tort" and "breach of contract."

Most tort and breaches of contract cases aren't based on laws passed by a legislative body. They are based on principles of fairness that have evolved in the American legal system over the years—principles known as the "common law."

What is a tort?

A tort occurs when a party violates a duty owed to another, causing injuries or property damage.

Consider the following example. A man negligently crashes a car into a homeowner's front porch, causing damage. Under tort law, the driver owes a legal duty to the homeowner to drive in a "reasonable" manner. Obviously, the driver didn't adhere to this duty—so he committed a tort.

The homeowner has a "cause of action" against the driver for operating the car negligently and may use the courts to be compensated for the damages. In a civil action to recover for the property damage, the homeowner would be the plaintiff and the driver would be the defendant.

A party usually must have acted either "negligently" or "intentionally" for a tort to occur. To prove negligence in court—to prove that someone breached his or her duty of care toward another—it isn't necessary that the defendant actually have foreseen a danger. It only requires that a reasonably careful or "prudent" person would have foreseen that reckless driving could cause damage and would therefore have avoided the crash.

This is the basic process for analyzing whether someone committed a tort. The Glossary at the end of the book defines many terms relating to civil courts.

What are other examples of torts?

Common torts are negligently failing to repair a car or properly erect a structure, driving a car negligently or recklessly, negligently or intentionally mishandling weapons, negligently treating a patient, negligently or intentionally leaving hidden or even obvious dangers on private property, and manufacturing faulty products. When these and other "tortious" acts cause injury or property damage, the plaintiff has a "cause of action" against the defendant.

Is a tort a crime?

Not necessarily. When a plaintiff sues, he or she rarely does so to obtain satisfaction for a crime even though an act can be a crime as well as a tort. The plaintiff is generally looking for money.

If the act also is a crime—if the act violates a public law—the state's attorney can prosecute for it. In other words, the state can bring a separate case or "charge" against the defendant. This happens all the time.

What are some examples of torts that are also crimes?

Vandalism, for example. Damaging another's property is against the law even if the damage isn't major. It is also a tort, so the property owner can bring a civil action against the vandal.

Another example is rape. A rapist obviously commits a serious crime, but rapists also cause severe emotional trauma. Rapists can be sued in civil court for the tort of intentionally inflicting emotional stress on their victims, and juries don't hesitate to assign a dollar value to this type of damage.

What is breach of contract?

A breach of contract occurs when a party to an agreement fails to perform according to its terms, thereby causing loss to the other party to the agreement. For example, a person breaches a contract if he or she agrees to sell a motorcycle, accepts full payment from the buyer, then refuses to deliver it. Here the buyer is the potential plaintiff and the seller is the potential defendant.

For more about contracts see Chapter Sixteen.

What are some other examples of breach of contract?

Very common examples are failing to pay rent or make a mortgage payment, failing to pay off a credit card bill, failing to make prompt delivery of an order of manufactured products, and failing to complete construction of a building on schedule.

What forms of relief can courts award in civil actions?

Money is the most common form of relief in both tort and contract cases. But courts can also issue "injunctions," which order a defendant to stop doing something that causes constant harm to the plaintiff.

MINORS AS PLAINTIFFS

Can a minor be a plaintiff?

Yes. A minor can be a plaintiff or a defendant and can sue or be sued for almost all the same reasons as an adult.

But minors lack the legal capacity to file lawsuits on their own, and for this reason an adult files in the minor's behalf. This long-standing rule is meant to protect minors from their own lack of knowledge of the court system (and the world at large). The adult representative might be the minor's parent, guardian, or so-called next friend—an individual appointed by the judge to protect the minor's interests.

A teen, for example, could sue a negligent driver for injuries and car damages resulting from an accident. The teen would sue through a parent or next friend. A young person could also be a plaintiff in a lawsuit resulting from carelessness at school or work.

(It would be difficult for a minor to sue on his or her own for another basic reason. Hiring a lawyer can be an expensive proposition. Payments to lawyers are discussed later in this chapter.)

Can a minor sue his or her parents?

For certain wrongdoings, yes. In the United States, the first lawsuit by a child against a parent took place in 1891. As soon as this happened, states feverishly began passing laws to protect parents *against* lawsuits by their children. In 1905, a Washington court went so far as to prohibit a civil lawsuit by a 15-year-old who had been raped by a parent—it refused to hear the lawsuit out of a concern for family harmony!

Today almost every state permits minors to sue their parents for certain torts. The most common is a suit for personal injuries resulting from a parent's negligent driving. (The child's representative in this type of suit is often an insurance company.) Also, almost every state permits minors to sue one or both parents for personal injuries *intentionally inflicted*. A few permit children to sue for emotional injury caused by bad parenting.

Can a minor sue an aunt, uncle, grandparent, or other relative?

Yes. These individuals have the same status as unrelated persons.

If a minor's parent is killed by a third party, can the minor sue the killer for money?

Most states have ''wrongful death'' statutes which permit certain survivors to sue a person who negligently causes a family member's death. Those who can sue usually are the decedent's spouse and minor children. It doesn't matter whether the death was deliberate or accidental.

Some states limit damages in wrongful death cases to the loss of the deceased parent's services at home and the value of his or her future earnings. This means a dependent child might be able to recover for the estimated dollar value of a deceased mother's services as a parent.

Many states also permit survivors to recover damages for mental anguish endured as a result of a wrongful death. When a court permits recovery for mental anguish, the jury is asked to place a dollar value on the survivors' emotional pain and suffering.

If a child is born with a severe handicap, can the child sue the mother's doctor?

In an increasing number of states, yes. In these cases, called "wrongful life" actions, the child's lawyer argues that the mother could have had an abortion if her doctor had discovered through genetic testing that the child might be severely handicapped. If the child wins in the lawsuit, his or her compensation would include expenses for special medical care and pain and suffering to be endured throughout life.

MINORS AS DEFENDANTS

Can a minor be a defendant?

A minor can be sued for torts and sometimes for breach of contract.

Minors who commit torts usually are held to a lower "standard of care" than adults. What this means is that instead of measuring a minor's actions against the level of care of a reasonable adult, courts hold them to a degree of care that a young person of the same age and maturity would be expected to exercise.

Most teens are measured against a standard of care very close to that of adults.

How does a minor go about defending a case?

Again, the minor has an adult representative, who assists the attorney. The representative must act in the minor's best interests and isn't required to take orders from the minor.

Who pays the damages when a jury decides a minor committed a tort?

In theory, the minor. But minors usually don't have much money—in legal jargon, they are "judgment proof." For this reason, parents often are jointly responsible for the torts of their minor children, particularly in cases in which the minor wasn't properly supervised when the tort occurred.

For example, if a parent left a handgun where anyone could reach it and a minor child managed to wound someone, the minor and the parents could be sued jointly. They would be "co-defendants." The minor could be sued for negligence and the parents would be sued for negligent supervision.

LAWYERS

How important is a lawyer?

In most civil cases and in all criminal cases a lawyer is critical. Anyone who wants to file a lawsuit should consider talking to a lawyer first. A lawyer can determine whether a person has a valid legal claim in tort or contract, whether the person has a chance of winning, and whether the estimated damages are worth the effort and expense of going to court.

Does a person need a lawyer to go to court?

No. Individuals can file lawsuits and go to court without legal representation. For better or worse, this happens all the time. Even so, court is exceedingly complex—it befuddles most nonlawyers (and many lawyers). As a rule, the more complex the case, the more important it is to have legal representation.

Would a lawyer talk privately to a teen about a case the minor wants to file?

A lawyer would undoubtedly urge a minor to bring a parent or other adult along, even for a first office meeting. In addition, the lawyer's availability might depend on whether the minor had any money. Most attorneys charge by the hour, and an hourly rate of $125 isn't at all unusual.

Are lawyers always paid by the hour?

No. Their fee usually depends on the type of case. For tort actions, the plaintiff's lawyer usually charges a "contingency fee," which means his or her pay is a percentage of the amount recovered from the defendant. Under contingency fee arrangements, the lawyer doesn't get paid *unless* and *until* the plaintiff collects.

A contingency fee usually is one-third of the amount recovered. If the plaintiff loses and the case is appealed, the percentage goes up. In addition to the contingency fee, the plaintiff usually pays filing fees and other standard court charges, regardless of the outcome of the case.

In tort actions the *defendant's* lawyer is paid by the hour.

SMALL CLAIMS COURT

What is small claims court?

It is a court that only hears cases in which the damage claim doesn't exceed a certain dollar amount, usually $5,000. Claims for unpaid bills or minor property damage often end up before a small claims judge.

Small claims courts are in the nature of "people's courts" because the parties rarely use lawyers. Sometimes state law prohibits parties in small claims court to have any legal representation at all.

Can a minor take a case to small claims court?

Only if state law permits minors to file lawsuits. Minors lack the legal capacity to file most civil suits on their own.

BRINGING A LAWSUIT

How does a plaintiff begin a civil case?

By filing a "complaint," which is a court document in which a plaintiff explains his or her claim against a defendant and requests a specific type of relief. As a rule, the plaintiff must always set forth enough information in the complaint to put the defendant on notice of the substance of the claim. If there isn't enough information given, the defendant can ask the judge to dismiss it.

Most courts charge a filing fee to open a case, and the amount depends on the state and also the type of court. The filing fee usually can be excused if the plaintiff can't afford it.

Can a plaintiff file in any court?

No. Courts have the legal power or "jurisdiction" to hear certain cases but not others. A court's jurisdiction depends on several factors, including the residence of the parties, the damages in dispute, the subject of the case, and the legal concepts upon which the plaintiff's claims are based.

There are federal, state, city, municipal, traffic, and tax courts. To find out the appropriate court for a particular case, ask the chief clerk of court at any state or county court.

What is the difference between state court and federal court?

Basically, their respective jurisdictional powers. Federal courts, which are in every state, have jurisdiction over cases in which—

1. The United States government is a party;
2. An issue concerning the federal Constitution or federal statute is raised;
3. The dispute involves more than $10,000 *and* is between two states, a state and citizens of another state, or citizens of different states; or
4. The defendant is charged with a federal crime.

State courts usually deal with controversies between a state's residents and property owners, and with crimes based on state law. County courts are part of the state court system.

Can there be more than one plaintiff in a case?

There can be multiple plaintiffs and multiple defendants.

How does a person find out that he or she is a defendant in a lawsuit?

The person receives a ''summons'' which states that a case naming that person as a defendant has been filed. The law allows the defendant a reasonable time, usually 20 or 30 days in most states, to prepare and file his or her ''answer.''

What should the defendant's answer contain?

It must admit or deny the statements in the complaint, and it may also state why the defendant believes he or she didn't do anything wrong and shouldn't be found responsible.

In a nutshell, the answer is the defendant's ''defense'' to a complaint.

What happens if the defendant doesn't answer?

A ''default judgment'' can be entered for the plaintiff; this basically means the plaintiff wins. At that point the plaintiff must present evidence to the judge concerning the damages he or she claims to have suffered. Once the judge calculates the damages (plus lawyer's fees), the plaintiff has an enforceable ''judgment'' against the defendant in a particular dollar amount.

If the defendant answers, will the case always go to trial?

No. Most lawsuits settle before trial. In the long run, settling a case often is less expensive than going to trial, especially if one party's case is weak.

PREPARING A CIVIL CASE

If the parties don't settle their dispute, what happens between the date the answer is filed and the first day of trial?

The parties conduct "discovery," which is the overall process by which they learn more about one another's positions.

Why don't the parties wait until trial to learn more about each other's case?

Because today's court rules encourage parties to discover as much as possible about one another's claims or defenses and settle as many issues as they can out of court. Judges only want to hear issues that the parties can't resolve on their own. This philosophy encourages better use of the court's time and, because the lawyer's fees mount up fast once a case goes to trial, always saves money.

Can the defendant ask to see documents in the plaintiff's possession that are likely to damage the plaintiff's case?

Yes, and the plaintiff can obtain damaging documents from the defendant. Prior to trial, a party must produce copies of any documents in his or her control relating to the case that the other party specifically requests.

Are documents in one party's control ever considered confidential?

Yes. Such items, called "privileged" communications, don't have to be turned over to the opposing party. They are protected because they occur in relationships in which honesty and trust are of critical importance. A privileged communication usually takes the form of a personal letter or memorandum, a private conversation, or a medical report.

The attorney-client relationship is a type of privileged relationship—hence, the "attorney-client privilege." A party who claims this privilege may refuse to produce material generated during the course of the relationship, and his or her lawyer *must* refuse. Other examples of privileged relationships are the relationship of husband and wife, the doctor-patient relationship, and the priest-confessor relationship.

Can a party force a person to testify?

Yes. The party would do so by asking the court to "subpoena" the person. A subpoena is a court order directing a certain person to appear as a witness. Often a party requests a subpoena if there is reason to believe the witness won't show up. If the witness ignores the subpoena, the judge declares him or her to be "in contempt of court." If the witness still won't appear, he or she can be fined or even jailed.

TRIALS

How does a trial begin?

Each party presents its "opening statement," which carefully explains what each will attempt to prove during trial.

What happens after the opening statements?

Each of the plaintiff's witnesses takes the stand and testifies. The plaintiff's lawyer conducts his or her "direct examination" of the plaintiff's witnesses. After the direct examination, the defendant's lawyer has an opportunity to "cross-examine."

What exactly is cross-examination?

Cross-examination occurs when a witness for one party is questioned by the lawyer for the other party. The cross-examiner will always attempt to test the truth or reliability of the witness's direct testimony but may also develop additional facts supporting his or her client's position.

What happens after all the plaintiff's witnesses have testified and been cross-examined?

The defendant's lawyer calls the defense witnesses. One by one he or she questions them, and one by one the plaintiff's lawyer cross-examines them.

How does material other than in-court testimony come into evidence?

Each party's lawyer can request that items such as letters, memos, photos, weapons, bills, and results of scientific tests be considered. The judge rules on the admissibility of each item as it is offered into evidence.

Can a young person testify?

Anyone who can remember significant events or evidence, express them clearly, and understand the duty to tell the truth is "competent" to testify. Minors often are placed on the stand.

In some states, if a minor is 10 years old (12 in other states) or younger, his or her ability to testify isn't taken for granted. If a party to a case believes a minor won't be able to offer reliable testimony, the judge will talk to the minor in private to determine whether he or she can understand questions, respond in court, remember important events, and comprehend the difference between true and false.

When determining a minor's competency to testify, age is often less significant than maturity. Judges have permitted children as young as 3 years old to testify in open court.

What is an "objection"? Why would a lawyer raise an objection in court?

A lawyer will object when an item of evidence, a question asked by the opposing party's lawyer, or a certain court procedure appears inappropriate. If a lawyer makes an objection, he or she must be ready to explain to the judge why the question, evidence, or procedure is out of line. If the judge agrees, he or she will "sustain" the objection. If the judge disagrees, it will be "overruled."

What happens after all the witnesses testify?

The lawyers present their "closing arguments." Each summarizes his or her client's case and tells the jury why it should decide the case in that party's favor.

What does a jury do?

It listens to the testimony of the witnesses, reviews the evidence, considers the applicable laws and earlier court cases dealing with similar legal issues, then decides the outcome. In essence, it decides what really happened in the parties' case.

The jury's decision is its "verdict." When the jury brings in its verdict, one party wins and the other loses. The winner receives a judgment.

Is a case always argued to a jury?

No. The parties can agree to argue their case to the judge. When this happens—and it often does in complex business cases—the judge decides what actually happened and renders a decision on his or her own.

How does a jury know what legal principles to apply to a case?

After the closing arguments the judge gives the jury its "instructions," which advise the jury what laws and earlier cases to apply to the dispute between the parties.

What is a "hung jury"?

A jury is "hung" when it tries to reach a decision but can't. Since the jury is hung, no judgment is awarded, and the case must be reargued to another jury.

Is a jury's verdict always final?

No. The losing party can ask the court—can "motion" the court—to grant a new trial. However, a judge will only grant a new trial if he or she believes that no reasonable jury could have reached the verdict that the jury returned.

DAMAGES

If the plaintiff wins, who decides how much the defendant will have to pay?

If the case is tried to a jury, the jury decides. Otherwise the judge decides. There aren't any hard and fast rules for deciding how much a plaintiff's injuries or other damages are "worth," and juries have considerable leeway in setting damage amounts, particularly in tort cases.

To calculate damages for a personal injury tort, a jury would consider evidence presented by the plaintiff's attorney regarding his or her client's medical expenses and loss of income. It might place a dollar value on both the plaintiff's pain and suffering and future employment opportunities lost because of the injury. If the damage was to property such as a car, the jury would consider the cost to repair the damage or replace the property altogether.

To determine damages in a breach of contract case, the jury would calculate the financial loss resulting from the defendant's failure to fulfill his or her side of the agreement.

APPEALING A COURT DECISION

What is an appeal? Who can appeal?

An appeal is a court review of certain issues previously decided at trial. The review is conducted by a higher court, called a court of appeals. In an appeal, the losing party—the "appellant"—claims a mistake was made by the judge or jury during the trial, causing the appellant to lose.

Is an appeal just a repeat of the trial?

No. Courts of appeal don't take testimony or accept additional evidence—they only review matters that are brought up for review. An appeals court considers the arguments of both parties on these issues, reviews the written summaries or "briefs" of their arguments, examines the applicable law, then decides to "affirm" or "reverse" the trial court's decision.

If a party loses an appeal, can he or she take the case to a still higher court?

In some cases, yes. The federal court system and most state court systems provide two levels of appeal. In federal court, the first level is the Federal Court of Appeals, and next is the United States Supreme Court. In state courts, the first level is the state court of appeals and the second is the state supreme court. A state supreme court may refuse to hear a party's appeal, except in states (such as Wyoming) in which there is no appeals court sandwiched between its trial courts and supreme court.

The United States Supreme Court only hears select appeals, usually from the federal courts. In limited circumstances it will hear the appeal of a party who loses in a state supreme court. In Supreme Court cases the issue on appeal will involve a constitutional right or other important issue under federal law that earlier cases haven't clarified.

FOR FURTHER READING

Archer, Jules. *You and the Law.* New York: Harcourt Brace Jovanovich, 1978.

Elias, Stephen, et al. *Legal Breakdown: 40 Ways to Fix Our Legal System.* Berkeley, California: Nolo Press, 1990.

Goldberg, Steven H. *The First Trial: Where Do I Sit? What Do I Say?* St. Paul, Minnesota: West Publishing, 1982.

Levin, Harvey. *The People's Court: How to Tell It to the Judge.* New York: Quill, 1985.

Warner, Ralph. *Everybody's Guide to Small Claims Court.* 4th ed. Berkeley, California: Nolo Press, 1990.

Zerman, Melvyn Bernard. *Beyond a Reasonable Doubt: Inside the American Jury System.* New York: Thomas Y. Crowell, 1981.

— 18 —

How to Find the Law

How would a young person go about finding the law for a given situation?

The first thing to do is go to a public library and ask to see a set of your state's laws, also called your state "statutes." Most laws governing important day-to-day activities are in state statutes, and for that reason every public library has a complete set.

Statutes aren't hard to use. Each set has a complete topic index. The index usually cites to the statute number, not the page number. If you can't find the particular statute you're looking for, ask a reference librarian to help. Large public libraries have legal specialists on hand (sometimes called "government document specialists") to assist further.

For instance, if capital punishment is permitted in your state and you want to find out if your state authorizes capital punishment for minors, look up "capital punishment" in the statute index. The index entry might look like this:

CAPITAL PUNISHMENT

    Adults, (Statute Number)

    Appeal of Sentence, (Statute Number)

    Due Process Hearing for, (Statute Number)

    Methods, (Statute Number)

    Minors, (Statute Number)

    Offenses, (Statute Number)

Next look up the statute for "Minors" and read what it says.

Follow the same process to locate a particular *city law*, or "ordinance," such as a local curfew law.

Federal laws are located the same way, but the indexes are complicated, mainly because federal law is complicated. Always ask a librarian for help locating a federal law (such as a law regulating age discrimination at the national level). Federal statutes are in the United States Code Annotated, or "USCA"—people often refer to it as the "Federal Code."

Aren't laws practically impossible to read?

No, although sometimes reading them can be rough going. The best way to understand what a law says is to read it over a number of times. Once usually isn't enough—any lawyer will tell you that. It's wise to photocopy the statute or ordinance after you've looked it up, then take the copy home and read it a few more times, carefully.

Isn't there an easier way to learn about the law?

Oftentimes, yes. Libraries frequently have books on various legal topics and many are written for young people. The sections at the end of each chapter entitled "For Further Reading" and Table 7 list many legal books for young readers.

How do you find out what a court case says?

You may have to go to the local law library to locate a court case— such as *Miranda v. Arizona* (regarding the *Miranda* warning) or *Roe v. Wade* (legalizing abortion). Most larger counties have a county law library, and every law school in the country has one. To find a case, ask the law librarian and, again, make a copy of it. You'll probably have to read it over more than once—some cases are long and complicated.

How do you find the Constitution?

Ask any librarian. The U.S. Constitution often is printed in the back of a good dictionary. State constitutions usually are at the front of the state statutes. The subject matter of state constitutions is indexed along with the statutes.

Who else can help a young person find the law?

Organizations such as those listed in Table 7. If you call or write to them, they will send you information about their special areas of concern.

Table 7
National Organizations Assisting Young People in Legal Matters

National Center for Youth Law
1663 Mission Street, 5th Floor
San Francisco, CA 94103
415-543-3307

National Juvenile Law Center
3701 Lindell Boulevard
PO Box 14200
St. Louis, MO 63178
314-652-5555

Children's Defense Fund
Legal Division
1520 New Hampshire Avenue, NW
Washington, DC 20036
202-483-1470

American Civil Liberties Union
Children's Rights Project
132 W 43 Street
New York, NY 10035
212-944-9800

Student Press Law Center
1735 Eye Street, NW
Washington, DC 20006
202-466-5242

Center for Law and Education
236 Massachusetts Avenue, NE
Washington, DC 20002
202-546-5300

ADDITIONAL BOOK SOURCES
Belli, Melvin, and Allen D. Wilkinson. *Everybody's Guide to the Law*. New York: Gramercy Publishing, 1989.
Davis, Samuel M., and Mortimer D. Schwartz. *Children's Rights and the Law*. Lexington: The Free Press, 1987.
Dolan, Edward F. *Protect Your Legal Rights: A Handbook for Teenagers*. New York: Julian Messner, 1983.
Englebardt, Leland S. *You Have a Right: A Guide for Minors*. New York: Lothrop, Lee and Shepard, 1979.
Epstein, Sam, and Beryl Epstein. *Kids in Court: The ACLU Defends Their Rights*. New York: Four Winds Press, 1982.
Gilbert, Sara D. *Get Help: Solving the Problems in Your Life*. New York: Morrow Junior Books, 1989.
Guggenheim, Martin, and Alan Sussman. *The Rights of Young People*. 2nd ed. Carbondale: Southern Illinois University Press, 1985.
Weiss, Ann E. *The Supreme Court*. Hillside: Enslow Publishers, 1987.
Zimring, Franklin E. *The Changing Legal World of Adolescents*. New York: The Free Press, 1982.

In addition, state and county "bar associations" usually have easy-to-read information available on a variety of legal subjects. (A bar association is a professional association of lawyers.) Also, many bar associations have recorded telephone information on dozens of legal topics. Phone numbers of state and county bar associations are in the phone book.

Bar associations often sponsor special programs to educate young people about the law, and often the lawyers who participate in them speak to student groups. The programs are very informative and easy to follow, so it's important to watch for them.

Couldn't a young person just call and ask a lawyer to explain a particular area of law?

That shouldn't be your first line of attack. Lawyers often have a difficult time cutting away for phone calls from people other than clients, and usually they are paid by the hour for their work, including phone calls. A lawyer would probably refer you to the library or local bar association anyway.

Glossary

Abandonment Voluntarily giving up one's parental rights. Abandonment usually is established by actions of a parent showing an intent to abandon a minor child and forfeit parental rights.

Accomplice A person who voluntarily helps another commit or attempt to commit a crime.

Adoption A process under state law in which a family court terminates a minor's legal rights and duties toward his or her birth parents and establishes similar rights and duties with respect to the minor's adoptive parents.

Advisory Hearing A hearing in juvenile court at which a minor is formally charged with a delinquent act.

Affirm An action of an appeals court in which a decision of a trial court is upheld.

Age of Majority The age at which a young person is legally entitled to manage his or her personal affairs and enjoy the rights associated with adulthood. The age of majority is 18 in most states.

Appeals Court A panel of judges with the power to review and change a judgment, verdict, or other order of a trial court. Appeals courts are also called "appellate courts."

Arbitrary A decision made by a court or jury that is not based on sound judgment. *The appeals court set aside the jury's decision because the appellate judges believed it was arbitrary.*

Arrest A police action that takes away a person's freedom, usually when the person is believed to have broken the law.

Attorney A person authorized to practice law in a particular state and therefore authorized to perform legal services for clients. An attorney's services may include giving legal advice, drafting legal documents, and representing clients in court. Attorneys are also referred to as "lawyers."

Battery Any intentional and harmful application of force to another. Examples of battery include injuring a person and giving a person medical treatment without legal permission in a nonemergency.

Beyond a Reasonable Doubt The level of proof needed to convict a defendant in a criminal case. When this level of proof is required, the jury must be firmly convinced that the defendant is guilty of the offense as charged.

Breach of Contract The failure of a contracting party to fulfill the terms of a contract.

Burden of Proof The duty of a plaintiff (or the duty of the state in a criminal proceeding) to prove a point or establish a fact supporting his or her case. In tort actions, the plaintiff's burden of proof is to establish his or her case by a "preponderance of the evidence." In criminal cases, the state's burden of proof is to prove its case "beyond a reasonable doubt."

Capital Punishment The death penalty.

Cause of Action Specific facts which give rise to a case against a defendant.

Child Labor Law A state or federal law limiting the type of work a minor may legally perform and the number of hours a minor may legally work per week.

Child Protection Proceeding A legal action, usually in state family court, in which a child protective agency requests court permission to protect a minor from neglect or abuse.

Child Protective Agency A government agency possessing the legal power to protect a minor from neglect or abuse, including sexual abuse.

Civil Action (also called *civil proceeding*) A court case brought by a plaintiff to enforce a private legal right. Generally, civil actions include all actions which are not criminal actions. Tort actions are a type of civil action.

Compensation Money a civil court orders a defendant to pay a plaintiff for an injury or other loss.

Conflict of Interest A clash between a lawyer's interest as a servant of the court and his or her private monetary interest in a particular legal matter. When a conflict of interest arises, the lawyer usually withdraws from the case.

Conservator See *property guardian*.

Constitution A written instrument from which a governing body derives its authority and which describes the limits on its powers. In America the federal government is subject to the U.S. Constitution. State and local governments and laws are subject to both the U.S. Constitution and also their respective state constitutions.

Contraceptive Any device or substance (such as birth control pills or condoms) that prevents a woman from becoming pregnant.

Contract An agreement between two or more persons creating a legal duty to perform a certain act. For example, a contract to purchase a car is an agreement in which one person agrees to turn a car over to another in return for the second person's promise to pay for it. Once the parties have fulfilled the duties promised under the contract, it is said to be "executed."

Controlled Substance Any illegal drug.

Corporal Punishment Any type of punishment inflicted on a person's body.

Crime An act committed by a person which violates a federal, state, or local law.

Criminal Act See *crime.*

Criminal Action (also called *criminal proceeding*) A court case in which an adult charged with a crime is brought to trial.

Cross-Examine In-court examination of a witness by the party other than the party producing the witness. The purpose of cross-examination is to test the reliability of the witness's original or "direct" testimony.

Cruel and Unusual Punishment Punishment that is so severe, given the seriousness of the crime, that it shocks the moral sense of the community.

Curfew A law forbidding persons (usually minors) from being on the streets at night.

Custodial Parent The parent who is in charge of the care of a minor child after a divorce.

Custody Responsibility for another person.

Damages Money awarded by a court to a person who sustained a loss or injury as a result of a breach of contract or tort.

Date Rape Forced sexual intercourse in a casual dating situation.

Debauchery Extreme sexual immorality in light of community standards.

Decedent A dead person.

Decedent's Estate The property a person owns at death.

Defamatory Statement A spoken or written statement that injures another's reputation and is untrue.

Defendant A person against whom damages are sought in a civil action or against whom punishment is sought in a criminal action.

Defense Attorney An attorney who represents a civil or criminal defendant.

Delinquent A minor who has broken a criminal law or engaged in indecent or immoral conduct. Such a person is also called a "juvenile delinquent."

Delinquent Act An act of a minor which would have been a crime under federal, state, or local law if committed by an adult.

Desegregation Order A court order forbidding skin color to serve as the basis for limiting an individual's right to hold a certain job or attend the school of his or her choice.

Detention Hearing A juvenile court hearing to determine whether a minor should be confined to a shelter or placed in foster care until a formal hearing in juvenile court takes place.

Disability A physical or mental condition that limits a person's ability to perform at the same level as persons who do not have the same condition.

Disaffirm To back out of a contract.

Discriminate To give rights or privileges to certain persons while denying them to others. Laws limiting the right of minors to purchase alcoholic beverages legally discriminate, but laws which discriminate in school or at work on the basis of gender, race, nationality, religion, age (over 40), or disability violate the federal Constitution.

Disposition Hearing A hearing in juvenile court at which the judge orders a delinquent minor into treatment or disposes of the case in some other way.

Due Process Hearing A type of legal hearing at which a person has a chance to present his or her side in a dispute involving personal or property rights. See *due process of law*.

Due Process of Law A course of action, usually in a legal proceeding, in which a person receives proper notice and has a chance to present his or her side in a dispute regarding legal rights. Formally defined, "due process of law" means that no person may legally be deprived of life, liberty, or property unless the matter is reviewed in a legal proceeding.

DWI An offense committed by a person who operates a vehicle while under the influence of alcoholic beverages or illegal drugs.

Emancipation Acts which cause parents to lose their authority over a minor child. An emancipation may be ordered by a court or be implied from conduct of either the minor or the parents.

Establishment Clause The provision in the First Amendment of the federal Constitution prohibiting the federal government or any state from passing laws which aid religion, giving a preference to a particular religion, or enforcing a religious belief.

Estate All the property a person owns.

Exclusionary Rule A rule of criminal law making evidence obtained in violation of the federal Constitution inadmissible against a criminal defendant in court. For example, evidence obtained in an unreasonable search is legally inadmissible.

Family Court   A state court with the power to decide child abuse and neglect cases, determine paternity with respect to children born out of wedlock, and terminate parental rights.

Federal Court   United States courts (as opposed to state courts) which handle cases relating to federal law and cases between persons of different states.

Federal System   A division of power between the United States government and the governments of the 50 states. States have their own legal powers, such as the power to create a public school system. The federal government has separate powers, such as control over foreign trade. Both have powers in the areas of taxation and public health.

Felony   A crime of a more serious nature than a misdemeanor. Under federal law and in most states, a felony is any offense punishable by imprisonment for more than one year, or death.

Fetus   An unborn child. Usually this term is used to describe an unborn child whose major body parts have begun to form.

Formal Hearing   A juvenile court trial.

Foster Home   A private home where a minor child resides after being removed from his or her parents' home by court order.

Foster Parent   An adult person who takes a minor child into his or her home, either temporarily or permanently, after the child has been removed from the custody of his or her parents by a court.

Freedom of Expression   A right set forth in the First Amendment of the federal Constitution guaranteeing the right of individuals to speak freely and openly.

Free Exercise Clause   The provision in the First Amendment of the federal Constitution prohibiting the federal government or any state government from outlawing or controlling the practice of religion.

Gender Bias   A preference in the workplace or elsewhere based solely on an individual's sex.

Guardian   A person with the legal power to care for another or manage another's legal and financial affairs. Usually a guardian is appointed if a person is too young, too old, or otherwise unable to make important personal and financial decisions.

Guardianship   A relationship existing between a guardian and the person under the guardian's legal protection. In such a relationship the protected person is sometimes called the ''ward.''

Health Insurance   A written agreement in which an insurance company promises to pay expenses associated with a certain individual's injuries, sickness, or death.

Homicide An act in which a person takes the life of another, either deliberately or accidentally.

Inadmissible Evidence that cannot be legally introduced in court to prove a party's case because it is false or unreliable, or was improperly obtained.

Indeterminate Sentencing A sentence for a period of time determined by the agency supervising the sentenced person and not fixed by the trial court.

Injury Damage to another's person, property, individual rights, or reputation.

Insurance A written agreement in which one party agrees to pay the other for a type of loss or damage specifically described in the insurance agreement. The party who is insured against loss or damage is the "insured," and the party who must pay in the event of a loss or damage is the "insurer."

Joint Custody A type of custody awarded by a divorce court in which the responsibility for the care and control of a minor child is awarded to both parents.

Jury A group of persons selected from the community to decide the facts of a case and determine the truth of a matter at trial.

Juvenile Court A state court with the legal authority to decide cases involving delinquent, abused, or neglected minors.

Juvenile Delinquent See *delinquent.*

Larceny The legal term for theft.

Lawyer An attorney.

Legal Guardian See *guardian.*

Liability A legal obligation or responsibility to do something or pay a specified amount of money. A *debt* is a type of liability.

Liability Insurance Insurance that covers the cost of damage caused by the insured person to another person or another's property.

Libel Printed material which is untrue and injures the personal or business reputation of another.

Majority See *age of majority.*

Material and Substantial Disruption A level of disruption that, in the opinion of a reasonable person, interferes with daily activities to the point that they cannot proceed at a normal pace.

Maternal Preference A tendency in the law to favor the mother over the father, particularly in child custody matters. The maternal preference may be applied when parents divorce or in cases involving children born outside marriage.

Medicaid A welfare program sponsored jointly by the federal and state governments which provides medical care for low-income persons.

Minor A person under the age of legal majority, which is 18 in most states.

Miranda **Warning** A constitutional rule requiring that before questioning a person who is in police custody, the police must warn (a) that the person has a right to remain silent, (b) that any statement the person makes may be used against him or her, (c) that the person has a right to a lawyer; and (d) that if the person can't afford a lawyer, one will be appointed to assist him or her.

Misdemeanor An offense which is less serious than a felony, usually punishable by a fine or less than one year in prison. In most states misdemeanors are grouped according to their seriousness (such as Class A and Class B misdemeanors).

Necessaries Food, drink, clothing, medical attention, and a suitable place to live.

Negligence A failure to perform an act that a reasonable person would do, or the performance of an act that a reasonable person would not do.

Opinion A written statement of a judge or appeals court setting forth the reasons for reaching a decision in a given case.

Ordinance A law of a city government, such as a traffic or parking ordinance.

Pain and Suffering A type of damage in a civil tort action that compensates a plaintiff for pain and suffering endured or to be endured as the result of the tort.

Paternity Suit A civil court action to prove that a certain person is the father of a particular child. If proof of paternity is established, the court will require the father to support the child financially.

Petition A complaint filed in juvenile court which begins a case against a minor suspected of committing a delinquent act. Often a juvenile court petition is called a "formal petition."

Plaintiff A person who brings a civil action against a defendant.

Preponderance of the Evidence The level of proof needed in a civil action to obtain a judgment against a defendant. When this level of evidence is required, the evidence presented by the plaintiff at trial must have greater weight than the evidence offered against it by the defendant.

Prior Restraint A law or rule preventing a statement or other First Amendment expression from ever being made.

Probable Cause Facts suggesting that a certain person committed a crime. When probable cause exists, a police officer has a right to arrest and search the person.

Probate   A system under state law providing for the orderly distribution of a person's property after death.

Probation   A system of allowing a juvenile delinquent to avoid treatment in an institution after a juvenile court conviction. While on probation, the juvenile delinquent is usually under the strict supervision of a probation officer.

Probation Officer   A person who works with and supervises the activities of a minor on probation.

Property Guardian   A person appointed by a family court to manage the property of an individual who is incapable of managing his or her property because of minority, old age, or a physical or mental disabilty.

Prosecuting Attorney   A attorney who conducts criminal prosecutions against persons charged with breaking a federal, state, or local law.

Public Policy   An approach to a matter of general concern that is believed by the community to promote its overall health, safety, and security.

Punitive Damages   Money awarded a plaintiff in a civil action over and above the actual damages suffered. An award of punitive damages is designed to punish the person causing the damages.

Rape   Forced sexual relations.

Reasonable Doubt   The amount of doubt justifying the dismissal of a criminal action or juvenile court action against a defendant. To convict a person, his or her guilt must be established in both adult and juvenile court "beyond a reasonable doubt."

Reasonable Person   A person who exercises ordinary or reasonable prudence.

Reasonable Suspicion (of criminal activity)   An amount of suspicion needed to arrest a minor. Reasonable suspicion is less suspicion than probable cause; it is also the amount of suspicion needed by a police officer to "stop and frisk" a person on the street. "Reasonable suspicion" and "reasonable cause" are synonymous.

Recklessness   Paying no attention to the fact that an act could seriously endanger the safety or life of another.

Reverse (a court decision)   An action of an appeals court in which a decision of a trial court is revoked. *The appeals court reversed the trial court's decision to convict a man of intentional homicide after deciding that the trial court refused to admit evidence regarding the man's lack of intent.*

Revocation Hearing   A juvenile court hearing held to decide whether a juvenile delinquent's probation should be set aside.

Search Incident to an Arrest   A personal search that a police officer may legally make at the time of arrest. No search warrant is necessary to make a search incident to an arrest.

Search Warrant A written order, issued by a judge or other court employee (such as a magistrate), authorizing the search of a person or place in order to uncover evidence of a crime.

Sexually Transmitted Disease (STD) A type of disease passed from one person to another during sexual activity.

Sibling A brother or sister.

Slander Making false oral statements about another which result in damage to the person's reputation.

Social Security A national program in which payments are paid to a former worker or his or her family to replace a portion of earnings lost by the worker as a result of retirement, death, or disability.

State Action Action taken by the federal government, a state or local government, or any division of such government bodies.

State Court A court system established under the laws of a state to hear civil and criminal cases arising under that state's laws.

State Supreme Court The highest appeals court in a state court system.

Statutory Rape A crime occurring when a person above a certain age has sexual relations with a minor, regardless of whether the minor may have consented.

Stop-and-Frisk Search A patdown of a person's clothing by a police officer to check for weapons.

Subpoena An order issued by a court commanding a particular person to appear at a certain time and place to give testimony in court.

Supreme Court The highest court in the United States; the Court to which certain state supreme court cases and all federal appeals court cases may be appealed.

Symbolic Speech Unspoken expression of an idea, such as an insignia or armband.

Taking Losing a valuable personal or property right under a particular law or regulation. In the United States, such "takings" cannot occur without due process of law.

Teen (or teenager) A person between 13 and 19, and generally under the age of majority.

Tort an act caused by a person's lack of care that causes emotional injury or property damage. In tort actions in civil court, plaintiffs recover "compensation" or "damages" from defendants for injuries or losses resulting from their torts.

Unconstitutional A law or action which violates either the federal Constitution or a state constitution.

United States Supreme Court See *Supreme Court.*

Vagrancy Loitering in a public place without a means of support and with the intention of begging or committing an immoral act such as prostitution.

Verdict A decision of a jury in a trial.

Viable Being able to exist or survive independently. This term is often applied to describe an unborn child that is able to live outside the mother's womb.

Visa A legal document or a mark in a passport indicating that the visa holder may legally enter or stay in a particular country.

Waiver Intentional surrender of a legal right or legal privilege. *The man waived his right to remain silent after receiving the* Miranda *warning, and then confessed to the robbery.*

Warrant A written order issued by a judge or other court employee (such as a magistrate) authorizing an arrest or search.

Workers' Compensation A program under state law which pays employees or their dependents for employment-related accidents and diseases regardless of who is at fault for the accident or disease.

Index

Abandonment of child, 55

Abortion and abortion rights, 99–104; counseling, 101; judicial bypass, 100; parental consent, 100; partner's consent, 101; public assistance for, 101; *Roe v. Wade*, 99, 100, 101

Abuse. *See* Child abuse; Child protection proceedings; Sexual abuse

Accidents: arrest following, 10, 141; refusal to produce identification, 5; responsibility for, 5–6; search of auto, 11, 154; what to do at the scene, 5. *See also* Traffic offenses

Acquired immunodeficiency syndrome. *See* HIV/AIDS

Adoption: child of teenage parent, 112–13; following termination of parental rights, 57; foster child by foster parents, 135; foster parents by foster child, 134–35; right to inherit from adoptive parent, 188; right to inherit from natural parent, 188–89

Adult books and adult videos, 53

Adult court. *See* Drugs and drug offenses; Juvenile court

AFDC (Aid to Families with Dependent Children), 113–14

Affirmative action, 72, 175

Age discrimination, 71, 171

Age of majority: defined, 53; minor's control of his or her own property, 187; parents' support obligations beyond, 54; rights gained, 53–54; state drinking laws, 53–54

Aid to Families with Dependent Children (AFDC), 113–14

AIDS. *See* HIV/AIDS

Alcohol. *See* Drinking

Aliens: employment of, 64–65, 176; right to public education, 44

Alimony, 92

Allowance, 49

Americans with Disabilities Act (ADA), 70–71

Apartments, 80

Appeals: from adult court, 211; from juvenile court, 162; of school disciplinary decision, 35–36

Armed forces: conscientious objector status, 81; emancipation, 79; homosexuals in, 183; national draft, 80–81; registration, 80–81; volunteering for, 81; women in, 80

Army. *See* Armed forces

Arrest: defined, 147, 149; following stop-and-frisk search, 154; juvenile suspect,

Arrest (*continued*)
147–48, 151–53; minor traffic violation, 10, 141; probable cause standard,
148; at school, 34–35; search at time
of arrest, 153–55. *See also Miranda*
rights and *Miranda* warning; Searches
and seizures
Attendance at school. *See* School
Automobile: curfews, 11–12; insurance,
6–10; loan to purchase, 13; offenses,
10–11, 141; purchase by minor, 12–
13; rental by minor, 13; search, 11,
153–55; weapon in auto, 11, 150–51.
See also Accidents; Drinking; Traffic
offenses
Automobile insurance: coverage and teen
marriage, 110–11; coverage for minor,
7; defined, 6–7; liability insurance, 7;
no-fault insurance, 8–10; premium, 7;
as proof of financial responsibility, 7;
purchase by minor, 7; risks covered,
7–8

Babysitting. *See* Employment
Bank accounts, 186, 190
Bar associations, 215, 216
Battery, 130
Bible readings, 29, 30
Birth control: counseling, 98–99; legal
status of, 97–98; parental consent to
obtain, 99; prescription and nonpre-
scription, 98; privacy rights, 97–98,
99, 100, 101; sex education, 29–30,
99; sterilization, 99; use by teens, 98.
See also Abortion and abortion rights
Blood tests, 39
Book banning, 26
Books: adult books, 53; American Li-
brary Association Bill of Rights, 27;
banned from curriculum, 26–27;
banned from school library, 26; *Board
of Education v. Pico*, 26–27
Breach of contract. *See* Contracts
Breathalyzer test, 141
Brown v. Board of Education, 172–74
Burden of proof: child protection proceed-
ings, 128–29; juvenile court, 161;

school disciplinary hearing, 34–35;
school dress codes, 84; termination of
parental rights, 56

Capital punishment, 163, 165
Car searches, 11, 154
Cases. *See* Finding the law
Child abuse: cleanliness of home, 131; defined, 117; distinguished from child neglect, 118; emergency situations, 124,
128; hotlines and hotline numbers,
118; parent abuses drugs or alcohol,
131–32; parent cohabits with unmarried adult, 131; parent is homosexual,
132; removal of minor from home,
124–25; report and investigation,
118–24; statistics, 117–18. *See also*
Child protection proceedings; Sexual
abuse
Child custody: beyond age of majority,
55, 89; child snatching, 93; choice of
custodial parent by minor, 88; divorce
of parents by child, 89; during child
protection proceedings, 124–25; factors
considered in awarding custody,
87–88; following parents' divorce,
87–90; homosexual parent, 181; joint
custody, 88–89; legal custody defined,
87; maternal preference, 88, 112; parent cohabits with unmarried adult, 90;
physical custody defined, 87; separating siblings, 90; visitation rights,
89–90; while parental rights are under
review, 56. *See also* Child support; Parenting by teens
Child labor laws, 61–64, 65–66
Child pornography, 53
Child protection proceedings: attorney for
minor, 126; attorney for parents,
125–26; burden of proof, 126–27;
criminal prosecution of abuser,
126–29; custody before and during proceedings, 124–25; testimony of minor,
125, 128–29. *See also* Child abuse;
Sexual abuse
Child snatching, 93
Child support: alimony compared, 92;
amount, 90–91; beyond age of major-

ity, 91; when both parents work, 91; defined, 90–91; enforcement of support orders, 92; insufficiency of, 91, 94 n.2; support obligations of teenage parents, 111. *See also* Parenting by teens

Cigarettes, 52

City laws, 214

Civil actions. *See* Lawsuits

Civil rights. *See* Discrimination

Civil Rights Act of 1964, 70–73

Clothing: dress codes, 25–26, 83–85; parental authority over minor's dress and hairstyle, 83; public nudity, 85–86; as symbolic speech, 19, 25–26

Competency testing, 43

Confessions. *See Miranda* rights and *Miranda* warning

Conservators. *See* Property of minor

Constitution and constitutional rights. *See specific topics throughout this index*

Contraceptives. *See* Birth control

Contracts: adult co-signer, 196; breach of contract, 195, 196, 201; civil court action, 199–200, 201; contract for auto purchase, 12–13, 197; damages or compensation for breach, 201, 210–11; defined, 195; disaffirmance by minors, 12–13, 196–97; injunction against, for breach, 201; misrepresentation of age, 197; necessaries, 130, 197; reason for rule of disaffirmance, 12–13, 196; restitution, 196–97; writing requirement, 195–96

Corporal punishment: at home, 49; in juvenile institution, 167; at school, 36–37

Courts. *See* Lawsuits

Curfews and curfew laws, 11–12

Curriculum: books banned from, 26; religious instruction in public school, 29–31; sex education, 30, 99

Custody. *See* Child custody

Date rape. *See* Rape

Death of minor: inheritance of minor's property, 190–91; validity of minor's will, 190

Death of parent: adopted child, 188; child born outside marriage, 190; inheritance of property by child, 187–90; inheriting from stepparent, 190; intestacy, 188; management of property by guardian, 186–87, 190; parent dies without will, 188; if parent leaves will, 187–90; parent's right to disinherit child, 188; probate court proceedings, 188; trust arrangements, 190

Death sentence, 163, 165, 169 n.1

Defamatory statements, 21

Defendants. *See* Lawsuits

Desegregation, 175

Detention, 157–58, 164–65

Disabilities and handicaps: at school, 44–45; at work, 70–71

Disaffirming contracts. *See* Contracts

Discipline. *See* Grandparents; Parents; School

Discrimination: affirmative action, 72, 175; age, 71, 171; Civil Rights Act of 1964, 70–73; competency testing, 43; desegregation, 175; examples of illegal gender discrimination, 176; examples of illegal race discrimination, 172; examples of legal discrimination, 174–75; handicapped students, 44–45; homosexuals, 183–84; housing, 80; illegal when state action involved, 172, 174–75; interracial marriages, 110; language barriers in public schools, 44; race, 172–76; reverse discrimination, 70–74, 175–76; separate-sex classes, 43–44; sex or gender, 41–42, 43–44, 176–77; sports, 41–42; students with hepatitis B, 45; students with HIV/AIDS, 45; tracking, 42–43. *See also* Age discrimination; Employment; Race discrimination; School; Sex discrimination

Distribution of materials on campus, 22–24

Divorce of parents: alimony compared, 92; by child, 89; child snatching, 93; child support, 90–92; discipline of minor following, 52; and emancipation of child, 78; lawyer for child, 88, 92; le-

Divorce of parents (*continued*)
gal separation compared, 93; statistics,
94 n.1; visitation rights, 89–90. *See
also* Child custody; Child support
Domestic partner laws, 181
Draft, 80–81
Dress codes. *See* Clothing
Drinking: alcohol in auto, 142; arrest for,
140–41; blood alcohol content (BAC),
141, 145 n.2; breathalyzer test, 141;
and driving (DWI), 10–11, 140–42;
employment of minor where alcohol
served, 140; field sobriety tests, 141;
fines and punishment, 10; at home,
139–40; impound of car, 11, 154; legal age, 139; marriage and purchase of
alcohol, 140; minor stopped, 10–11,
142; purchase of alcohol across state
lines, 140; random car stops, 142; right
to attorney, 142; roadblocks and checkpoints, 142; statistics, 140–41; treatment for alcoholism, 130
Driver's education, 1–4
Driver's license: driving without license,
1; learner's permit, 1–4; legal age, 1–
4; parental consent not required, 4–5;
parental consent to obtain, 1–5; proof
of financial responsibility, 5, 7. *See
also* Drinking
Drugs and drug offenses: arrest of minor,
144; elements of offense, 143; juvenile
court hearing, 144, 162, 164; minors
in adult court, 144, 162; possession
and sale compared, 143; search for
drugs, 37–38, 39, 70, 143–45; stop-
and-frisk search, 154; treatment for
drug abuse, 144–45, 130, 164; use at
home, 59; as violation of school rule,
34–35, 37–39, 144–45. *See also* Arrest; Searches and seizures
Drug testing: at school, 39; at work, 70
Due process of law: appeal of disciplinary decision, 35–36; burden of proof,
34–35, 161–62; child abuse cases, corporal punishment, 36–37, 167; defined, 36–37; expulsion from school,
32–33; and extracurricular activities,
35; *Goss v. Lopez,* 32; grade lowered,
32–33; juvenile court cases, 158–62;

Miranda warning, 35, 149–51; off-campus activities, 34; private schools,
46–47; school disciplinary matters,
31–36; 38–39; school rules, 31–32;
searches, 11, 37–39, 41; student handbook, 31–32; suspension from school,
33–34; termination of parental rights
cases, 56–58

Earnings of minor. *See* Employment
Emancipation: defined, 77–78; enlistment
in armed forces as, 79; homosexual
teens and, 180; marriage and, 79; medical care and, 130; parents' divorce
and, 78; rights received upon, 78–79;
runaway child and, 78; and school attendance, 18
Emergency medical treatment, 55, 118,
128
Employment: affirmative action, 72; age
requirements, 61; of aliens, 64; Americans with Disabilities Act, 70–71; babysitting, 61, 64, 69–70; child labor
laws, 61–64, 65–66; discrimination,
70–74, 171; dress codes, 20, 84–85;
drug testing, 70; duties of employee to
employer, 66; earnings of minor, 50,
65–66; employee-at-will, 68–69; employment certificates, 63–64; fringe
benefits, 66–68; full-time employment,
63, 65–66; hairstyle, 70, 84–85; health
insurance, 67; HIV/AIDS testing, 70;
hours of work permitted, 63; job
safety, 74; job testing, 71; loss of job,
68–69; maternity leave, 72; minimum
wage, 65; of minor where alcohol
served, 140; Occupational Safety and
Health Act, 74; overtime pay, 65; part-
time employment, 49, 63; paternity
leave, 72; pension plans, 66–67; pregnancy, 72; search of employee, 70; sexual harassment, 73–74; Social Security
card, 64; summer jobs, 49, 63; taxation of earnings, 69–70; tips, 65; types
of work permitted, 61; unemployment
compensation, 68–69; urine tests, 70;
visas, 64; workers' compensation, 67–
68
Employment certificates, 63–64

Expulsion. *See* Due process of law
Extracurricular activities and clubs: discipline and due process, 35; gay and lesbian, 28–29; religious, on campus, 30

Field sobriety tests, 141
Finding the law, 213–15
Food stamps, 114
Foster care and foster homes: adoption of foster child by foster parents, 135; adoption of foster parents by foster child, 134–35; payment to foster parents, 135; reasons for, 133; reuniting with natural family, 134; rights of foster child, 133; rights of foster parents, 134–35; rights of natural parents, 134; visitation rights, 134
Free expression. *See* Freedom of expression
Free speech. *See* Freedom of expression
Freedom of assembly: extracurricular clubs, 28–29, 30; gay and lesbian rights clubs, 28–29, 181–82; material and substantial disruption, 28–30; protest marches and sit-ins, 28; *Tinker v. Des Moines Independent School District* and, 28
Freedom of association. *See* Freedom of assembly
Freedom of expression: book banning, 26; clothing, 25–26; criticism of teachers, 20–21, 25; defamatory statements, 21; demonstrations, 27–29; distribution of materials on school grounds, 22–24; leafletting, 22–24; libel, 21; libraries, 26; material and substantial disruption, 19–21, 22, 23, 28–29; newspapers, 24–25; obscene language, 21–22; prior approval, 23–24; regulation of time, place, and manner, 23; slander, 21; symbolic speech, 19, 25–26, 182; *Tinker v. Des Moines Independent School District*, 19–20, 24, 25–26; underground newspapers, 20, 25. *See also* Freedom of assembly
Freedom of religion: bible readings in school, 29, 30; Establishment clause, 29, 30–31; Free exercise clause, 30; moment of silence in school, 29;

Pledge of Allegiance, 31; prayer at graduation ceremony, 30–31; prayer at school athletic event, 30–31; "release-time" programs, 29–30; saluting the American flag, 31; "Star Spangled Banner," 31; use of public school assembly halls, 30
Fringe benefits, 66–68

Gay and lesbian teens. *See* Homosexuals and homosexual activity
GED, 18
Gender discrimination. *See* Discrimination; Sex discrimination
Grades: lowered for absences or misconduct, 17; lowered insurance premium, 7
Graduate equivalency degree (GED), 18
Graduation ceremonies, 18, 30–31
Graffiti, 192
Grandparents: discipline of minor grandchild, 52; visitation rights following divorce, 92–93
Guardians: legal, 54–55; property, 186, 187, 190
Guns. *See* Weapons

Hairstyle, 83, 84, 85
Handicapped students. *See* School
Hazelwood School District v. Kuhlmeier, 24–25
Health insurance, 67
Hepatitis B, 45
Hitchhiking, 11
HIV/AIDS: counseling and treatment, 104, 130; at school, 18–19, 45; testing at work, 70
Homosexuals and homosexual activity: in armed forces, 183; custody of minor child, 132, 181; discrimination in housing, 183; domestic partner laws, 101; emancipation and, 180; gay and lesbian rights clubs, 28–29, 181–82; harassment by students or teacher, 182–83; homosexual parent's visitation rights, 181; legality of homosexual activities, 179–80; open displays of affection, 182; parents' right to forbid, 180; same sex marriages, 181; same sex prom

Homosexuals and activity (*continued*)
date, 182; sodomy, 179; statutory rape,
180; at work, 183
Hotlines and hotline numbers, 118
Human immunodeficiency virus. *See*
HIV/AIDS

Income taxes, 69–70
Inheriting property. *See* Death of parent
Injunctions, 201
Insanity defense, 161–62
Insurance. *See* Automobile insurance
Intake. *See* Juvenile court
Interracial marriages, 110
Intestacy and intestate succession. *See*
Death of parent

Job discrimination: homosexuality, 183;
marital status, 72; pregnancy, 72; race,
70–72; reverse discrimination, 71; sex
discrimination, 72–73; sexual harassment, 73
Job safety, 74
Job testing, 70
JOBS program, 114
Joint custody, 88–89
Jury. *See* Juvenile court; Lawsuits
Juvenile court: advisory hearing, 156,
157; appeal, 162; attorney for minor,
156, 157–58, 159, 162, 164; conviction on confession alone, 161; death
sentence, 163, 165; disposition hearing, 163–65; fines and restitution,
164–65; guilty plea, 157; how minor is
charged, 156–57; indeterminate sentencing, 166; insanity defense, 161–62;
institutional treatment, 166–67; intake,
155–57; juvenile delinquent, 158; newspaper coverage, 168–69; not guilty
plea, 157; petition, 158–59; pretrial detention, 157–58; probation, 165–66; records, 167–68; right to jury trial, 159;
right to remain silent, 161; sentencing,
163–67; state's burden of proof, 161;
testimony of minor, 161; trial of minor
as adult, 162–63; trial or formal hearing, 158–62; types of treatment, 166–
67
Juvenile delinquent. *See* Juvenile court

Larceny, 191
Last will and testament. *See* Wills
Law. *See specific topics throughout this
index*
Law libraries, 214
Laws. *See* Finding the law
Lawsuits: appeals, 211; appellant, 211; attorney-client relationship, 207–8; cause
of action, 199–201; closing arguments,
209; confidentiality issues, 207–8;
cross-examination, 208; damages or
compensation, 199, 200, 201, 210–11;
default judgment, 206; defendant, 199,
201, 203, 205, 206, 207, 208, 210; discovery of opponent's case, 207; evidence, 208–9; federal court, 205, 206;
filing a complaint, 205; filing an answer, 206–7; filing fee, 205; hung
jury, 210; judgment, 209; juries, 209–
10; lawsuit against parents, 202; lawsuit against relatives, 202; minors as
parties, 201–4, 209; objections, 209;
opening statement, 208; parties, 199;
plaintiff, 199, 201, 205, 206, 208,
210; reasonably prudent person, 200,
201–4, 206; representation by attorney,
204–5; settlement of case, 207; small
claims court, 205; subpoenas, 208;
summons, 205; testimony of minor,
209; torts, 200–201; United States
Supreme Court, 211; verdict, 20;
wrongful death lawsuit, 202–3; wrongful life lawsuit, 203. *See also*
Contracts
Lawyers: attorney-client relationship,
207–8; bar associations, 215–16; con-
sulting with minor, 216; contingency
fees, 204–5; need for, 204; payment
to, 204–5; representation of minor,
201–4
Leafletting, 22–24
Learner's permit, 1–4
Legal guardian. *See* Guardians
Legal research, 213–16
Legal separation, 93
Lesbian and gay teens. *See* Homosexuals
and homosexual activity
Liability insurance, 7
Libel, 21

Libraries, 26
Lockers and desks, 38

Marriage: and auto insurance coverage, 110–11; and emancipation, 79; interracial, 110; instability of teen marriages, 107; legal age, 107–9; and medical care, 130; out-of-state marriages, 109–10; parental consent for, 107–10; and public welfare, 110; and purchase of alcohol, 110; same-sex marriages, 101; and school attendance, 18
Maternal preference, 88, 112
Maternity leave, 72
Medicaid, 113–14
Medical care: battery, 130; court ordered treatment for minor, 129–30; emergency care, 124, 128; health insurance, 67; Medicaid, 113–14; minor arranging for offspring's care, 111; minor arranging for own care, 130; minor arranging for parent's care, 55; necessaries, 130, 197; opposition to, for religious reasons, 129–30; sexually transmitted diseases, 104, 130. See also Mental illness
Mental illness: as reason to terminate parental rights, 58; teen arranging for own care, 132; treatment in mental hospital, 132
Military service. See Armed forces
Minimum wage, 65
Minor. See specific topics throughout this index
Miranda rights and Miranda warning: confession after warning, 151; failure of police to recite, 149–51; minor's right to warning, 149; nature of rights and elements of warning, 149; and routine police questioning, 151; at school, 35; stop-and-frisk search, 154; timing of warning, 149–51; waiver of right, 151; withdrawal of waiver, 151
Miranda v. Arizona. See Miranda rights and Miranda warning

Necessaries, 130, 197
Neglect. See Child abuse
Negligence. See Lawsuits

News coverage, of juvenile case, 168–69
Newspapers, school and underground, 24
No-fault insurance, 8–10
Nudity, 85–86

Obscene language, 21–22
Occupational Safety and Health Act (OSHA), 74
Overtime pay, 65

Parenting by teens: change in custody, 112; child born outside marriage, 111–13; consent to child's medical care, 111; custody by teenage father, 112; maternal preference, 112; placing child for adoption, 112–13; proof of paternity, 113, 190; obligations and rights, 111; statistics, 114 nn.2, 3; visitation of child born outside marriage by noncustodial parent, 112; welfare for teenage parents, 113–14. See also Parents
Parents: abandonment of child, 55; abortion consent, 101; authority over minor child, 49, 83, 111; consent for minor child to use birth control, 98; consent to minor child's marriage, 107–9; corporal punishment, 49; divorced parents, 87–94; emancipation of minor child, 77–78; foster parents, 130–35; homosexual parent, 132, 181; lawsuit of minor child against parent, 202; minor arranging medical care for, 55; minor child's driver's license, 1–4, 5; obligation to educate minor child, 15; obligation to support minor child, 50–51, 111–13; parents' discipline obviously too harsh, 52; responsibility for negligent acts, 5–6, 200–201, 202–3; right to discipline minor child, 49; right to minor child's earnings, 50, 65–66; unmarried parents, 111–14; use of minor's property, 187. See also Child abuse; Death of parent; Divorce of parents; Parenting by teens; Sexual abuse; Termination of parental rights
Part-time employment. See Employment
Paternity: leave, 72; proof of, 113, 190
Pension plans, 66–67

Personal appearance. *See* Clothing
Plaintiffs. *See* Lawsuits
Pledge of Allegiance, 31
Police questioning: at police station, 155; at scene of suspected crime, 149–51, 153, 155; on school property, 40–41. *See also Miranda* rights and *Miranda* warning
Pornography, 53
Prayer. *See* Freedom of religion
Pregnancy: discrimination on basis of, 72, 177; maternity leave, 72; medical care for, 130; school attendance and, 18
Private schools, 46
Probate court proceedings, 188
Probation, 165–66
Property crimes. *See* Graffiti; Robbery; Shoplifting; Trespassing
Property of minor: at age of majority, 187; bank accounts, 186; conservators, 186, 187, 190; earnings of minor, 50, 65–66; gift by minor, 187; inherited property, 187–90; jointly owned property, 185–86, 187; at minor's death, 190–91; parents as legal custodians, 186; parents' use of, 187; personal items, 185; power to sell, 186; property guardians, 186, 187, 190; search at school, 37–39, 41; trust arrangements and trust property, 190; Uniform Transfers to Minors Act, 186
Protest marches, 27–29
Public office, 81

Race discrimination: affirmative action, 72, 175; against whites, 70–74, 175–76; *Bakke v. California*, 175; *Brown v. Board of Education*, 172, 174; busing, 175; Civil Rights Act of 1964, 70–73; desegregation, 175; examples of illegal race discrimination, 172, 176; interracial marriages, 110; reverse discrimination, 70–74, 175–76; state action requirement, 172, 174–75; tracking, 42–43. *See also* Discrimination; School

Rape: date rape, 104; proving, 104–5; statutory, 105
Religion. *See* Freedom of religion
Report of child abuse. *See* Child abuse
Reverse discrimination, 70–74, 175–76
Robbery, 191
Roe v. Wade, 99, 100, 101
Runaways: emancipation, 78; medical care, 129–31; statistics, 135 n.6

Same-sex marriages, 181
School: age limits, 15; aliens, 44; appeal of disciplinary decision, 35–36; attendance requirements, 15; Bible readings, 29, 30; blood and urine tests, 39; clothing, 19, 25–26, 83–84; competency testing, 43; corporal punishment, 36–37; criticism of teachers, 20–21; curriculum issues, 26–27; demonstrations, 27–29; disciplinary hearings, 31–39; discipline, 31–39; discipline for off-campus activities, 34–35; distribution of materials on campus, 22–24; dress codes, 19, 25–26, 83–84; drug search, 37–38; drug testing, 39; due process of law, 31–39; expulsion, 32–35; extracurricular activities, 28–29, 30, 35; flunking out, 18; free expression, 19–26; gay and lesbian rights clubs, 28–29, 181–82; grade lowered for absences or misconduct, 15–18; graduate equivalency degree (GED), 18; graduation ceremonies, 18, 30–31; handicapped students, 44–45; HIV/AIDS students, 18–19, 45; leafletting, 22–24; libel, 21; lockers and desks, 38, 41; married students, 18; mass searches, 39; *Miranda* warning, 35; *New Jersey v. T.L.O.*, 37, 38; obscene language, 21–22; Pledge of Allegiance, 31; police on campus, 40–41; prayer, 29–31; prayer at athletic event, 31; prayer at graduation ceremony, 30–31; pregnant students, 18; private schools, 46; protest marches, 27–29; punishment, 32–35; records, 45–46; "release-time" programs, 29–30; right to free public education, 15, 44; salut-

ing the American flag, 31; school newspapers, 24–25; searches at school,
37–39, 41; separate-sex classes,
41–42, 43–44; sex discrimination,
43–44, 176–77; sex education, 30, 99;
slander, 21; sports, 41–42; strip
searches, 38–39; student handbook,
34; students with children, 18; suspension, 32–35; tracking and testing,
42–43; underground newspapers,
24–25; use of improperly obtained evidence, 41; weapons, 39–40
Search incident to arrest, 153–55
Search warrants, 11, 153–54, 155
Searches and seizures: blood and urine
tests, 39; consent to warrantless search,
155; at school, 37–39, 41; search incident to arrest, 153–55; search of auto,
11, 153, 154, 155; stop-and-frisk
searches, 154; suppression of evidence,
149–51, 154; at work, 70. See also
Search warrants
Separate-sex classes, 41–42, 43–44
Separation, 93
Sex: abortion, 99–104; AIDS, 18–19,
45, 70, 104, 130; birth control, 97–99;
education, 30, 99; legal sexual acts,
97, 179–80; rape, 104–5; sexual harassment, 73–74; sterilization, 99. See
also Homosexuals and homosexual activity; Sex discrimination; Sexual abuse
Sex Discrimination: against homosexuals,
183–84; examples of illegal sex discrimination, 176–77; lawful sex discrimination, 176; separate-sex classes,
41–42, 43–44; sexual harassment,
73–74; sports, 41–42; at work, 70–74;
Sex education, 30, 99
Sexual abuse: both parents charged, 127;
criminal punishment for, 127; criminal
trial, defined, 127; hearsay testimony,
128–29; how to get help, 128; teen
charged, 127–28; testimony of minor,
125, 128–29. See also Child abuse
Sexual harassment, 73–74
Sexually transmitted diseases (STDs),
counseling and treatment for teens,
104, 130. See also HIV/AIDS

Shoplifting, 191
Siblings, 90
Single parents. See Parenting by teens
Sit-ins, 27–29
Slander, 21
Social Security card, 64
Social Security payments, 66
Sodomy, 22
Sports: discrimination in, 41; nonparticipa-
tion in, as punishment, 35; prayer at
sports event, 31
Statutes. See Finding the law
Statutory rape: age limits, 105; defined,
105; homosexuals, 180
STDs. See Sexually transmitted diseases
Stepparents: inheriting from, 190; rights
and obligations of, 92–93
Sterilization, 99
Stop-and-frisk search, 154
Strip searches, 38–39
Summer jobs, 49, 63
Suspension. See Due process of law
Symbolic speech. See Freedom of ex-
pression

Taxes. See Income taxes
Teenage Parents. See Parenting by teens
Teens. See specific topics throughout this
index
Termination of parental rights: assistance
to family prior to, 56–57; "best interests of the child," 56, 58; burden of
proof, 56; child and parent separated
prior to, 57; crime of parent as basis
for, 57; lawyer for minor, 57; mental
illness of parent not necessarily basis
for, 58; poverty not necessarily basis
for, 57; voluntary termination, 57
Testimony of minor: child protective proceedings, 125, 128–29; civil actions,
209; juvenile court, 161; sexual abuse
hearing, 128–29
Testing. See School
Tinker v. Des Moines Independent School
District, 19–20, 24, 25–26
Tips, 65
Tobacco, 52
Torts. See Lawsuits

Tracking, 42–43
Traffic offenses: arrest, 10, 142; driving while intoxicated (DWI), 10, 140–42; habitual violators, 10; impound of auto, 11, 154; search warrant unnecessary, 153, 154; traffic court, 10, 142; weapon in auto, 11
Trespassing, 191–92
Trials. *See* Juvenile court; Lawsuits
Trust arrangements and trust property, 190

Underground newspapers, 24–25
Unemployment compensation, 68–69
Uniform Transfers to Minors Act, 186
United States Supreme Court, 211
Urine tests, 39, 70

Visitation and visitation rights: following parents' divorce, 89–90; by grandparents, 92; by homosexual parent, 181; by natural parents of foster children, 134; by parent of child born outside marriage, 112; by stepparent, 93
Voting, 81

Walk-outs, 28
Warrants. *See* Search warrants
Weapons: in auto, 11; parental permission to carry, 58–59; at school, 39, 40
Welfare for teenage parents, 113–14
WIC program, 114
Wills, 187–90
Workers' compensation, 67–68

X-rated movies, 53

About the Author

KATHLEEN A. HEMPELMAN is an attorney in private practice in Phoenix, Arizona.